Real-Resumes for Financial Jobs

Anne McKinney, Editor

PREP PUBLISHING

FAYETTEVILLE, NC

PREP Publishing
1110½ Hay Street
Fayetteville, NC 28305
(910) 483-6611

Library of Congress Cataloging-in-Publication Data

Real-resumes for financial jobs / Anne McKinney, editor.
        p. cm. -- (Real-resumes series)
     ISBN 1-885288-15-8 (pbk.)
     1. Résumés (Employment) 2. Financial services industry. I. McKinney, Anne, 1948- II. Series.

    HF5383 .R39585 2001
    808'.06665--dc21   2001018503
                                                           CIP

Printed in the United States of America

By PREP Publishing

Business and Career Series:

RESUMES AND COVER LETTERS THAT HAVE WORKED

RESUMES AND COVER LETTERS THAT HAVE WORKED FOR MILITARY PROFESSIONALS

GOVERNMENT JOB APPLICATIONS AND FEDERAL RESUMES

COVER LETTERS THAT BLOW DOORS OPEN

LETTERS FOR SPECIAL SITUATIONS

RESUMES AND COVER LETTERS FOR MANAGERS

REAL-RESUMES FOR TEACHERS

REAL-RESUMES FOR STUDENTS

REAL-RESUMES FOR CAREER CHANGERS

REAL-RESUMES FOR SALES

REAL ESSAYS FOR COLLEGE & GRADUATE SCHOOL

REAL-RESUMES FOR MEDICAL JOBS

REAL-RESUMES FOR COMPUTER JOBS

REAL-RESUMES FOR FINANCIAL JOBS

Judeo-Christian Ethics Series:

SECOND TIME AROUND

BACK IN TIME

WHAT THE BIBLE SAYS ABOUT...Words that can lead to success and happiness

A GENTLE BREEZE FROM GOSSAMER WINGS

BIBLE STORIES FROM THE OLD TESTAMENT

Fiction:

KIJABE...An African Historical Saga

Table of Contents

Real-Resumes

For Financial Jobs

A WORD FROM THE EDITOR:
ABOUT THE REAL-RESUMES SERIES

This book is dedicated to individuals seeking employment in the financial field. We hope the superior samples will help you manage your career so that you will find satisfying and challenging jobs!

Welcome to the Real-Resumes Series. The Real-Resumes Series is a series of books which have been developed based on the experiences of real job hunters and which target specialized fields or types of resumes. As the editor of the series, I have carefully selected resumes and cover letters (with names and other key data disguised, of course) which have been used successfully in real job hunts. That's what we mean by "Real-Resumes." What you see in this book are *real* resumes and cover letters which helped real people get ahead in their careers.

The Real-Resumes Series is based on the work of the country's oldest resume-preparation company known as PREP Resumes. If you would like a free information packet describing the company's resume preparation services, call 910-483-6611, e-mail us at preppub@aol.com, or write to PREP at 1110½ Hay Street, Fayetteville, NC 28305. If you have a job hunting experience you would like to share with our staff at the Real-Resumes Series, please contact us at preppub@aol.com or visit our website at http://www.prep-pub.com.

The resumes and cover letters in this book are designed to be of most value to people already in a career change or contemplating a career change. If we could give you one word of advice about your career, here's what we would say: Manage your career and don't stumble from job to job in an incoherent pattern. Try to find work that interests you, and then identify prosperous industries which need work performed of the type you want to do. Learn early in your working life that a great resume and cover letter can blow doors open for you and help you maximize your salary.

As the editor of this book, I would like to give you some tips on how to make the best use of the information you will find here. Because you are considering a career change, you already understand the concept of managing your career for maximum enjoyment and self-fulfillment. The purpose of this book is to provide expert tools and advice so that you *can* manage your career. Inside these pages you will find resumes and cover letters that will help you find not just a job but the type of work you want to do.

Overview of the Book

Every resume and cover letter in this book actually worked. And most of the resumes and cover letters have common features: all are one-page, all are in the chronological format, and all resumes are accompanied by a companion cover letter. The book is divided into three parts. **Part One** provides some advice about job hunting. Step One begins with a discussion of why employers prefer the one-page, chronological resume. In Step Two you are introduced to the direct approach and to the proper format for a cover letter. In Step Three you learn the 14 main reasons why job hunters are not offered the jobs they want, and you learn the six key areas employers focus on when they interview you. Step Four gives nuts-and-bolts advice on how to handle the interview, send a follow-up letter after an interview, and negotiate your salary. At the end of Part One, you'll find advice about how to research and locate the companies and organizations to which you want to send your resume.

Since the cover letter plays such a critical role in a career change, **Part Two** of the book is entitled Cover Letters for Job Hunting. You will learn from the experts how to format your cover letters and you will see suggested language to use in particular job-hunting situations. It has been said that "A picture is worth a thousand words" and, for that reason, you will see numerous examples of effective cover letters used by real individuals to change fields, functions, and industries. Part Two ends with answers to six of the most commonly asked questions about cover letters and job hunting, and the answers are provided in the form of actual cover letters.

Parts One and Two lead up to the most important part of the book, which is Real-Resumes—**Part Three, Part Four, and Part Five.** In those sections you will see people in varying types of job hunts. Part Three is **Students Seeking to Enter the Financial Field.** Part Four is **Junior Financial Managers.** Part Five is **Senior Financial Managers and Executives.**

Whatever your circumstances, you'll find resumes and cover letters that will "show you the ropes" in terms of successfully finding jobs in the financial field. Bear in mind that you can learn a lot from any of the resumes in this book. You will find resumes and cover letters of college students entering the financial field for the first time, and you will see how students show off experience such as "tutor" and summer jobs in order to sell their potential to excel in the financial field. You will also find resumes of experienced professionals seeking to advance in the financial field and sometimes seeking to transfer their skills to other industries. There are resumes and cover letters of people who wanted a change from the functional area in which they had been working but who probably wanted to remain in their industry. Some of you will be especially interested by the resumes and cover letters of individuals who knew they definitely wanted a career change but had no idea what they wanted to do next. Other resumes and cover letters show individuals who knew they wanted a new challenge and had a pretty good idea of what they wanted to do next.

Before you proceed further, think about why you picked up this book.

- Are you dissatisfied with the type of work you are now doing?
- Would you like to change careers, change companies, or change industries?
- Are you satisfied with your industry but not with your niche or function within it?
- Do you want to transfer your skills to a new product or service?
- Even if you have excelled in your field, have you "had enough?" Would you like the stimulation of a new challenge?
- Are you aware of the importance of a great cover letter but unsure of how to write one?
- Are you preparing to launch a second career after retirement?
- Have you been downsized, or do you anticipate becoming a victim of downsizing?
- Do you need expert advice on how to plan and implement a job campaign that will open the maximum number of doors?
- Do you want to make sure you handle an interview to your maximum advantage?
- Would you like to master the techniques of negotiating salary and benefits?
- Do you want to learn the secrets and shortcuts of professional resume writers?

The "direct approach" is the style of job hunting most likely to yield the maximum number of job interviews.

Using the Direct Approach
As you consider the possibility of a job hunt or career change, you need to be aware that most people end up having at least three distinctly different careers in their working lifetimes, and often those careers are different from each other. Yet people usually stumble through each job campaign, unsure of what they should be doing. Whether you find yourself voluntarily or unexpectedly in a job hunt, the direct approach is the job hunting strategy most likely to yield a full-time permanent job. The direct approach is an active, take-the-initiative style of job hunting in which you choose your next employer rather than relying on responding to ads, using employment agencies, or depending on other methods of finding jobs. You will learn how to use the direct approach in this book, and you will see that an effective cover letter is a critical ingredient in using the direct approach.

Using references in a skillful fashion in your job hunt will inspire confidence in prospective employers and help you "close the sale" after interviews.

Lack of Industry Experience Not a Major Barrier to Entering New Field
"Lack of experience" is often the last reason people are not offered jobs, according to the companies who do the hiring. If you are changing careers, you will be glad to learn that experienced professionals often are selling "potential" rather than experience in a job hunt. Companies look for personal qualities that they know tend to be present in their most effective professionals, such as communication skills, initiative, persistence, organizational and time management skills, and creativity. Frequently companies are trying to discover "personality type," "talent," "ability," "aptitude," and "potential" rather than seeking actual hands-on experience, so your resume should be designed to aggressively present your accomplishments. Attitude, enthusiasm, personality, and a track record of achievements in any type of work are the primary "indicators of success" which employers are seeking, and you will see numerous examples in this book of resumes written in an all-purpose fashion so that the professional can approach various industries and companies.

The Art of Using References in a Job Hunt
You probably already know that you need to provide references during a job hunt, but you may not be sure of how and when to use references for maximum advantage. You can use references very creatively during a job hunt to call attention to your strengths and make yourself "stand out." Your references will rarely get you a job, no matter how impressive the names, but the way you use references can boost the employer's

confidence in you and lead to a job offer in the least time. You should ask from three to five people, including people who have supervised you, if you can use them as a reference during your job hunt. You may not be able to ask your current boss since your job hunt is probably confidential. A common question in resume preparation is: "Do I need to put my references on my resume?" No, you don't. And even if you create a page of references at the same time that you prepare your resume, you don't need to mail your references page with the resume and cover letter. The potential employer is not interested in your references until he meets and gets interested in you, so the earliest you need to have references ready is at the first interview. An excellent attention-getting technique is to take to the first interview not just a page of references (giving names, addresses, and telephone numbers) but an actual letter of reference written by someone who knows you well and who preferably has supervised or employed you. A professional way to close the first interview is to thank the interviewer, shake his or her hand, and then say you'd like to give him or her a copy of a letter of reference from a previous employer. Hopefully you already made a good impression during the interview, but you'll "close the sale" in a dynamic fashion if you leave a letter praising you and your accomplishments. For that reason, it's a good idea to ask employers during your final weeks in a job if they will provide you with a written letter of recommendation which you can use in future job hunts. Most employers will oblige, and you will have a letter that has a useful "shelf life" of many years. Such a letter often gives the prospective employer enough confidence in his opinion of you that he may forego checking out other references and decide to offer you the job in the next few days. Whom should you ask to serve as references? References should be people who have known or supervised you in a professional, academic, or work situation. References with big titles, like school superintendent or congressman, are fine, but remind busy people when you get to the interview stage that they may be contacted soon. Make sure the busy official recognizes your name and has instant positive recall of you! If you're asked to provide references on a formal company application, you can simply transcribe names from your references list. In summary, follow this rule in using references: If you've got them, flaunt them! If you've obtained well-written letters of reference, make sure you find a polite way to push those references under the nose of the interviewer so he or she can hear someone other than you describing your strengths. Your references probably won't ever get you a job, but glowing letters of reference can give you credibility and visibility that can make you stand out among candidates with similar credentials and potential!

With regard to references, it's best to provide the names and addresses of people who have supervised you or observed you in a work situation.

The approach taken by this book is to (1) help you master the proven best techniques of conducting a job hunt and (2) show you how to stand out in a job hunt through your resume, cover letter, interviewing skills, as well as the way in which you present your references and follow up on interviews. Now, the best way to "get in the mood" for writing your own resume and cover letter is to select samples from the Table of Contents that interest you and then read them. A great resume is a "photograph," usually on one page, of an individual. If you wish to seek professional advice in preparing your resume, you may contact one of the professional writers at Professional Resume & Employment Publishing (PREP) for a brief free consultation by calling 1-910-483-6611.

Part One: Some Advice About Your Job Hunt

What if you don't know what you want to do?

Your job hunt will be more comfortable if you can figure out what type of work you want to do. But you are not alone if you have no idea what you want to do next! You may have knowledge and skills in certain areas but want to get into another type of work. What *The Wall Street Journal* has discovered in its research on careers is that most of us end up having at least three distinctly different careers in our working lives; it seems that, even if we really like a particular kind of activity, twenty years of doing it is enough for most of us and we want to move on to something else!

Figure out what interests you and you will hold the key to a successful job hunt and working career. (And be prepared for your interests to change over time!)

That's why we strongly believe that you need to spend some time figuring out *what interests you* rather than taking an inventory of the skills you have. You may have skills that you simply don't want to use, but if you can build your career on the things that interest you, you will be more likely to be happy and satisfied in your job. Realize, too, that interests can change over time; the activities that interest you now may not be the ones that interested you years ago. For example, some professionals may decide that they've had enough of retail sales and want a job selling another product or service, even though they have earned a reputation for being an excellent retail manager. We strongly believe that interests rather than skills should be the determining factor in deciding what types of jobs you want to apply for and what directions you explore in your job hunt. Obviously one cannot be a lawyer without a law degree or a secretary without secretarial skills; but a professional can embark on a next career as a financial consultant, property manager, plant manager, production supervisor, retail manager, or other occupation if he/she has a strong interest in that type of work and can provide a resume that clearly demonstrates past excellent performance in *any* field and *potential* to excel in another field. As you will see later in this book, "lack of exact experience" is the last reason why people are turned down for the jobs they apply for.

How can you have a resume prepared if you don't know what you want to do?

"Lack of exact experience" is the last reason people are turned down for the jobs for which they apply.

You may be wondering how you can have a resume prepared if you don't know what you want to do next. The approach to resume writing which PREP, the country's oldest resume-preparation company, has used successfully for many years is to develop an "all-purpose" resume that translates your skills, experience, and accomplishments into language employers can understand. What most people need in a job hunt is a versatile resume that will allow them to apply for numerous types of jobs. For example, you may want to apply for a job in pharmaceutical sales but you may also want to have a resume that will be versatile enough for you to apply for jobs in the construction, financial services, or automotive industries.

Based on 20 years of serving job hunters, we at PREP have found that **an all-purpose resume** and **specific cover letters tailored to specific fields** is sometimes your best approach to job hunting rather than trying to create different resumes for different employers. Usually, you will not even need more than one "all-purpose" cover letter, although the cover letter rather than the resume is the place to communicate your interest in a narrow or specific field. An all-purpose resume and cover letter that translate your experience and accomplishments into plain English are the tools that will maximize the number of doors which open for you while permitting you to "fish" in the widest range of job areas.

Your resume will provide the script for your job interview.
When you get down to it, your resume has a simple job to do: Its purpose is to blow as many doors open as possible and to make as many people as possible want to meet you. So a well-written resume that really "sells" you is a key that will create opportunities for you in a job hunt.

This statistic explains why: The typical newspaper advertisement for a job opening receives more than 245 replies. And normally only 10 or 12 will be invited to an interview.

But here's another purpose of the resume: it provides the "script" the employer uses when he interviews you. If your resume has been written in such a way that your strengths and achievements are revealed, that's what you'll end up talking about at the job interview. Since the resume will govern what you get asked about at your interviews, you can't overestimate the importance of making sure your resume makes you look and sound as good as you are.

So what is a "good" resume?
Very literally, your resume should motivate the person reading it to dial the phone number you have put on the resume. (If you are relocating, that's one reason you should think about putting a local phone contact number on your resume, if possible, when your contact address is several states away; employers are much more likely to dial a local telephone number than a long-distance number when they're looking for potential employees.)

If you have a resume already, look at it objectively. Is it a limp, colorless "laundry list" of your job titles and duties? Or does it "paint a picture" of your skills, abilities, and accomplishments in a way that would make someone want to meet you? Can people understand what you're saying?

How long should your resume be?
One page, maybe two. Usually only people in the academic community have a resume (which they usually call a *curriculum vitae*) longer than one or two pages. Remember that your resume is almost always accompanied by a cover letter, and a potential employer does not want to read more than two or three pages about a total stranger in order to decide if he wants to meet that person! Besides, don't forget that the more you tell someone about yourself, the more opportunity you are providing for the employer to screen you out at the "first-cut" stage. A resume should be concise and exciting and designed to make the reader want to meet you in person!

Should resumes be functional or chronological?
Employers almost always prefer a chronological resume; in other words, an employer will find a resume easier to read if it is immediately apparent what your current or most recent job is, what you did before that, and so forth, in reverse chronological order. A resume that goes back in detail for the last ten years of employment will generally satisfy the employer's curiosity about your background. Employment more than ten years old can be shown even more briefly in an "Other Experience" section at the end of your "Experience" section. Remember that your intention is not to tell everything you've done but to "hit the high points" and especially impress the employer with what you learned, contributed, or accomplished in each job you describe.

Your resume is the "script" for your job interviews. Make sure you put on your resume what you want to talk about or be asked about at the job interview.

The one-page resume in chronological format is the format preferred by most employers.

Once you get your resume, what do you do with it?

You will be using your resume to answer ads, as a tool to use in talking with friends and relatives about your job search, and, most importantly, in using the "direct approach" described in this book.

When you mail your resume, always send a "cover letter."

A "cover letter," sometimes called a "resume letter" or "letter of interest," is a letter that accompanies and introduces your resume. Your cover letter is a way of personalizing the resume by sending it to the specific person you think you might want to work for at each company. Your cover letter should contain a few highlights from your resume—just enough to make someone want to meet you. Cover letters should always be typed or word processed on a computer—never handwritten.

Never mail or fax your resume without a cover letter. If possible, e-mail the cover letter, too, when you e-mail your resume.

1. Learn the art of answering ads.

There is an "art," part of which can be learned, in using your "bestselling" resume to reply to advertisements.

Sometimes an exciting job lurks behind a boring ad that someone dictated in a hurry, so reply to any ad that interests you. Don't worry that you aren't "25 years old with an MBA" like the ad asks for. Employers will always make compromises in their requirements if they think you're the "best fit" overall.

What about ads that ask for "salary requirements?"

What if the ad you're answering asks for "salary requirements?" The first rule is to avoid committing yourself in writing at that point to a specific salary. You don't want to "lock yourself in."

What if the ad asks for your "salary requirements?"

There are two ways to handle the ad that asks for "salary requirements."

First, you can ignore that part of the ad and accompany your resume with a cover letter that focuses on "selling" you, your abilities, and even some of your philosophy about work or your field. You may include a sentence in your cover letter like this: "I can provide excellent personal and professional references at your request, and I would be delighted to share the private details of my salary history with you in person."

Second, if you feel you must give some kind of number, just state a range in your cover letter that includes your medical, dental, other benefits, and expected bonuses. You might state, for example, "My current compensation, including benefits and bonuses, is in the range of $30,000-$40,000."

Analyze the ad and "tailor" yourself to it.

When you're replying to ads, a finely-tailored cover letter is an important tool in getting your resume noticed and read. On the next page is a cover letter which has been "tailored to fit" a specific ad. Notice the "art" used by PREP writers of analyzing the ad's main requirements and then writing the letter so that the person's background, work habits, and interests seem "tailor-made" to the company's needs. Use this cover letter as a model when you prepare your own reply to ads.

Date

Mr. Arthur Wise
Chamber of Commerce of the U.S.
9439 Goshen Lane
Dallas, TX 22105

Dear Mr. Wise:

I would appreciate an opportunity to show you in person, soon, that I am the energetic, dynamic individual you are looking for as your Accounting Manager for the Chamber of Commerce in Texas.

Here are just three reasons why I believe I am the effective young professional you seek:

- *I myself am "sold" on the Chamber of Commerce* and have long been an admirer of its goal of forming a cohesive business organization to promote the well-being of communities and promote business vigor. As someone better known that I put it long ago, "the business of America is business." I wholeheartedly believe that the Chamber's efforts to unite, solidify, and mobilize American business can be an important key in unlocking the international competitiveness and domestic vitality of our economy. I am eager to contribute to that effort.

- *I am a proven financial professional* with a demonstrated ability to handle all functional areas related to financial management. In my current position I oversee 15 employees who include accounts payable and receivable specialists as well as professionals involved in capital investment planning and strategic forecasting.

- *I offer strong management skills and a proven ability to train and develop others.* I recently led a highly motivated team of 15 individuals in installing new software applications which boosted profitability and efficiency while producing the highest customer satisfaction index in the company's history.

You will find me, I am certain, a friendly, good-natured person whom you would be proud to call part of the Chamber's "team." Although I have worked primarily in profit-making environments, I am confident that I could enthusiastically and gracefully transition my skills into a trade association environment. I would enjoy the opportunity to share my extensive financial knowledge with other professionals.

I hope you will call or write me soon to suggest a convenient time when we might meet to discuss your needs further and how I might serve them.

Yours sincerely,

Your Name

Employers are trying to identify the individual who wants the job they are filling. Don't be afraid to express your enthusiasm in the cover letter!

2. Talk to friends and relatives.

Don't be shy about telling your friends and relatives the kind of job you're looking for. Looking for the job you want involves using your network of contacts, so tell people what you're looking for. They may be able to make introductions and help set up interviews.

About 25% of all interviews are set up through "who you know," so don't ignore this approach.

3. Finally, and most importantly, use the "direct approach."

The "direct approach" is a strategy in which you choose your next employer.

More than 50% of all job interviews are set up by the "direct approach." That means you actually send a resume and a cover letter to a company you think might be interesting to work for.

To whom do you write?

In general, you should write directly to the *exact name* of the person who would be hiring you: say, the president of the company, or the vice-president of finance or management information systems. If you're in doubt about to whom to address the letter, address it to the president by name and he or she will make sure it gets forwarded to the right person within the company who has hiring authority in your area.

How do you find the names of potential employers?

You're not alone if you feel that the biggest problem in your job search is finding the right names at the companies you want to contact. But you can usually figure out the names of companies you want to approach by deciding first if your job hunt is primarily geography-driven or industry-driven.

In a **geography-driven job hunt,** you could select a list of, say, 50 companies you want to contact **by location** from the lists that the U.S. Chambers of Commerce publish yearly of their "major area employers." There are hundreds of local Chambers of Commerce across America, and most of them will have an 800 number which you can find through 1-800-555-1212. If you and your family think Atlanta, Dallas, Ft. Lauderdale, and Virginia Beach might be nice places to live, for example, you could contact the Chamber of Commerce in those cities and ask how you can obtain a copy of their list of major employers. Your nearest library will have the book which lists the addresses of all chambers.

In an **industry-driven job hunt,** and if you are willing to relocate, you will be identifying the companies which you find most attractive in the industry in which you want to work. When you select a list of companies to contact **by industry,** you can find the right person to write and the address of firms by industrial category in *Standard and Poor's, Moody's,* and other excellent books in public libraries. Many Web sites also provide contact information.

Many people feel it's a good investment to actually call the company to either find out or double-check the name of the person to whom they want to send a resume and cover letter. It's important to do as much as you feasibly can to assure that the letter gets to the right person in the company.

At the end of Part One, you will find some advice about how to conduct library research and how to locate organizations to which you could send your resume.

What's the correct way to follow up on a resume you send?

There is a polite way to be aggressively interested in a company during your job hunt. It is ideal to end the cover letter accompanying your resume by saying, "I hope you'll welcome my call next week when I try to arrange a brief meeting at your convenience to discuss your current and future needs and how I might serve them." Keep it low key, and just ask for a "brief meeting," not an interview. Employers want people who show a determined interest in working with them, so don't be shy about following up on the resume and cover letter you've mailed.

STEP THREE: Preparing for Interviews

It pays to be aware of the 14 most common pitfalls for job hunters.

But a resume and cover letter by themselves can't get you the job you want. You need to "prep" yourself before the interview. Step Three in your job campaign is "Preparing for Interviews." First, let's look at interviewing from the company's point of view.

What are the biggest "turnoffs" for companies?

One of the ways to help yourself perform well at an interview is to look at the main reasons why companies *don't* hire the people they interview, according to companies that do the interviewing.

Notice that "lack of appropriate background" (or lack of experience) is the *last* reason for not being offered the job.

The 14 Most Common Reasons Job Hunters Are Not Offered Jobs *(according to the companies who do the interviewing and hiring)*:

1.   Low level of accomplishment
2.   Poor attitude, lack of self-confidence
3.   Lack of goals/objectives
4.   Lack of enthusiasm
5.   Lack of interest in the company's business
6.   Inability to sell or express yourself
7.   Unrealistic salary demands
8.   Poor appearance
9.   Lack of maturity, no leadership potential
10. Lack of extracurricular activities
11. Lack of preparation for the interview, no knowledge about company
12. Objecting to travel
13. Excessive interest in security and benefits
14. Inappropriate background

Department of Labor studies have proven that smart, "prepared" job hunters can increase their beginning salary while getting a job in *half* the time it normally takes. (4½ months is the average national length of a job search.) Here, from PREP, are some questions that can prepare you to find a job faster.

Are you in the "right" frame of mind?

It seems unfair that we have to look for a job just when we're lowest in morale. Don't worry *too* much if you're nervous before interviews. You're supposed to be a little nervous, especially if the job means a lot to you. But the best way to kill unnecessary fears about job hunting is through 1) making sure you have a great resume and 2) preparing yourself for the interview. Here are three main areas you need to think about before each interview.

Do you know what the company does?
Don't walk into an interview giving the impression that, "If this is Tuesday, this must be General Motors."

Research the company before you go to interviews.

Find out before the interview what the company's main product or service is. Where is the company heading? Is it in a "growth" or declining industry? (Answers to these questions may influence whether or not you want to work there!)

Information about what the company does is in annual reports as well as newspaper and magazine articles. Just visit your nearest library and ask the reference librarian to guide you to materials on the company. Internet searches will yield valuable information. At the end of Part One you will find many suggestions about how to research companies.

Do you know what you want to do for the company?
Before the interview, try to decide how you see yourself fitting into the company. Remember, "lack of exact background" the company wants is usually the last reason people are not offered jobs.

Understand before you go to each interview that the burden will be on you to "sell" the interviewer on why you're the best person for the job and the company.

How will you answer the critical interview questions?
Put yourself in the interviewer's position and think about the questions you're most likely to be asked. Here are some of the most commonly asked interview questions:

Anticipate the questions you will be asked at the interview, and prepare your responses in advance.

Q: *"What are your greatest strengths?"*
A: Don't say you've never thought about it! Go into an interview knowing the three main impressions you want to leave about yourself, such as "I'm hard-working, loyal, and an imaginative cost-cutter."

Q: *"What are your greatest weaknesses?"*
A: Don't confess that you're lazy or have trouble meeting deadlines! Confessing that you tend to be a "workaholic" or "tend to be a perfectionist and sometimes get frustrated when others don't share my high standards" will make your prospective employer see a "weakness" that he likes. Name a weakness that your interviewer will perceive as a strength.

Q: *"What are your long-range goals?"*
A: If you're interviewing with Microsoft, don't say you want to work for IBM in five years! Say your long-range goal is to be *with* the company, contributing to its goals and success.

Q: *"What motivates you to do your best work?"*
A: Don't get dollar signs in your eyes here! "A challenge" is not a bad answer, but it's a little cliched. Saying something like "troubleshooting" or "solving a tough problem" is more interesting and specific. Give an example if you can.

Q: "What do you know about this company?"

A: Don't say you never heard of it until they asked you to the interview! Name an interesting, positive thing you learned about the company recently from your research. Remember, company executives can sometimes feel rather "maternal" about the company they serve. Don't get onto a negative area of the company if you can think of positive facts you can bring up. Of course, if you learned in your research that the company's sales seem to be taking a nose-dive, or that the company president is being prosecuted for taking bribes, you might politely ask your interviewer to tell you something that could help you better understand what you've been reading. Those are the kinds of company facts that can help you determine whether you want to work there or not.

Q: "Why should I hire you?"

A: "I'm unemployed and available" is the wrong answer here! Get back to your strengths and say that you believe the organization could benefit by a loyal, hard-working cost-cutter like yourself.

In conclusion, you should decide in advance, before you go to the interview, how you will answer each of these commonly asked questions. Have some practice interviews with a friend to role-play and build your confidence.

Go to an interview prepared to tell the company why it should hire you.

STEP FOUR: Handling the Interview and Negotiating Salary

Now you're ready for Step Four: actually handling the interview successfully and effectively. Remember, the purpose of an interview is to get a job offer.

A smile at an interview makes the employer perceive of you as intelligent!

Eight "do's" for the interview

According to leading U.S. companies, there are eight key areas in interviewing success. You can fail at an interview if you mishandle just one area.

1. Do wear appropriate clothes.
   You can never go wrong by wearing a suit to an interview.

2. Do be well groomed.
   Don't overlook the obvious things like having clean hair, clothes, and fingernails for the interview.

3. Do give a firm handshake.
   You'll have to shake hands twice in most interviews: first, before you sit down, and second, when you leave the interview. Limp handshakes turn most people off.

4. Do smile and show a sense of humor.
   Interviewers are looking for people who would be nice to work with, so don't be so somber that you don't smile. In fact, research shows that people who smile at interviews are perceived as more intelligent. So, smile!

5. Do be enthusiastic.
   Employers say they are "turned off" by lifeless, unenthusiastic job hunters who show no special interest in that company. The best way to show some enthusiasm for the employer's operation is to find out about the business beforehand.

6. Do show you are flexible and adaptable.

An employer is looking for someone who can contribute to his organization in a flexible, adaptable way. No matter what skills and training you have, employers know every new employee must go through initiation and training on the company's turf. Certainly show pride in your past accomplishments in a specific, factual way ("I saved my last employer $50.00 a week by a new cost-cutting measure I developed"). But don't come across as though there's nothing about the job you couldn't easily handle.

7. Do ask intelligent questions about the employer's business.

An employer is hiring someone because of certain business needs. Show interest in those needs. Asking questions to get a better idea of the employer's needs will help you "stand out" from other candidates interviewing for the job.

8. Do "take charge" when the interviewer "falls down" on the job.

Go into every interview knowing the three or four points about yourself you want the interviewer to remember. And be prepared to take an active part in leading the discussion if the interviewer's "canned approach" does not permit you to display your "strong suit." You can't always depend on the interviewer's asking you the "right" questions so you can stress your strengths and accomplishments.

An important "don't": Don't ask questions about salary or benefits at the first interview.
Employers don't take warmly to people who look at their organization as just a place to satisfy salary and benefit needs. Don't risk making a negative impression by appearing greedy or self-serving. The place to discuss salary and benefits is normally at the second interview, and the employer will bring it up. Then you can ask questions without appearing excessively interested in what the organization can do for you.

"Sell yourself" before talking salary
Make sure you've "sold" yourself before talking salary. First show you're the "best fit" for the employer and then you'll be in a stronger position from which to negotiate salary.

Interviewers sometimes throw out a salary figure at the first interview to see if you'll accept it. Don't commit yourself. You may be able to negotiate a better deal later on. Get back to finding out more about the job. This lets the interviewer know you're interested primarily in the job and not the salary.

Now...negotiating your salary
You must avoid stating a "salary requirement" in your initial cover letter, and you must avoid even appearing **interested** in salary before you are offered the job.

Never bring up the subject of salary yourself. Employers say there's no way you can avoid looking greedy if you bring up the issue of salary and benefits before the company has identified you as its "best fit."

When the company brings up salary, it may say something like this: "Well, Mary, we think you'd make a good candidate for this job. What kind of salary are we talking about?"

Never name a number here, either. Give the ball back to the interviewer. Act as though you hadn't given the subject of salary much thought and respond something like this: "Ah, Mr. Jones, salary. . .well, I wonder if you'd be kind enough to tell me what salary you had in mind when you advertised the job?" Or ... "What is the range you have in mind?"

Don't worry, if the interviewer names a figure that you think is too low, you can say so without turning down the job or locking yourself into a rigid position. The point here is to negotiate for yourself as well as you can. You might reply to a number named by the interviewer that you think is low by saying something like this: "Well, Mr. Lee, the job interests me very much, and I think I'd certainly enjoy working with you. But, frankly, I was thinking of something a little higher than that." That leaves the ball in your interviewer's court again, and you haven't turned down the job, either, in case it turns out that the interviewer can't increase the offer and you still want the job.

Salary negotiation can be tricky.

Last, send a follow-up letter.

Finally, send a letter right after the interview telling your interviewer you enjoyed the meeting and are certain (if you are) you are the "best fit" for the job. The people interviewing you will probably have an attitude described as either "professionally loyal" to their companies or "maternal and proprietary" if the interviewer also owns the company. In either case, they are looking for people who want to work for *that* company in particular. The follow-up letter you send might be just the deciding factor in your favor if the employer is trying to choose between you and someone else.

Sample follow-up letters are shown in the next section. Be sure to modify the model letter according to your particular skills and interview situation.

A follow-up letter can help the employer choose between you and another qualified candidate.

Researching companies and locating employers

Figuring out the names of the organizations to which you want to mail your resume is part of any highly successful job campaign. Don't depend on only answering the ads you read in printed or electronic form, waiting for the ideal job to appear in **newspapers or magazines,** many of which are published online. If you are geographically oriented and need to find work in a particular city or town, check out the Sunday advertisements in the classified sections which suit you best, such as "administrative" or "professional" or "technical." Also aggressively research possible employers. Here is some information which you can use in researching the names of organizations for which you might be interested in working.

In electronic and printed form, most libraries have a variety of information available on various organizations throughout the U.S. and worldwide. If your local library has computers, you will probably have access to a vast network of information. Many printed materials might be available only for use in the reference room of the library, but some items may be checked out. Listed below are some of the major sources to look for, but be sure and check at the reference desk to see if there are any resources available in a printed or online form related to the specific types of companies you wish to investigate.

The Worldwide Chamber of Commerce Directory

Most chambers of commerce annually produce a "list of major employers" for their market area (or city). Usually the list includes the name, address, and telephone number of the employer along with information about the number of people employed, kinds of products and services produced, and a person to contact about employment. You can obtain the "list of major employers" in the city where you want to work by writing to that chamber. There is usually a small charge.

The *Worldwide Chamber of Commerce Directory* is an alphabetical listing of American and foreign chambers of commerce. It includes:

All U.S. Chambers of Commerce (with addresses and phone numbers)
American Chambers of Commerce abroad
Canadian Chambers of Commerce
Foreign Chambers of Commerce in principal cities worldwide
Foreign Embassies and Consulates in the U.S.
U.S. Consulates and Embassies throughout the world

Standard and Poor's Register of Corporations, Directors, and Executives

Standard and Poor's produce three volumes annually with information concerning over 77,000 American corporations. They are:

Volume 1—**Corporations.** Here is an alphabetical listing of a variety of information for each of over 77,000 companies, including:
- name of company, address, telephone number
- names, titles, and functions of several key officers
- name of accounting firm, primary bank, and law firm
- stock exchange, description of products or services
- annual sales, number of employees
- division names and functions, subsidiary listings

Volume 2—**Directors and Executives.** This volume lists alphabetically over 70,000 officers, directors, partners, etc. by name. Information on each executive includes:
- principal business affiliation
- business address, residence address, year of birth
- college and year of graduation, fraternal affiliation

Volume 3—**Index.**

Moody's Manuals

Moody's Manuals provide information about companies traded on the New York and American Stock Exchanges and over the counter. They include:

Moody's Industrial Manual

Here, Moody's discusses detailed information on companies traded on the New York, American, and regional stock exchanges. The companies are listed alphabetically. Basic information about company addresses, phone numbers, and the names of key officers is available for each company listed. In addition, detailed information about the financial and operating data for each company is available. There are three levels of detail provided:

Complete Coverage. Companies in this section have the following information:
- *financial information* for the past 7 years (income accounts, balance sheets, financial and operating data).
- *detailed description of the company's business* including a complete list of subsidiaries and office and property sites.
- *capital structure information,* which includes details on capital stock and long-term debt, with bond and preferred stock ratings and 2 years of stock and bond price ranges.
- *extensive presentation of the company's last annual report.*

Full Measure Coverage. Information on companies in this section includes:
- *financial information for the past 7 years* (income accounts, balance sheets, financial and operating data).
- *detailed description of company's business,* with a complete list of subsidiaries and plant and property locations.
- *capital structure information,* with details on capital stock and long term debt, with bond and preferred stock ratings and 2 years of stock and bond price changes.

Comprehensive Coverage. Information on companies in this section includes:
- *5 years of financial information* on income accounts, balance sheets, and financial and operating ratios.
- *detailed description of company's business,* including subsidiaries.
- *concise capital structure information,* including capital stock and long term debts, bond and preferred stock ratings.

Moody's OTC Manual

Here is information on U.S. firms which are unlisted on national and regional stock exchanges. There are three levels of coverage: complete, full measure, and comprehensive (same as described above). Other Moody's manuals include: *Moody's Public Utility Manual, Moody's Municipal and Government Manual,* and *Moody's Bank and Finance Manual.*

Dun's Million Dollar Directory

Three separate listings (alphabetical, geographic, and by products) of over 120,000 U.S. firms. There are three volumes:

Volume 1—The 45,000 largest companies, net worth over $500,000.
Volume 2—The 37,000 next largest companies.
Volume 3—The 37,000 next largest companies.

U.S. industrial directories

Ask your librarian to guide you to your library's collection of industrial directories. Almost every state produces a manufacturing directory, for example, and many libraries maintain complete collections of these directories. You may find information on products and the addresses and telephone numbers of industrial companies.

Thomas' Register of Manufacturers

16 volumes of information about manufacturing companies.
Volumes 1-8—Alphabetical listing by product.
Volumes 9-10—Alphabetical listing of manufacturing company names, addresses, telephone numbers, and local offices.
Volumes 11-16—Alphabetical company catalog information.

Information About Foreign Companies

If you'd like your next job to be overseas or with an international company, you can find much helpful information in the library. You approach these companies in the same way as you would approach U.S.-based companies.

Directory of Foreign Manufacturers in the U.S.

Alphabetical listing of U.S. manufacturing companies which are owned and operated by parent foreign firms. The information provided includes the name and address of the U.S. firm, the name and address of the foreign parent firm, and the products produced.

Directory of American Firms Operating in Foreign Countries
Alphabetical listing of the names, addresses, chief officers, products, and country operated in of U.S. firms abroad.

International Firms Directory
This lists foreign corporations.

Hoover's Handbook of World Business
This lists corporations in Asia and Europe.

Principal International Businesses
This is a comprehensive directory of international businesses.

Information Available From The Internet

Information about companies is also available through the Internet. You can use all the search engines to help you in your search for company information and company website addresses. It is not the purpose of this book to recommend websites by name, but you can type in "jobs" or "employment" or "careers" as a key word using any search engine and you will be introduced to organizations that will allow you to post your resume online. You can also usually find an organization's website by typing in the following website addresses, just substituting the name of the company you want to find, such as "Dell," for "organizationname":

http://www.organizationname.com
http:/www.organizationname.org
http://www.organizationname.net

However, sometimes finding what you are looking for takes trial and error. For example, if you wanted to find Hewlett Packard's website, you would find it either by typing in "Hewlett Packard" as a key word or by typing in http://www.HP.com. Not all website addresses are perfectly obvious, straightforward, or intuitive, but the search engines usually perform in an excellent fashion when you type in key words in a trial-and-error "surfing" or fact-finding mode.

Many people are aware of the importance of having a great resume, but most people in a job hunt don't realize just how important a cover letter can be. The purpose of the cover letter, sometimes called a **"letter of interest,"** is to introduce your resume to prospective employers.

"A Picture Is Worth a Thousand Words."

As a way of illustrating how important the cover letter can be, we have chosen to show you on the next two pages the cover letter and resume of a woman who is seeking to reenter the job market after several years of full-time motherhood. What the cover letter allows her to do is to explain why she hasn't been working recently and what is "going on" with her that is motivating her to return to the work force.

The cover letter is the critical ingredient in a job hunt such as Brandy Sullivan's because the cover letter allows her to say a lot of things that just don't "fit" on the resume. For example, she can emphasize her commitment to the financial field and stress her many skills and technical knowledge as well as her outstanding track record of advancement with one institution.

Finally, the cover letter gives her a chance to stress the outstanding character and personal values which she feels will be an asset to her next employer.

You will see on the next two pages that the cover letter gives you a chance to "get personal" with the person to whom you are writing whereas the resume is a more formal document. Even if the employer doesn't request a cover letter, we believe that it is *always* in your best interest to send a cover letter with your resume. The aim of this book is to show you examples of cover letters designed to blow doors open so that you can develop your own cover letters and increase the number of interviews you have.

A cover letter is an essential part of a job hunt.

Please do not attempt to implement a job hunt without a cover letter such as the ones you see in Part Two and Part Three of this book. A cover letter is the first impression of you, and you can influence the way an employer views you by the language and style of your letter.

Your cover letter and resume are "companion" documents.

Date

Exact Name of Person
Exact Title
Exact Name of Company
Address
City, State, Zip

Experienced financial professional seeking to reenter the work force after motherhood

Dear Exact Name of Person (or Dear Sir or Madam if answering a blind ad):

With the enclosed resume, I would like to make you aware of my interest in exploring employment with your organization.

As you will see from my resume, I have acquired a variety of data entry and customer service skills while working in a banking environment for one employer, Atlanta Citizens Bank. After 20 years with the bank, I resigned from Atlanta Citizens in 2001 when my husband received a promotion with the Prudential Company and we relocated from Atlanta to Dallas.

We have settled into our new house in Dallas, and I am eager to resume my professional career. I am a reliable hard worker with skills in numerous areas, and I can provide outstanding references from both of the branch managers with whom I worked.

You will notice from my resume that I excelled in a track record of promotion at the bank, where I began as a Savings Clerk, was promoted to Customer Service Clerk and Senior Customer Service Clerk, and then to Financial Services Representative. I played a key role in helping the bank implement numerous changes related to automation and internal restructuring over the years, and I became known as a gracious and reliable professional. I am accustomed to working in an environment in which attention to detail and accuracy at all times is required.

If you can use a versatile and dependable professional in a part-time role, I hope you will call me soon to suggest a time when we might meet and discuss your organization's needs and how I could help meet them.

Sincerely,

Brandy Sullivan

BRANDY SULLIVAN

1110½ Hay Street, Fayetteville, NC 28305 • (910) 483-6611 • preppub@aol.com

---

OBJECTIVE

To benefit an organization that can use an experienced office professional with superior communication skills and outstanding references who offers a background related to data entry and computer operations, customer service and sales, as well as accounting and collections.

EDUCATION

Completed numerous professional development and technical training programs sponsored by Atlanta Citizens Bank which provided training related to:

customer service	operations management
loan processing	legal issues and regulatory matters
sales	data entry and computer operations

COMPUTERS

Familiar with Microsoft Programs and the Windows operating system; have utilized numerous customized banking and financial programs.

EXPERIENCE

Until I resigned in 2001 when my husband was promoted and we moved from Atlanta to Dallas, I worked for one employer for 20 years and I excelled in the following track record of advancement to increasing responsibilities: Atlanta Citizens Bank.

- Can provide outstanding references from both the Branch Managers for whom I worked:
  Fortuna McDonald   910-483-6611   *Terry Bradshaw*   910-483-6611

1996-01: FINANCIAL SERVICES REPRESENTATIVE. Handled new accounts and established loans for consumer goods; was given the authority to authorize unsecured loans up to $30,000 based on prescribed formulas and guidelines.

- Became skilled at making judgments about character and credit worthiness.
- Was involved in collection during special projects as requested by branch managers.
- Input new account data for loans and performed data entry; performed audit checks.
- Handled an extensive volume of correspondence.
- Was recognized for superior leadership skills and quality performance as well as for my strong oral communication skills.
- Played a role in implementing new efficiencies and new computer applications; my opinion was sought by reengineering personnel with respect to how changes would affect customer service and client relations.
- Frequently trained new customer service personnel; prepared internal control reports which accumulated data related to cash control, balancing of vaults, and other matters.
- Became known for my flexibility and willingness to work wherever I was needed; worked well with employees and branch managers at branches of different sizes.

1986-96: SENIOR CUSTOMER SERVICE REPRESENTATIVE. After being promoted to this position, trained new Customer Service Representatives.

1983-86: CUSTOMER SERVICE REPRESENTATIVE. Handled new accounts and established accounts related to checking, saving, Certificates of Deposit (CDs), and IRAs.

1981-82: SAVINGS CLERK. In my first job in the bank, specialized in serving customers of savings accounts.

- Opened new accounts, resolved customer problems; was promoted based on my ability to make sound decisions and interact with the public in a gracious manner.

PERSONAL

Enjoy reading in my spare time. Physically fit. Excellent references.

Date

**Addressing the
Cover Letter:** Get the exact name of the person to whom you are writing. This makes your approach personal.

Exact Name of Person
Exact Title of Person
Exact Address
City, State Zip

Dear Sir or Madam:

First Paragraph: This explains why you are writing.

With the enclosed resume, I would like to acquaint you with the considerable accounting, financial, and management skills I could put to work for your organization.

Second Paragraph: You have a chance to talk about whatever you feel is your most distinguishing feature.

As you can see from the enclosed resume, I am continuing to excel in a "track record" of promotion with a food industry corporation. I began with the company as an assistant manager, was promoted to store manager, and then advanced to my present position as supervisor overseeing multiple stores in five cities.

Third Paragraph: You bring up your next most distinguishing qualities and try to sell yourself.

While utilizing my strong communication and problem-solving skills in guiding store managers at 11 locations throughout New Hampshire, I am continuously involved in financial analysis and budget preparation. You will see from my resume that I hold an A.A.S. degree in Accounting, and I am completing my Bachelor's degree. I have learned from practical work experience as well as formal courses in program analysis, auditing, budget preparation, and quantitative analysis.

Fourth Paragraph: Here you have another opportunity to reveal qualities or achievements which will impress your future employer.

My computer operation skills are highly refined. I offer proficiency with numerous popular software products including Lotus 1-2-3 and offer the ability to troubleshoot and repair various types of equipment problems. While previously serving my country for two years in the U.S. Army, I received extensive training in computer operations and telecommunications operations/repair.

Final Paragraph: He asks the employer to contact him. Make sure your reader knows what the "next step" is.

You would find me in person to be a dynamic young professional who prides myself on my ability to rapidly become a contributing member of any team. I can provide outstanding personal and professional references at the appropriate time, and I hope I will have the opportunity to meet with you in person to discuss your needs and how I might meet them.

Sincerely,

Terrell A. Ferdinand

Alternate Final Paragraph: It's more aggressive (but not too aggressive) to let the employer know that you will be calling him or her. Don't be afraid to be persistent. Employers are looking for people who know what they want to do.

Date

Exact Name of Person
Title or Position
Name of Company
Address (number and street)
Address (city, state, and zip)

Dear Exact Name of Person: (or Dear Sir or Madam if answering a blind ad)

I would appreciate an opportunity to talk with you soon about how I could contribute to your organization through my education in finance and my reputation as a hardworking, knowledgeable, and dedicated professional.

As you will see from my enclosed resume, I recently received my Bachelor of Business Administration (B.B.A.) degree with a concentration in Finance from The University of Colorado at Boulder, where I funded my college education by working full time. I am especially proud that I excelled academically while simultaneously advancing in jobs which required expertise in managing human and material resources.

The majority of my experience with the retail giant Buy Mart has been in inventory control and support activities, but I have been given opportunities to demonstrate my finance and accounting knowledge. Selected for a six-month assignment as a Billing and Data Processing Supervisor, I was involved in conducting complex audits which required strong analytical and problem-solving skills.

Although I have established a track record of accomplishments in supervisory positions since the age of 20 with this national retailer, I am exploring employment opportunities which will allow me to apply my education in finance.

If you can use a self-confident and self-motivated individual who is persistent and assertive, I hope you will contact me to suggest a time when we might meet to discuss your needs and how I might help you. Thank you in advance for your time.

Sincerely,

Gisela Myshka

CC: Michael Smith

Exact Name of Person
Title or Position
Name of Company
Address (number and street)
Address (city, state, and zip)

**THE
DIRECT APPROACH**

**Question 1: What is the
"direct approach?"**
You need to master the
technique of using the
"direct approach" in
your job hunt. By
using the direct
approach, you create
an all-purpose letter,
such as the one on this
page, which you can
send to numerous
employers introducing
yourself and your
resume. The direct
approach is a
proactive, aggressive
approach to a job
campaign, and it sure
beats waiting around
until the "ideal job"
appears in the
newspaper (and 200
other people see it,
too). Figure out the
employers you wish to
approach either (1) by
geographical area or
(2) by industry and
directly approach them
expressing your
interest in their
company. Believe it or
not, most people get
their jobs through the
direct approach!

Dear Exact Name of Person: (or Dear Sir or Madam if answering a blind ad)

I would appreciate an opportunity to talk with you soon about how I could contribute to your organization through my extensive expertise in the financial field including my recent experience as a Financial Consultant.

As you will see from my resume, I hold the Series 7, Series 63, Series 24, and Series 65 licenses and am a Registered Member of numerous exchanges and associations of securities dealers. In 2000 I left a Wall Street firm to relocate to the South, where my wife and her family live. Since 2000 I have been working for Merrill Lynch, and after my training and licensing, I established 364 accounts and produced $5 million in managed money in my first six-month period of production. Although I am excelling in my job and have been offered a branch management position in another state, I wish to remain in the Norfolk area. Since I am not under contract with Merrill Lynch, I am exploring suitable opportunities with area firms.

Much of my rapid success as a Financial Consultant stems from my background in nearly all aspects of finance, credit, and collections, in addition to my entrepreneurial experience. As Managing Director, I owned and managed a lead-based company for Dun & Bradstreet. Subsequent to that, I worked with Wall Street firms in New York City until I met my wife and she decided she wanted us to relocate to Norfolk to be near her family. I offer an extensive background in working with high net worth individuals.

I can provide outstanding personal and professional references, and I would be delighted to make myself available at your convenience for a personal interview. Thank you in advance for your professional courtesies and consideration.

Yours sincerely,

Elias Johnson III

Exact Name of Person
Title or Position
Name of Company
Address (number and street)
Address (city, state, and zip)

Dear Exact Name of Person: (or Sir or Madam if answering a blind ad)

With the enclosed resume, I would like to make you aware of my interest in joining your organization in some capacity which could utilize my extensive experience related to consumer lending, credit, and collections. I am responding to your recent advertisement for a Loan Processor. I am somewhat familiar with your organization because I had the pleasure of working by telephone last year with several of your employees on matters related to skip tracing, and I was impressed with the professionalism of your personnel. Ms. Lenette Wilson, in particular, was especially helpful to me and gave me an outstanding impression of your organization.

My family and I have recently relocated to Little Rock from El Paso, TX, where I excelled in a track record of achievement as a Collections Officer. I began working for the Ft. Bliss Credit Union as a Teller, was quickly named "Teller of the Quarter," and then was promoted to handle complex responsibilities related to collections. I received numerous Customer Service Awards and achieved an extremely low delinquency rate on repossessed vehicles while maintaining the lowest possible ratios related to bankruptcies and written-off loans. I am skilled in every aspect of collections.

In addition to excelling as a Collections Officer, I became knowledgeable of consumer lending and banking while handling money orders, bank checks, IRA withdrawals, travelers checks, savings bonds, coin exchanges, night deposit posting, handling the closing of members' accounts, filing members' open-account cards, processing returned checks, as well as processing and filming checks to National Credit Union Headquarters.

If you can use a hardworking young professional who offers a reputation as a thorough, persistent, and highly motivated individual, I hope you will contact me to suggest a time when we might meet to discuss your needs and goals and how I could help you achieve them. I would be delighted to discuss the private details of my salary history with you in person, and I can provide outstanding personal and professional references.

Sincerely,

Athena Zibart

NAME DROPPING

Question 2: If I want to "drop a name" in a letter, what's the best way?
It's nice to play the "who you know" game socially and in business, and it can help you get in the door for interviews, too. If a current employee has recommended that you write to the organization, or if you have worked with members of the organization on some project, you can "drop a name" gracefully. In so doing, you will add warmth to a cover letter that will exude a very personalized tone.

Date

Exact Name of Person
Title or Position
Name of Company
Address (number and street)
Address (city, state, and zip)

APPLYING FOR INTERNAL OPENINGS

Question 3: How do I apply for internal openings?
We recommend sacrificing no formality when applying for internal promotions. As you see from this cover letter, you still need to "sell" your interest and qualifications, even when the insiders know you.

Dear Exact Name of Person: (or Dear Sir or Madam if answering a blind ad)

With the enclosed resume, I would like to make you aware of my interest in the position of **Financial Management Analyst II with the Vermont Department of Revenue.** As you will see from my enclosed resume, I offer a background as a seasoned accounting professional with exceptional analytical, communication, and organizational skills. In my current job, I perform essentially as a Financial Management Analyst in my role as a Field Auditor and Revenue Officer with the Vermont Department of Revenue.

With the Department of Revenue, I have advanced in a track record of increasing responsibilities. In my current position as a Field Auditor, I analyze financial reports of businesses and individuals, reconciling various general ledgers as well as investment and checking accounts in order to accurately determine tax liability. Earlier as a Revenue Officer, I consulted with taxpayers to assist them in determining the validity of deductions and calculating the amount of individual income tax owed. In both of these positions, I trained my coworkers, sharing my extensive knowledge of Internal Revenue Service and Vermont Department of Revenue codes and laws while educating department personnel on correct procedures related to professional auditing and collections.

I hold an Associate of Applied Science degree in Accounting from Central Berkshire Community College and a Bachelor of Science in Business Administration from the University of Oregon at Portland.

Please favorably consider my application for this internal opening, and please also consider my history of dedicated service to the Vermont Department of Revenue. I feel certain that I could excel in this job and could be a valuable asset to the department.

Sincerely,

Kevin Strafford

BY FAX TO: Human Resources Department
910-483-2439
Reference Job Code XYZ 9034

Dear Sir or Madam:

With the enclosed resume, I would like to make you aware of my interest in employment as a Financial Consultant. Grayson Timmons, one of your Financial Consultants, has recommended that I talk with you because he feels that I could excel in the position.

As you will see from my enclosed resume, I offer proven marketing and sales skills along with a reputation as a highly motivated individual with exceptional problem-solving abilities. Shortly after joining my current firm as a Mortgage Loan Specialist, I was named Outstanding Loan Officer of the month through my achievement in generating more than $20,000 in fees.

I believe much of my professional success so far has been due to my highly motivated nature and creative approach to my job. For example, when I began working for my current employer, I developed and implemented the concept of a postcard that communicated a message which the consumer found intriguing. The concept has been so successful that it has been one of the main sources of advertisements in our office and the concept has been imitated by other offices in the company.

In addition to my track record of excelling in the highly competitive financial services field, I gained valuable sales experience in earlier jobs selling copying equipment and sleep systems. I have also applied my strong leadership and sales ability in the human services field, when I worked in adult probation services. I am very proud of the fact that many troubled individuals with whom I worked told me that my ability to inspire and motivate them was the key to their becoming productive citizens.

If you can use a creative and motivated self-starter who could enhance your goals for market share and profitability, I hope you will contact me to suggest a time when we could meet in person to discuss your needs and goals and how I could meet them. I can provide strong personal and professional references at the appropriate time.

Yours sincerely,

Cheri Garcia

Date

TO: John Smith
    Elaine Bryant
    Meredith Kleinfield

**A LETTER OF
LEAVE TAKING**

**Question 5: How do I resign
— gracefully?**
A letter of resignation
can be a highly
emotional experience,
both for the person
sending it and for the
individuals receiving it. It
gives you a formal
opportunity to declare
your last day on the job
and to thank appropriate
people.

Dear Friends and Valued Colleagues:

It is with much sadness as well as with great personal affection for all of you that I wish to inform you that I will be leaving the Ford Motor Company. My final departure date can be worked out according to your wishes, but I would suggest Wednesday, December 20, 2001.

A sales position has become available at *The Schofield Gazette* and I believe the hours of employment will be better suited to my needs as a single parent.

Because I have been employed with Ford Motor Company since 1995, I feel as though I am "leaving home," and in that nostalgic frame of mind, it is my desire to tell you how much I have appreciated your training me, helping me, and giving me opportunities to try new things and gain new skills. I am very truly grateful to you, and I hope you know that I always gave my best effort.

I can assure you that I will continue to be a highly productive source of referrals for you even when I am gone, because I believe wholeheartedly in the products and the product line we all have represented. If I can ever help any of you individually in any way, too, please let me know.

In the meantime, please accept my sincere thanks for all the kindnesses and professional courtesies you have shown me.

Yours sincerely,

Mary Anne Murphy

Date

Exact Name of Person
Title or Position
Name of Company
Address (number and street)
Address (city, state, and zip)

Dear Exact Name of Person:

LETTER OF RESIGNATION

Question 6: How do I resign—gracefully?
Here's an example of a letter that will be an emotional experience for the people receiving it as it was for the person who signed it. Employers are often not happy when you leave them, so a great letter of resignation can ease the hurt.

It is with genuine sadness and many mixed feelings that I must inform you that I will be resigning from my position at Cranford, Sweeney & Co., CPAs, effective July 26.

The firm of Hill, Gilbert & Wilkins in Spokane, also a public accounting firm, has offered me a position as a CPA at a salary of nearly $50,000 annually, and I feel it is a time in my life when I must move on.

Leaving the firm of Cranford, Sweeney & Co., CPAs, is very difficult for me professionally and emotionally. After I passed the CPA Exam, you gave me my first job in the public accounting field, and I have thoroughly enjoyed the family atmosphere coupled with the professional style of both you and Mr. Cranford. You have taught me so much about how to solve problems, how to work more efficiently, and how to handle difficult clients. I am deeply grateful for your encouragement, professional mentoring, and strong personal example.

Although the decision to leave Cranford, Sweeney & Co., CPAs, is difficult, I really feel that I have no choice. As a single parent who provides full financial support of my daughter, I am driven by the desire to provide a gracious standard of living for my small family. I will be placing her in a Christian school in Spokane so that she can continue learning in the same Christian environment as she has had in Tacoma.

I hope you know that I have always given 110% to your firm in terms of my financial knowledge, intelligence, and problem-solving ability, and I hope you feel that I have made contributions to its reputation. I feel I am separating more from a family than from an employer, and I felt I wanted to put this information in writing to you as a first step because getting the words out verbally would be a difficult emotional experience for me.

Thank you from the bottom of my heart for all you have done for me professionally and personally.

Yours sincerely,

Elizabeth J. Ritchie

In this section, you will find resumes and cover letters of students who generally have more education than experience in the financial field. Students often have experience such as "Tutor" or "Youth Program Assistant" on the resume they use to obtain their first "real" job in the financial field. Students are selling mostly "potential" to do something they've never done before. If you are a student, don't be afraid to show off a high GPA. Employers know that a high GPA doesn't always translate into high productivity on the job, but high grade point averages are what recruiters often look for when they are recruiting individuals with little or no experience in the field.

Junior professionals have advantages over more experienced professionals.
In a job hunt, junior professionals often have an advantage over their more experienced counterparts. Junior professionals have usually not made a 15-year commitment to an industry or type of work, so prospective employers often view them as "more trainable" and "more coachable" than their seniors. This makes it easier for the junior manager to "change careers" and transfer skills to other industries.

Junior professionals may also have disadvantages compared to their seniors.
Almost by definition, the junior manager is less tested and less experienced than senior or mid-level professionals, so the resume and cover letter of the junior manager may often have to "sell" his or her potential to do something he or she has never done before. Lack of experience in the field she wants to enter can be a stumbling block to the junior manager, but remember that many employers believe that someone who has excelled in one field can excel in many other fields.

Some advice to junior professionals...
If senior professionals could give junior professionals a piece of advice about careers, here's what they would say: Manage your career and don't stumble from job to job in an incoherent pattern. Try to find work that interests you, and then identify prosperous industries which need work performed of the type you want to do. Learn early in your working life that a great resume and cover letter can blow doors open for you and help you maximize your salary.

Junior professionals are often still experimenting in their careers, and they have more freedom than older job hunters to try new fields and change careers. They are not "locked in" to a functional specialty.

Date

Exact Name of Person
Title or Position
Name of Company
Address (no., street)
Address (city, state, zip)

ACCOUNTING MAJOR

Dear Exact Name of Person: (or Dear Sir or Madam if answering a blind ad.)

Employers know that high grades do not always translate into exceptional work performance but, since there are no other certain predictors of future performance, they look for good grades. That's why this professional is emphasizing her outstanding academic track record.

I would appreciate an opportunity to talk with you soon about how I could contribute to your organization through my education in accounting as well as through my excellent math skills, adaptability, and reputation as a fast learner.

As you will see from my enclosed resume, I will receive my B.S. in Accounting from the University of North Carolina at Chapel Hill in December. I earned a full scholarship on the basis of my potential to excel academically and high SAT scores and have succeeded in maintaining a perfect 4.0 GPA throughout my college career. I was singled out to receive the Dean's Award for achieving the highest GPA of any student in the School of Business and Finance.

My work history outside the accounting field reveals my high level of creativity, resourcefulness, and adaptability.

Recently as a tutor in the university's writing center, I have been able to teach written communication skills and computer knowledge. My computer experience includes the most commonly used programs including Word, Lotus 1-2-3, and dBase IV, and I offer a proven ability to rapidly master new software and operating systems.

I am a highly motivated individual with a reputation for outstanding communication, motivational, and organizational skills along a high level of enthusiasm and energy.

I hope you will welcome my call soon to arrange a brief meeting at your convenience to discuss your current and future needs and how I might serve them. Thank you in advance for your time.

Sincerely yours,

Page Jasanoff

PAGE JASANOFF

1110½ Hay Street, Fayetteville, NC 28305 • preppub@aol.com • (910) 483-6611

OBJECTIVE

To contribute to an organization in need of a mature professional who can offer a keen eye for detail and high level of initiative as well as an education in accounting, excellent math skills, and the enthusiasm and energy needed to achieve superior results.

EDUCATION

Bachelor of Science (B.S.) degree in Accounting, University of North Carolina, Chapel Hill, NC; December 2001.

- Received the Chancellor's Scholarship Award, a full scholarship given on the basis of my SAT scores and potential to excel academically.
- Have maintained a perfect 4.0 GPA throughout my college career.
- Was honored with the Dean's Award for achieving the highest GPA of any student in the School of Business and Economics.
- Earned acceptance in Delta Mu Delta National Honor Sorority in recognition of my academic excellence.
- Completed specialized course work including the following:

cost accounting	marketing	auditing
accounting theory	tax accounting	business law
money and banking	fund accounting	corporate finance

EXPERIENCE

TUTOR. University of North Carolina, Chapel Hill, NC (2000-present).
Instructed other students in the university's writing center where assistance was given in the areas of essay writing, conducting research, and using computers.
- Built on my own knowledge of Word, Lotus, and Excel software programs by helping others increase their skills and familiarity with the software and equipment.

PIANIST. Grayson Methodist Church, Grayson, NC (1994-present).
Offer my musical talents to provide the church congregation with piano music during regularly scheduled services and for practices as well as occasionally for funerals.
- Used my musical knowledge and creativity to write music after listening to tapes when the sheet music was not available for a particular song.

BOOKKEEPER. Harwicke & Klingel Accountants, Chapel, Hill, NC (1999-present).
Learned the value of being professional, tactful, and courteous helping out in this busy accounting firm for a month over the Christmas holiday while filling in for regular employees on vacation.
- Demonstrated that I am capable of quickly mastering a job with no formal training and with no one to show me the way things "should" be done.

SPECIAL SKILLS

Type 50 wpm.
Familiar with Word and Excel; working knowledge of Lotus 1-2-3 and dBase IV.

LANGUAGES

Completely bilingual—speak, read, and write both English and German fluently.

PERSONAL

Well-organized individual with a creative flair. Offer a very outgoing and friendly personality. Enjoy helping others learn, live, and grow. Eager to tackle new challenges.

References available upon request

Date

Exact Name of Person
Title or Position
Name of Company
Address (no., street)
Address (city, state, zip)

Dear Exact Name of Person: (or Dear Sir or Madam if answering a blind ad.)

I would appreciate an opportunity to talk with you soon about how I could contribute to your organization through my proven abilities related to customer service, sales, management, and finance.

In the process of completing my B.S. degree in Economics with concentrations in Banking and Finance, I worked during the summers and Christmas seasons and held part-time jobs throughout the school year. While juggling those part-time jobs with a rigorous academic curriculum, I also found time to become a respected campus leader and was elected Treasurer of my residence hall in my junior year and President in my senior year. Although I am just 21 years old, I have been told often that I am "mature beyond my years." I am known for my responsible and hardworking nature.

In one summer job as an Assistant to a Financial Analyst with Merrill Lynch, I gained exposure to the operations of the stock market and acquired hands-on experience in working with customers of various financial services and financial instruments. I obtained my current job as Customer Service Representative with Blockbuster Video because the company created a position for me in Dalton when I moved from Albany, where I had become a valued employee and was a major contributor to achieving the fourth highest Christmas sales volume of all stores in the chain. I have been encouraged by both Merrill Lynch and Blockbuster to seek employment there after college graduation, and I feel certain I could become a valued part of your organization within a short period of time, too.

You would find me in person to be an outgoing individual who prides myself on my ability to remain poised in all customer service situations. I can provide outstanding personal and professional references, and I would cheerfully relocate and travel extensively according to your needs.

I hope you will call or write me soon to suggest a time convenient for us to meet and discuss your current and future needs and how I might serve them. Thank you in advance for you time.

Sincerely yours,

Daryl Urbanowicz

DARYL URBANOWICZ

1110½ Hay Street, Fayetteville, NC 28305 • preppub@aol.com • (910) 483-6611

OBJECTIVE	To contribute to an organization that can use a hardworking young professional who offers proven leadership ability and management potential along with a congenial personality, outstanding communication skills, and an ability to relate well to anyone.
EDUCATION	**Bachelor of Science (B.S.) degree** with a major in **Economics** and concentrations in **Banking** and **Finance**, Dalton College, Dalton, GA, 2001. • Worked part-time during the school year as well as every summer and Christmas season in order to finance my education; became a highly valued employee of every organization in which I worked and can provide outstanding references. • Was a popular and respected campus leader; was elected **President** of my residence hall, Bryant Hall, in my senior year and **Treasurer** of Bryant Hall in my junior year. • Active member of the Economics/Finance Club and the Illusions Modeling Club.
COMPUTERS	Familiar with MS Word, WordPerfect, Lotus 1-2-3 and PowerPoint. • Offer an ability to rapidly master new software and operating systems.
EXPERIENCE	**CUSTOMER SERVICE REPRESENTATIVE.** Blockbuster Video, Dalton and Albany, GA (1997-present). Worked in the Albany Blockbuster Store part-time while going to college and was commended for playing a key role in helping the Albany store achieve the fourth highest sales volume in the chain during the 2000 Christmas season; when I transferred to Dalton College to complete my degree in economics, Blockbuster Video persuaded me to stay with the company and found a similar spot for me in Dalton. • Handle thousands of dollars daily utilizing computer-assisted cash registers. • Train new personnel hired by the company; earned a reputation as a polite and gracious individual while assisting dozens of people daily in video selection. • Have been told I have a bright future in management with Blockbuster Corporation; have been encouraged to enter the company's management trainee program. **RESIDENCE MANAGER.** Bryant Hall at Dalton College, Dalton, GA (1998-present). In a part-time job simultaneous with the one above, work closely with the dorm director to ensure the efficient administration of this residence hall housing 400 students. • Supervise the conduct and activities of students living the dorm, and pride myself on setting an example for them in terms of my own morals and actions. • Solved a wide range of maintenance and administrative problems while also counseling students with financial matters and personal problems ranging from depression and loneliness to poor academic performance and insufficient motivation. • Acquired experience in mentoring others, most of whom were older than I am. **ASSISTANT TO FINANCIAL ANALYST.** Merrill Lynch, Albany, GA (Summer 1997). Was the "right arm" of a financial analyst with this worldwide investment company; prepared documents designed to persuade potential clients to transact business with Merrill Lynch, and also processed and filed accounts of current customers. • Gained insight into how selling and customer service occur within a brokerage firm. • Scored very high on a mock test administered by my supervisor to test my knowledge of stock market issues and facts. • Was commended for my hard work and financial aptitude, and was encouraged to seek employment with Merrill Lynch upon college graduation.
PERSONAL	Am skilled at remaining calm and courteous in all customer service situations.

Exact Name of Person
Title or Position
Name of Company
Address (no., street)
Address (city, state, zip)

ECONOMICS MAJOR

Dear Exact Name of Person: (or Dear Sir or Madam if answering a blind ad.)

Student resumes often have lengthy Education sections, since much of the experience and many of the honors thus far are related to the academic environment.

I would appreciate an opportunity to talk with you soon about how I could contribute to your organization through my education and knowledge in the area of economics.

In the process of completing my B.S. degree in Economics, I worked in a variety of jobs which permitted me to refine my communication and interpersonal skills. I enjoy helping others and you will notice that many of my summer and part-time jobs were in the social service and mental health field. I have learned the disciplines involved in teamwork, and I am eager to apply my hardworking nature within a professional team.

You will notice that I have been the recipient of numerous sports honors. Even in high school, I received the MVP award and was considered the star of the women's volleyball and basketball teams. In college, too, I earned numerous awards for athletic abilities and was named an All-American in two sports. I have learned much about people on the playing field and basketball court, and I am confident I can apply that knowledge for the benefit of my employer.

I can provide outstanding personal and professional references, and I would cheerfully relocate and travel extensively according to your needs.

I hope you will call or write me soon to suggest a time convenient for us to meet and discuss your current and future needs and how I might serve them. Thank you in advance for you time.

Sincerely yours,

Elizabeth Adams

ELIZABETH ADAMS

1110½ Hay Street, Fayetteville, NC 28305　　•　　preppub@aol.com　　•　　(910) 483-6611

OBJECTIVE　　To offer my ability to manage time and human resources as well as my organizational and planning skills and attention to detail to an organization that can use a fast learner who excels in relating to people from diverse backgrounds, ages, and socioeconomic levels.

EDUCATION　　Earned a **Bachelor's degree in Economics** from Hendrix College, Conway, AR, 2001; graduated **cum laude**.
- Was honored with a Chancellor's Award of Merit in recognition of my accomplishments in sports, academics, and family activities.
- Nominated by my peers, was elected president of the Economics and Finance Club, managed all funds for the Economics and Finance Club while also planning, implementing, and overseeing the club's fundraising activities.
- Earned numerous awards and honors for my athletic abilities as a member of the university's basketball and volleyball teams.
- Was named to the **All-Conference Teams,** honored as **Most Valuable Player,** and an **All-American** in both sports.
- Participated in a work-study program in a university office where my responsibilities included typing tests and research papers while gaining strong computer skills.
- Was nominated **"Woman of the Year"** in sports.

EXPERIENCE　　*Gained experience in positions where "people skills" and the ability to manage time and deal with problems professionally and calmly were of major importance while attending school full-time and working in demanding summer jobs to partially finance my education:*
YOUTH PROGRAM ASSISTANT. Workforce Temporary Agency, Conway, AR (summer, 2000). Worked as part of a team of professionals providing care for three mentally handicapped children while ensuring that daily care was provided according to policies.

MENTAL HEALTH TECHNICIAN. P.C. Contract Management Services, Conway, AR (summers, 1999 and 1998). Provided direct care to five mentally handicapped adults with an emphasis on implementing and carrying out behavior plans and behavior modification techniques.
- Taught self-help and independent living skills as well as maintaining documentation on each client's progress or lack of visible progress.
- Protected the well-being and legal rights of my clients.

HABILITATION TECHNICIAN. MSC of Arkansas and Procomm, Bitsburg, AR (summer, 1997). Provided direct care to profoundly mentally retarded clients; handled the expense accounts used in operating the group homes these clients lived in.
- Applied my knowledge of the legal rights of this class of clients and provided support for them so that their well being and legal rights were protected.
- Transported clients for and from activities such as recreational and social outings as well as medical and counseling appointments.

COMPUTERS　　Windows operating system with software including WordPerfect, Lotus, and MS Word.

ATHLETIC HONORS　　Graduated from Concordia Senior High School, Concordia, MI, 1997.
- Was the "star" of both the women's basketball and volleyball teams.
- Won the MVP Award for the Concordia District schools, 1996.

PERSONAL　　Am a highly self disciplined individual who always strives to give my greatest effort.

Exact Name of Person
Exact Title
Exact Name of Company
Address
City, State, Zip

FINANCE
MAJOR

Notice in the Education
section how this young
professional shows off a
team project which has
helped him refine his
analytical, problem-
solving, and strategic
thinking skills.

Dear Exact Name of Person (or Dear Sir or Madam if answering a blind ad):

With the enclosed resume, I would like to make you aware of the knowledge related to finance which I could put to work for you.

While completing my B.S. degree in Finance, I played a key role as a member of a team which analyzed the Harley-Davidson company and made strategic and operational recommendations for the company and industry as a whole. I have earned a reputation as an insightful analyst and problem-solver and I am certain I could make a significant contribution to the bottom line of a company that can use an astute young financier.

In jobs which I held to finance my college degree, I worked in several roles within Macy's Department Store, where I excelled in handling responsibilities as a Loss Prevention Detective, Supervisor, and handler of cash accounting. Although Macy's has strongly encouraged me to remain with the corporation after college graduation and seek internal promotions, I have decided to explore other opportunities.

I can assure you in advance that I have an excellent reputation and would quickly become a valuable asset to your organization. Please contact me if my considerable abilities interest you, and I will gladly make myself available for a personal interview at your convenience.

Sincerely,

David Yuen

DAVID YUEN

1110½ Hay Street, Fayetteville, NC 28305 • preppub@aol.com • (910) 483-6611

OBJECTIVE

To offer my education in finance as well as my analytical, sales, and communication skills to an organization that can benefit from my strong interest in financial planning and banking as well as my personal reputation for integrity, high moral standards, and a strong work ethic.

EDUCATION

Completing a **Bachelor's degree in Finance,** The University of Kentucky, Lexington, KY; degree expected spring 2002.
- Placed on the university's Dean's List in recognition of my academic accomplishments.
- Received an "A" on an intensive class project: performed a company analysis on Harley-Davidson including keeping records, analyzing price and volume data as well as technical data, gathering and analyzing information about the industry, and making determinations on the economic outlook for the company and industry.
- Completed specialized course work such as Finance 330 (principles of finance, stock valuation, options, etc.) and Finance 331 (real estate investing).

EXPERIENCE

Learned to manage time wisely while maintaining at least a 3.4 GPA in my college career and excelling in demanding part-time jobs including this track record of accomplishments with Macy's Department Store, Lexington, KY:
LOSS PREVENTION DETECTIVE. (2001-present). In only 18 months with the company, have progressed to the highest level available to a part-time employee based on my maturity, willingness to take on hard work, and communication skills.
- Increased apprehensions of shoplifters 50%, thereby greatly reducing losses from theft.
- Displayed the ability to remain calm and in control and act as an arbitrator under intense conditions.
- Provided security for the store premises, researched discrepancies in cash accounts, and generated surveillance programs.
- Learned the importance of confidentiality while guarding privileged information.

FRONT-LINE SUPERVISOR. (2000). Supervised approximately 50 employees in order to ensure that customers received the highest quality of service and satisfaction.
- Opened cash drawers and initiated changeovers while register contents were transferred as well as changing large denominations of bills for smaller ones as needed.
- Approved refunds, lay-a-ways, and purchases by associates.
- Conducted new employee orientation which included such areas as cash handling procedures, customer service techniques, and company policy.
- Was honored as **"Associate of the Quarter"** by management and other associates.

CASH OFFICE ASSOCIATE. (1999). Was given the opportunity to apply my knowledge gained in college in a real-life situation while handling day-to-day retail store office activities.

CASHIER. (1998). Became skilled in handling refunds and sales accurately and quickly while becoming responsible for large amounts of cash transactions.
- Was known for my ability to assist customers as well as my keen eye for possible theft.

TRAINING

Completed several seminars and training programs including a Lotus 1-2-3 workshop and loss prevention training (detecting losses, detaining suspects, and making reports).

PERSONAL

Keep up with stock market and read *"The Wall Street Journal"* regularly. Familiar with Windows, WordPerfect, and the Internet. Graduated from high school with honors.

Date

Exact Name of Person
Exact Title
Exact Name of Company
Address
City, State, Zip

Dear Exact Name of Person: (or Dear Sir or Madam if answering a blind ad):

With the enclosed resume, I would like to make you aware of my interest in seeking employment opportunities with your company and to acquaint you with my background as an articulate, well-educated, and mature young professional.

As you will see from my resume, I will be graduating from the University of Toledo in December 2001 and will receive a B.S. in Finance. Recognized on the university's Dean's List for my academic accomplishments, I have excelled in specialized course work which has included marketing, financial, personnel, and accounting management. Additional classes have covered the areas of international business, entrepreneurial activities, Management Information Systems, and managerial negotiations.

This semester I am involved in a team effort to develop a business plan, including a complete financial analysis and financial projections as well as marketing plans, for a new business. Working together, we are developing plans and standards for a successful entrepreneurial effort.

Presently refining sales and customer service skills in a part-time job in retail sales, I have become effective at managing my time productively while attending college full time. While handling sales and financial transactions, I excel at providing courteous and helpful assistance to customers. In an earlier job, I became experienced in dealing with the public with patience and courtesy while operating photographic equipment, handling cash transactions, and taking inventories of supplies and equipment. I was rehired each year for this seasonal job on the basis of my maturity and "people skills."

If you can use a dependable, mature, and reliable young professional with a reputation as a good listener who enjoys helping others, I hope you will welcome my call soon when I try to arrange a brief meeting to discuss your goals and how my background might serve your needs. I can provide outstanding references at the appropriate time.

Sincerely,

Ming Kao

MING KAO

1110½ Hay Street, Fayetteville, NC 28305   •   preppub@aol.com   •   (910) 483-6611

OBJECTIVE   To benefit an organization that can use an articulate, resourceful, and reliable young professional who offers a proven ability to deal effectively with people in team settings and business situations while also demonstrating initiative when working independently.

EDUCATION   **B.A. in Finance**, University of Toledo, Toledo, OH; December 2001.
- During fall semester 2001, am developing a Business Plan for my entrepreneurship course as part of a team; our project is to start a drive-through coffee shop and develop standards which could be copied by small business owners; the plan includes a complete financial analysis and financial projections.
- Have placed on the university Dean's List twice with a GPA above 3.5.
- Transferred from Toledo State University after changing my major.

Graduated from Toledo High School, Toledo, OH, December 1997.
- As a journalist for *The Bulldog* newspaper, produced copy for one of the state's largest high schools; was a sports reporter.
- Placed on the Honor Roll and was a member of the National Honor Society.
- Was a member of Tri Chi service society, the Spanish Club, and basketball team.

COMPUTERS   Working knowledge of Word, Excel, and Access.

LANGUAGES   Basic working knowledge of Spanish.

EXPERIENCE   **SALES REPRESENTATIVE & CASHIER.** The Shoe Department, Toledo, OH (2000-present). Am refining time management and customer service skills working approximately 26 hours a week for this chain store where my main responsibilities are to operate the automated cash register system, stock shoes and accessories, and assist customers in finding the correct fit and style.
- As a business major, have been applying my knowledge to make suggestions about changes which would allow the store to operate more efficiently and which are being considered for implementation by management.
- Upon college graduation, have been encouraged to consider the company's management training program but have decided to pursue other options.
- Am gaining valuable sales experience as well as an opportunity to make practical applications of what has been learned in the college classroom.

PHOTOGRAPHER and **CASHIER.** Bluebird Photography Studio, Cleveland, OH (seasonal work and summers). While still in high school, worked in a seasonal job taking children's portraits operating a stationary camera.
- Impressed the owners with my maturity and pride in the quality of my work and was rehired each year.
- Collected payments and operated a cash register.
- Took inventories of photographic and office supplies.

PERSONAL   Attend Sylvester Memorial Baptist Church; Youth Choir member. Am highly conscious of environmental issues. Offer a reputation as a good listener who enjoys helping others. Excellent personal and professional references are available upon request.

Date

Exact Name of Person
Exact Title
Exact Name of Company
Address
City, State, Zip

Dear Exact Name of Person (or Dear Sir or Madam if answering a blind ad):

TRUST MANAGEMENT WITH MINOR IN FINANCIAL PLANNING

This young professional is seeking his first job in trust management in the financial services arena. He will probably approach banks and other financial institutions including mortgage bankers, credit unions, and savings and loan associations.

With the enclosed resume, I would like to express my interest in exploring employment opportunities with your company.

While earning my B.B.A. degree, I excelled academically and received a prestigious scholarship. The program I attended has one of the strongest concentrations in Trust Management in the country, and I have become knowledgeable of financial planning and trust instruments.

You will see from my resume that I have worked since I was a youth. I began working as a farm worker at the age of 11 or 12, and I quickly advanced into management roles which made me responsible for migrant workers.

If you can use a young professional with strong communication and analytical skills, I hope you will contact me to suggest a time when we might meet to discuss your needs and how I might serve them.

Sincerely,

Liam McDonald

LIAM MCDONALD

1110½ Hay Street, Fayetteville, NC 28305 • preppub@aol.com • (910) 483-6611

OBJECTIVE

I want to contribute to a financial institution that can use a dedicated young professional who seeks a career in personal trust management with an emphasis in estate planning and investments.

EDUCATION

Completing **Bachelor of Business Administration (BBA) in Trust Management** with a Minor in Financial Planning and a Trust certificate from Beloit College, Beloit, WI, May 2000.
- Excelled academically with a 3.55 GPA in my major.

Scholarships:
- Received the Mason Williams Scholarship valued at approximately $13,000 because of my outstanding academic record in high school.
- Also received the President's Scholarship valued at $600.00.

Extracurricular Activities:
- Member of the Trust Club.
- Member of the Society for the Advancement of Management.
- Participant in the Stock Market Game.

Courses:
- Courses have included Estate and Gift Tax, Qualified Retirement Plans, Estate Planning, Management Trust Departments, Trust Law, and Investments.

EXPERIENCE

FARM WORKER. Donald Produce Farms, Carson, WI (1998-present). As the son of a successful entrepreneur in the agricultural business, worked on a farm throughout my childhood and learned the business.
- Established "from scratch" a business which I operated for profit during the summer months during high school and college; made a profit of $15,000 annually while only working a few months a year.
- Developed a niche business which concentrated on chemical applications to improve the production of produce, and which made volume sales to retailers.
- Personally approached retailers; handled all sales and marketing for the business.
- Refined my time management and strategic planning skills.

FARM EMPLOYEE. Donald Farms, Carson, WI (1992-present). Since childhood, have been actively involved in my father's business, and have gained valuable management skills while assisting him in the management of a multifaceted family farm which includes 2,500 head of swine and 130 cattle.
Handled veterinary work in addition to being trained in management skills.

COMPUTERS

Proficient in using computers including Lotus 1-2-3, Word, and Excel.

PERSONAL

Single and willing to relocate or travel to meet the needs of my employer. Can provide outstanding personal and professional references upon request. Enjoy hunting, snow skiing, fishing, and spending time with family and friends.

In this section, you will find resumes and cover letters of professionals who have somewhat more experience than the professionals in the previous section. You will meet individuals who have already invested considerable time in one or more functional areas of finance, such as accounting. Looking over their resumes may give you some ideas about the types of work you'd like to perform in the financial area.

If you have been working in a certain area for some time and have begun to feel that the work is getting "stale" or repetitious, you may feel the urge to diversify your base of knowledge and find new and different pastures. Many of the people in this section transferred skills from one area of finance to another, or from one industry to another.

Need a little encouragement to try something new in the financial field? Looking over the resumes and cover letters in this section may give you clues and insights into what you'd like to do next.

Most people have three distinctly different careers in their lifetimes. It's important to keep yourself stimulated mentally and often that means diversifying into new areas of finance.

Date

Exact Name of Person
Title or Position
Name of Company
Address (number and street)
Address (city, state, and zip)

Dear Exact Name of Person: (or Dear Sir or Madam if answering a blind ad.)

This is a young professional who had advanced to an accounting position with the Army and Air Force Exchange Service in Germany. She left her great job because her husband got transferred. Now she is in a small town where accounting jobs are not plentiful. PREP tried to make her resume and cover letter as versatile as possible since she may have to take a job outside her accounting field.

With the enclosed resume, I would like to make you aware of my strong accounting, office management, and finance experience as well as my desire to put my expertise to work within your organization.

With a background which includes knowledge of numerous software programs as well as experience in both retail and industrial accounting, I have become known as a versatile and adaptable young professional. As you will see from my enclosed resume, my most recent experience was as an Accounting Manager for the Army and Air Force Exchange System (AAFES), the retail store system which supports military personnel and families throughout the world. After receiving several performance awards as a Lead Accounting Clerk, I was promoted ahead of older and more experienced personnel to supervise 52 employees and provide financial advice, guidance, and support for 105 facilities.

My husband has recently resigned from military service, and we are making our permanent home in Bessemer, Oregon, where he grew up and where most of his family lives. I am eager to make Bessemer my personal and professional home, too. A dedicated hard worker known for attention to detail and unflagging commitment to excellence, I can provide outstanding references. It is my hope that I can find an employer to whom I can make a long-term contribution.

I hope you will welcome my call soon to arrange a brief meeting to discuss your current and future needs and how I might serve them. Thank you in advance for your time.

Sincerely,

Orietta Hallock

ORIETTA HALLOCK

1110½ Hay Street, Fayetteville, NC 28305 • preppub@aol.com • (910) 483-6611

OBJECTIVE	To offer a reputation as a highly knowledgeable and dedicated manager with expertise in finance and accounting to an organization which can benefit from my attention to detail, initiative, enthusiasm, and dedication to excellence.
EDUCATION	Completed schooling in Germany which is the equivalent of two years of college coursework in the U.S., 1989-91. Earned certification as a commercial employee in a two-year apprenticeship program with a concentration in economics and social studies, Chamber of Industry and Commerce, Wuerzburg and Schweinfurt, Germany, 1993.
EXPERIENCE	*Advanced to a managerial role in an international organization, AAFES (the Army and Air Force Exchange System), based on my knowledge, skills, and abilities, Wuerzburg, Germany:* **ACCOUNTING MANAGER.** (2000-present). Officially evaluated as a key player in the implementation of new programs and consolidation of support facilities, was promoted to this job supervising 52 employees in March 1997 ahead of more experienced employees.

* Provided financial advice and guidance to 105 facilities while inspecting and balancing their accounts as well as reconciling accounts payable and receivable.
* Earned praise for my attention to detail and time management skills while handling the hiring and training of personnel for a new accounting office at an outlying site.
* Attended corporate-sponsored workshops on subjects which included EEO (Equal Employment Opportunity) for managers and how to deal with a diverse work force.
* Was recognized with a second "Sustained Superior Accomplishment Award" for my role in implementing and supervising four accounting offices.

LEAD ACCOUNTING CLERK. (1996-00). During a period of rapid change due to military post closings and the consolidation of many services, earned several superior service awards in recognition of my support for a multimillion-dollar retail store and 105 additional stores.

* Became aware of problems in the Purchase-in-Transit procedures which led to their identification by the national headquarters and resulted in their revamping.
* Received a "Sustained Superior Accomplishment Award" as well as Service and Excellence Awards in recognition of my professionalism, sound judgment, and five years of devoted service.

Began as a student apprentice and was hired on a permanent basis by Weifenbach of Germany, a mechanical engineering company:
PAYROLL AND ACCOUNTING SPECIALIST. (1995). Assigned to the payroll office to assist in payroll and direct labor cost accounting, used automated data processing systems while adjusting differences using the attendance lists and production figures to find and correct discrepancies.

* Learned procedures for calculating large corporation payroll and labor costs.
* **INTERN.** (1991-94). Excelled in a training program which acquainted me with the inner workings of every type of commercial business in a large industrial firm from purchasing, to operations, to sales, to financial control.

PERSONAL	Bilingual in German and English. Supportive and concerned manager.

Date

Exact Name of Person
Exact Title
Exact Name of Company
Address
City, State, Zip

ACCOUNT MANAGER

Dear Exact Name of Person (or Dear Sir or Madam if answering a blind ad):

Notice the fourth paragraph. In a gracious way, this junior professional is announcing her desire to become a part of an organization which will use her in financial management roles. Here's a tip about employers: they like people who know what they want to do, because if you are in a job doing what you want to do, you are more likely to excel — and make money for the company.

I would appreciate an opportunity to talk with you soon about how I could contribute to your organization through my demonstrated skills in financial management as well as my exceptional communication, organizational, and time management abilities.

As you will see from my enclosed resume, I am presently excelling as a Corporate Account Manager with Quality Rent-a-Car. When I assumed responsibility for corporate accounts, monthly sales were an average of $45,000. Due to my initiative in developing new accounts and maximizing existing accounts, sales have risen to $160,000 per month, and I have received numerous awards for sales excellence.

Joining this national company three weeks after graduating from college, I quickly mastered all aspects of branch management, customer service, sales, and administration during the management training program. As Assistant Branch Manager, I was the top seller in the region in both outside and inside sales, and my branch was the top office in the region in Customer Satisfaction scores. In addition, two employees whom I trained were promoted through two levels of advancement, to Assistant Branch Manager positions. Since joining this company, I have earned a reputation as a talented and articulate sales professional with strong managerial abilities.

Although I am highly respected in my present job and achieving results in all areas of performance, I feel my abilities would be better utilized in a financial management role than in the sales positions for which Quality is grooming me.

If you can use an intelligent, enthusiastic, and results-oriented professional, I hope you will contact me to suggest a time when we might meet to discuss your needs. I can assure you in advance that I could rapidly become an asset to your organization.

Sincerely,

Elizabeth Hyland

ELIZABETH HYLAND

1110½ Hay Street, Fayetteville, NC 28305 • preppub@aol.com • (910) 483-6611

OBJECTIVE   To benefit an organization that can use an articulate young management professional with exceptional communication, financial, and organizational skills along with a background in multiunit management and staff development.

EDUCATION   **B.S., Psychology and Finance,** University of Las Vegas, 1996.
- Maintained a cumulative 3.5 GPA while working 30 hours per week and completing this rigorous degree program in three years.
- Was elected Panhellenic Chairwoman (1995) and Pledge Class Vice President (1993), Psi Alpha chapter of Chi Omega Sorority.
- Played first-string goalie on women's water polo team; participated on the women's cross country team; counseled a special needs child with Tourette's Syndrome; placed 2nd in a scholarship pageant.

EXPERIENCE   *Am advancing in a track record of promotion with Quality Rent-a-Car (1995-present):*
CORPORATE ACCOUNT MANAGER. Las Vegas, NV (2000-present). Design and sell corporate account programs to business and government clients; increased monthly sales to $160,000 from $45,000 since taking over corporate accounts for this 12-store area.
- Provide government and private industry representatives with information on the advantages of a corporate rental car program in their travel plans.
- Generate business through a combination of client visits and employee referrals.
- Prepare and submit bids used in obtaining federal, state, and local government contracted business from 12 rental car offices throughout Nevada.
- Created and implemented a corporate business training manual; responsible for all corporate training for 52 current employees and new hires.
- Organize and coordinate corporate presence at events such as corporate trade shows, business expos, and career fairs.
- Was recognized with the **Employee Excellence Award** in December 2000.
- Received the **#1 Corporate Class Performance Award** for the western region in March 2000.

ASSISTANT BRANCH MANAGER. Tempe, AZ (1996-00). Set sales records in several areas while also supervising a staff of four full-time and three part-time employees.
- Earned recognition as "Top Seller" in both inside and outside sales for the Arizona region and established the highest number of corporate accounts of any manager in the area.
- Trained and motivated manager trainees in daily branch rental business.
- Managed and collected branch receivables and vehicle repossessions.
- Devised a new method for the reservations process which streamlined branch operations and increased productivity.
- Provided exceptional customer service which enabled the branch to place first in customer satisfaction scores for the region in 1997.

MANAGEMENT TRAINEE. Monterey, CA (1995-96). Mastered all aspects of branch office management, customer service, sales, and administration; achieved sales in the top 5% of my training groups.
- Orchestrated a branch delivery service project which involved a staff of 12 and 225 vehicles.

PERSONAL   Affiliations and professional memberships include the Las Vegas Chamber of Commerce, Las Vegas Business Network, and National Defense Transportation Association. Excellent personal and professional references on request.

Date

Exact Name of Person
Title or Position
Name of Company
Address (number and street)
Address (city, state, and zip)

ACCOUNTANT

Dear Exact Name of Person: (or Dear Sir or Madam if answering a blind ad.)

As every experienced professional knows, it is a sobering reality that often one must change companies in order to increase one's pay and range of responsibilities. This CPA is seeking a larger firm which can offer her a wider range of involvements.

With the enclosed resume, I would like to indicate my interest in your organization and my desire to explore employment opportunities.

As you will see from my enclosed resume, I have excelled in my first job as a Staff Accountant after passing the CPA exam, and I have worked with corporations, partnerships, sole proprietors, pension and profit-sharing plans, and individuals. Although I am held in high regard by my current employer, I am selectively exploring opportunities with larger firms involved in more diversified accounting activities.

I hope you will welcome my call soon to arrange a brief meeting at your convenience to discuss your current and future needs and how I might serve them. Thank you in advance for your time.

Sincerely yours,

Joan Mackler

Alternate last paragraph:
I hope you will call or write me soon to suggest a time convenient for us to meet and discuss your current and future needs and how I might serve them. Thank you in advance for your time.

JOAN MACKLER

1110½ Hay Street, Fayetteville, NC 28305 • preppub@aol.com • (910) 483-6611

OBJECTIVE

To contribute to an organization that can use a resourceful CPA candidate with excellent problem-solving skills as well as a background in accounting and financial planning.

EDUCATION

B.S. in Business Administration with a concentration in Accounting, University of San Diego, CA. A.A., San Diego Community College, San Diego, CA.

LICENSURE

Passed CPA exam, November 2000.
Enrolled in Certified Financial Planner program, The American College, Bryn Mawr, PA.

EXPERIENCE

STAFF ACCOUNTANT. Cary & Sharp CPAs, Anchorage, AK (2000-present). Compile financial statements, prepare payroll and sales tax reports, and prepare tax returns for corporations, partnerships, sole proprietors, pension and profit-sharing plans, and individuals.
* Set up companies on QuickBooks accounting software.
* Prepare year-end tax projections for clients; conduct audits of nonprofit organizations.
* For one company, identified and resolved client recordkeeping discrepancies which resulted in a reduction of taxable income to client; designed and implemented a new "daily report" system to monitor sales, receivables, and expenses, simplifying verification of cash flow and providing accountability.
* Identified illegal acts occurring within one client's accounting office, designed internal control procedures for implementation by management.

FINANCE MANAGER. Barrington, Wells, and Company, San Diego, CA (1995-00). Contributed knowledge and problem-solving skills in ways which increased cash flow and the effectiveness of financial support operations in this dealership while handling the full range of financial activities including accounts payable and receivable and payroll accounting for 15 employees.
* Solved cash flow problems after investigating auto parts department procedures: designed and implemented inventory and accounts receivable activities.
* On my own initiative, mastered computer applications unique to this industry such as dealership warranties, sales reporting, and marketing programs.
* Handled bank reconciliations, sales tax processing for the dealership and a separate auto parts business, vehicle warranty repair administration, and employee insurance.
* Maintained daily reports, ledgers, and computer records on dealership operations.

CLIENT CONTACT SPECIALIST. USPA & IRA, San Diego, CA (1990-95). Became recognized as a top-notch communicator and sales/customer service professional while calling on prospective and existing clients of this financial planning company which supports a clientele made up predominantly of military officers with a full range of financial planning and investment services.
* Received recognition from the highest levels of the company as part of one of the most productive teams of Brokers, Administrative Assistants, and Client Specialists.
* Made it possible for two agents to set new sales records due to the increased level of appointments made through my skill in describing the company's services.

Highlights of earlier experience: Gained versatile skills and abilities in previous jobs:
* As **PROJECT ACCOUNTANT,** handled the costing of an average of $25 million worth of construction projects.
* As **ACCOUNTING MANAGER,** supervised two employees while handling retail accounting including inventory, accounts receivable and payable, general ledger, financial statements, payroll, and sales tax.

PERSONAL

Offer excellent analytical skills and the ability to develop workable strategies.

Date

Exact Name of Person
Exact Title
Exact Name of Company
Address
City, State, Zip

ACCOUNTANT Dear Exact Name of Person (or Dear Sir or Madam if answering a blind ad):

With the enclosed resume, I would like to make you aware of my versatile background with an emphasis on accounting and office management as well as of my reputation as an innovative, customer-service oriented professional.

As you will see from my resume, I offer a diverse background in construction, manufacturing, and service environments and have always earned respect for my ability to adapt to change, pressure, and deadlines. Having studied Business and Accounting in college, I am building a track record of effectiveness in dealing with people ranging from office and accounting clerks, to temporary workers, to management professionals, to accounts and corporate financial officers. With a knack for quickly learning and mastering advances in computer technology, I am proficient in creating databases and in using automated systems for accounting, data processing, and purchasing activities.

In my present job as Staff Accountant and Office Manager for Ready Mixed Concrete, I have been credited with developing creative ideas for streamlining procedures. In addition to preparing payroll for 106 employees at five plants, I process and manage a wide range of tax and accounting activities including overseeing Worker's Compensation, OSHA compliance reporting, and health insurance plan support. Among my accomplishments has been reducing the time needed to process payroll from three days to one and taking the financial report process which had been six months behind to a point where it is now consistently completed on time.

In earlier jobs in accounts payable and payroll processing, I was recruited by one construction company to handle their accounts payable for multimillion-dollar projects and process payroll for more than 200 employees. For a large temporary services firm with eight branches, I worked in the corporate office processing weekly payroll for approximately 3,000 people. Earlier I earned promotion from Accounts Receivable and Collections Specialist to Department Secretary with Tom's Food, Inc., a manufacturer of snack foods with plants throughout the country.

If you can use an experienced and mature professional who has long been recognized as a reliable and honest individual with high personal standards, I hope you will contact me soon to suggest a time when we might meet to discuss your needs. I can assure you in advance that I can provide outstanding references.

Sincerely,

Catherine Dabbs

CATHERINE DABBS

1110½ Hay Street, Fayetteville, NC 28305 • preppub@aol.com • (910) 483-6611

OBJECTIVE

To offer a background of accomplishments and reputation as a results-oriented professional with strong knowledge of accounting and office management to an organization that can use an enthusiastic, energetic professional with experience in collections and customer service.

EDUCATION

Studied **Business and Accounting,** Columbus College, Columbus, GA.

COMPUTERS & SPECIAL SKILLS

Knowledgeable of Microsoft Access and database creation; utilize automated systems while handling purchasing, accounting, and data processing activities.

Proficient with software programs including the following:

QuickBooks Pro	PeachTree Accounting
Word	Excel
MS Front Page 98, Excel, Outlook, and Works	

Broad experience in office operations and customer service; use standard office machines.

EXPERIENCE

STAFF ACCOUNTANT and **OFFICE MANAGER.** Metro Products & Construction Company dba Ready Mixed Concrete, Columbus, GA (2001-present). Excelling in handling diverse responsibilities, have been credited with making changes which have significantly improved operating procedures while supervising three people including accounting clerks and office staff for a business with five separate plant locations.

- Streamlined operations in the accounting department and have implemented changes which have reduced the time needed to complete support activities; for instance, payroll processing which had taken three days is now completed in one.
- Improved the process for producing monthly and yearly financial reports for the CPAs and owners – a function which had been six months behind is now consistently on time.
- Applied knowledge in database creation to establish a new system for tracking equipment purchases and status of computers, printers, vehicles, and other equipment.
- Prepare payroll for up to 106 employees in the company's five plants.
- Manage Worker's Compensation claims and yearly audits, preparation of forms for OSHA, and monthly approval of employee health insurance; prepare daily bank deposits; post payroll and accounts payable check numbers; issue and then post manual checks; prepare the petty cash sheet; process state and federal tax payments.
- Verify data between the general ledger, accounts payable, and accounts receivable.

ACCOUNTS PAYABLE AND PAYROLL TECHNICIAN. Metric Constructors, Columbus, GA (1999-01). Was recruited by this commercial construction company to handle accounts payable for multimillion-dollar projects and to process payroll for 200 employees.

- Assisted in purchasing support for large projects; prepared weekly and monthly reports for Project Managers and Supervisors.

PAYROLL TECHNICIAN. Mega Force, Columbus, GA (1999). Processed weekly payroll for approximately 3,000 people at the corporate office of a company with eight branches.

- Polished data entry skills inputting daily employee information and job orders.

Advanced with Tom's Food, Inc., Columbus, GA while earning a reputation as a detail-oriented, positive, and enthusiastic professional:
ACCOUNTS RECEIVABLE AND COLLECTIONS SPECIALIST. (1991-98). Dealt with more than 1,100 accounts which included distributors and grocery store chains.

- Researched past due accounts and made weekly and monthly reports.

PERSONAL

Creative individual who thrives under the challenge of deadlines. Notary Public.

Date

Exact Name of Person
Exact Title
Exact Name of Company
Address
City, State, Zip

ACCOUNTANT   Dear Exact Name of Person: (or Dear Sir or Madam if answering a blind ad):

With the enclosed resume, I would like to make you aware of my background as an articulate, focused professional with exceptional analytical and problem-solving skills who offers experience in accounting and office management in nonprofit, government, and entrepreneurial environments.

As you will see from my resume, I majored in Accounting while earning my Bachelor of Science in Business Administration from the University of Arizona at Tucson.

I am currently excelling as Chief Accountant for the North and South Carolina Divisions of the Salvation Army, where I provide oversight for all aspects of the local financial and business operations. My pride in my work and strong attention to detail have led me to succeed in a diverse range of challenging environments, from bringing order and accountability to a local small business, to running the office of a senior executive.

Although I am highly regarded by my present employer and can provide exceptional personal and professional references upon request, I feel that there is a good "fit" between my skills and your company's needs. I trust that you will hold my letter of interest in strictest confidence until after we have had a chance to meet.

If you can use a meticulous, highly skilled accounting professional with a solid reputation as a competent, reliable team player whose integrity is beyond reproach, I hope you will welcome my call soon when I try to arrange a brief meeting to discuss your goals and how my background might serve your needs.

Sincerely,

Patricia Meyer

Alternate Last Paragraph:
I hope you will write or call me soon to suggest a time when we might meet to discuss your needs and goals and how my background might serve them. I can provide outstanding references at the appropriate time.

PATRICIA MEYER

1110½ Hay Street, Fayetteville, NC 28305   •   preppub@aol.com   •   (910) 483-6611

OBJECTIVE

To offer experience in accounting and office administrative environments to an organization that can benefit from my strong computer, decision-making, customer service, and time management skills as well as my reputation as a quick and accurate professional.

EDUCATION

B.S. in **Business Administration**, The University of Arizona, Tucson, 2000.
Majored in **Accounting** and excelled in specialized course work such as cost and managerial accounting, advanced and intermediate accounting, advanced federal taxation, and principles of auditing as well as human relations and management policies.

SPECIAL SKILLS

Able to quickly adapt and learn new software or operational systems, am proficient with Microsoft Word, PowerPoint, Windows 3.1/95, and Excel as well as DOS, Harvard Graphics, and Buildsoft Construction Management Systems proprietary software.

EXPERIENCE

CHIEF ACCOUNTANT. The Salvation Army, North and South Carolina Division, Columbia, SC (2001-present).
Provide oversight for all aspects of the financial and business functions for the local social services, shelter, thrift store, and community center programs with responsibility for ensuring a stable financial base for all areas of operations.
- Was placed in charge of a special project to transfer all data from an EDP system to CASA, a FoxPro-based proprietary accounting system.
- Plan, develop, manage, and control accounting, finance, and personnel functions.
- As liaison and financial advisor to the local unit, advisory board, and divisional and territorial headquarters, report on financial status and research discrepancies.
- Manage and monitor general ledger, purchasing, budgetary, and personnel functions.
- Ensure compliance with corporate, local, state, and federal regulations as well as with the accuracy, completeness, timeliness, and integrity of financial reporting.

FULL-CHARGE BOOKKEEPER. Showcase Construction, Castleton, VT (2000).
Originally hired as Bookkeeper for Rental Management, rapidly advanced to hold increased responsibilities as Senior Bookkeeper while training the new Rental Management Book-keeper.
- Provided the owner with overhead and cash flow figures needed to facilitate an efficient decision-making process; handled payroll, taxes, and accounts receivable/payable.
- Managed the use of the computer system so that all accounting information followed generally accepted accounting principles.

FULL-TIME STUDENT. The University of Arizona, Tucson (1997-00).

Gained experience in working as a contributor to team efforts while serving in the U.S. Air Force, Davis-Monthan AB, AZ (1993-97):
ASSISTANT SUPERVISOR. (1995-97). Supervised two subordinates in the office of a high-ranking senior military executive; was described as providing "expert management" for the diverse functions of an operations center in the senior supervisor's absence.
- Maintained and controlled a $67,000 government equipment and computer account.

PERSONNEL OFFICE SUPERVISOR. (1993-95). Completely mastered all functions of the personnel office while restructuring procedures which improved customer service.

PERSONAL

Possess a reputation as a reliable professional. Enjoy mastering new concepts.

Exact Name of Person
Exact Title
Exact Name of Company
Address
City, State, Zip

ACCOUNTANT   Dear Exact Name of Person (or Dear Sir or Madam if answering a blind ad):

With the enclosed resume, I would like to make you aware of my interest in exploring employment opportunities in financial and accounting management with your organization. Although I am held in the highest regard by my current employer and can provide outstanding references at the appropriate time, I would appreciate your holding my interest in your company in confidence.

As you will see from my resume, I currently work as a Staff Accountant for The Pantry, Inc., in Columbia. As a Staff Accountant, I have resolved numerous software problems causing "hidden" problems in general ledgers and accounts receivables. In addition to my regular job as a Staff Accountant, I was asked by the company to assume the position as Acting Manager of Credit Accounting when the manager left after giving a one-week's notice. As acting manager for six months while the company found a replacement, I trained and sharpened the accounting and problem-solving skills of the seven individuals on the accounts receivable team. As a Staff Accountant, I have expertly directed a variety of special projects, and I handle 56 general ledger accounts related to 748 convenience stores which never close. On one occasion, I took one account from $1 million in "hidden" errors on the AS400 to $46,000.

In my previous position as a Budget Analyst, I managed 10 employees at a fast-paced government office. Prior to that, I worked as an Accountant for a petroleum company which operated eight convenience stores, and I prepared financial statements and audited control systems on a daily basis.

My computer skills are very strong, and I am accustomed to working on PCs, UNIX-based systems, and the AS400 with a variety of software. I am experienced at identifying software glitches which result in financial and accounting problems.

Although I enjoy my work and colleagues at The Pantry and am considered a very valuable employee, I would like to be more involved in work related to the preparation of financial statements and play a key role in the overall financial control of operations. I have much to offer an organization, and I hope you will contact me if my skills and talents interest you.

Yours sincerely,

Jennifer Nicols

JENNIFER NICOLS

1110½ Hay Street, Fayetteville, NC 28305 • preppub@aol.com • (910) 483-6611

OBJECTIVE   To benefit a company seeking a professional skilled in controllership, accounting, budget preparation, and financial management with strong communication, management, and organizational abilities.

EDUCATION   **Associate's degree in Accounting**, Columbia Technical Community College, Columbia, SC, 1993; graduated with a 3.97 GPA.
Extensive coursework towards Associate's degree in Business Computer Management.

EXPERIENCE   **STAFF ACCOUNTANT & ACTING MANAGER, CREDIT ACCOUNTING.** The Pantry, Inc., Columbia, SC (2001-present). For a company on the New York Stock Exchange with 748 convenience stores doing $1.5 million daily in credit card transactions alone, handle gasoline taxes and licenses for eight states (NC, SC, GA, VA, MD, IN, KY, and TN) and resolve accounting and software problems.

- Upon the resignation and one-week notice of the Manager of Credit Accounting, assumed the position during the six-month period when the company searched for a replacement; worked in a 58-person office and managed seven people on the accounts receivable team. Am now training the new Manager of Credit Accounting.
- Directed audits of store-level transactions related to accounts receivable and financial reports.
- As Staff Accountant, handle a variety of special projects such as accounts which had never been reconciled; handle 56 general ledger accounts related to 748 convenience stores which never close.
- Am highly regarded for my skill in identifying software problems causing "hidden" problems in general ledgers and accounts receivables.
- Continuously in a problem-solving mode, took one account from $1 million in hidden errors on the AS400 to $46,000; identified this problem on my own initiative and persisted in resolving it.

ACCOUNTING MANAGER and **BUDGET ANALYST MANAGER.** Non-Appropriated Funds (NAF) Accounting Office, Pope AFB, NC (1994-01). Utilized my outstanding financial and planning skills while providing a wide range of services at this fast-paced government office; hired, trained, supervised, and evaluated 10 employees.

- Oversaw operation of total accounting services, including planning work schedules to ensure deadlines were met; formulated training plans, handled employee cross-training, and supervised and evaluated employees. Developed employee training programs.
- Used accrual accounting for assets, liabilities, equity, income, and expense accounts.
- Provided procedural guidance, developed written accounting procedures.
- Prepared financial statements and conducted audits.
- Maintained subsidiary journals and processed monthly reconciliation to general ledger controlling accounts, in addition to researching discrepancies, analyzing effects, and overseeing corrective action; reviewed trial balances with management prior to finalization of financial statements.

ACCOUNTANT. Fortune Petroleum Company, Columbia, SC (1992-94). Oversaw accounting procedures for eight convenience stores; handled accounts payable/receivable.

SKILLS   IBM-compatible computers, Lotus 1-2-3, Excel, Enable software packages, Unix operating system, AS400; Resource Management System by PDI; Monarch, FTP Client, PowerPoint; Word; Windows 98; operate 10-key calculators and adding machines.

Exact Name of Person
Title or Position
Name of Company
Address (number and street)
Address (city, state, and zip)

ADJUSTER, AUTO DAMAGE

Dear Exact Name of Person: (or Dear Sir or Madam if answering a blind ad.)

There are many different formats for showing a track record of progression within a single company. Look at the first job on his resume and you will see one approach for showing a pattern of involvement in increasingly more complex assignments. He may be approaching competitors of his current employer, so notice how he emphasizes his desire for confidentiality.

With the enclosed resume, I would like to indicate my interest in your organization and my desire to explore employment opportunities.

As you will see from my enclosed resume, I am an expert appraiser and licensed insurance adjuster with a proven commitment to outstanding customer service. I also offer a reputation for unquestioned integrity and reliability. You will notice that I have excelled in a track record of advancement with my current employer.

Although I am held in high regard by my employer and enjoy both my work and my colleagues, I am selectively exploring opportunities in other companies which have earned a reputation for quality. Although I can provide excellent references at the appropriate time, please keep my interest in your company confidential until after we have a chance to talk.

I hope you will welcome my call soon to arrange a brief meeting at your convenience to discuss your current and future needs and how I might serve them. Thank you in advance for your time.

Sincerely yours.

Daniel Naidoo

Alternate last paragraph:
I hope you will call or write me soon to suggest a time convenient for us to meet and discuss your current and future needs and how I might serve them. Thank you in advance for your time.

DANIEL NAIDOO

1110½ Hay Street, Fayetteville, NC 28305 • preppub@aol.com • (910) 483-6611

OBJECTIVE	To benefit a company that can use an expert automobile appraiser and licensed insurance adjuster who offers a proven commitment to outstanding customer service along with a reputation for unquestioned honesty, strong negotiating skills, and technical knowledge.
LICENSE	Licensed by the state of South Carolina as an Auto Damage Adjuster and Auto Appraiser; also licensed as a Notary Public. • Was previously licensed in New York as an Automobile Damage Adjuster/Appraiser. • Hold a valid South Carolina Driver's License with a violation-free record.
EXPERIENCE	**AUTO DAMAGE ADJUSTER**. Nationwide Insurance Company, Columbia, SC (2000-present) and various locations in New York State (1986-present). Began with Nationwide as a part-time security guard on weekends, and was offered a chance to train as an adjuster; excelled in all schools and training programs, and have exceeded corporate goals and expectations in every job I have held within Nationwide. • *1995-present*: Was the first adjuster sent into South Carolina, and have played a key role in implementing the company's strategic plan to do more business inland selling auto policies; in a highly competitive market, opened the Columbia office "from scratch," which now includes two drive-in locations as well as a guaranteed repair shop which I monitor while averaging 100-125 claims monthly as the only adjuster within a 50-mile area. • *1991-95*: Built a six-adjuster territory into a 14-adjuster territory in Queens. • *1989-91*: Worked in Suffolk County, a huge territory 30 miles wide and 100 miles long, where I made a significant contribution to building the territory; when I left as the only adjuster in Suffolk County, I was replaced with four adjusters in this rapidly expanding territory where I had helped Nationwide earn a name for excellent service. • *1987-89*: Relocated to Nassau County, Long Island, where I trained new adjusters while also working the field and drive-in. • *1986-87*: After initial training as an adjuster, worked in Brooklyn and the Bronx, NY: averaged five claims per day while helping the company earn a reputation for outstanding customer service. *Technical knowledge*: Skilled at utilizing Mitchell Estimate System and CCC Total Loss Evaluation as well as guide books including NADA and the Red Book; routinely use equipment including a CRT and personal computer. • Known for my excellent negotiating skills and ability to settle claims quickly and fairly. • In the Columbia area, have improved customer relations and reduced loss ratio 15%. • Skilled at evaluating total losses, coordinating removal of salvage, and handling titles. **NAVAL PETTY OFFICER**. (1980-86). After joining the Navy, advanced rapidly through the ranks to E-5 in four years while managing people as well as inventories of ammunition, missiles, and nuclear fuel; was strongly urged to make a career out of the Navy because of my exceptional management ability, leadership skills, human relations knowhow, and technical knowledge of supply and logistics.
EDUCATION & TRAINING	Completed college course work in Business Administration and Management, Farmingdale State University, NY, 1991-92. Completed technical training in Risk & Insurance and Insurance Law as well as numerous courses conducted by companies such as General Motors and Honda pertaining to refinishing, principles of four-wheel steering, transmission repair, computer operation, other areas.
PERSONAL	Offer an unusual combination of exceptional organizational and communication skills, along with technical knowledge of auto adjusting and the insurance industry. Strongly believe in delivering outstanding customer service.

Exact Name of Person
Exact Title
Exact Name of Company
Address
City, State, Zip

AUDITOR, WORKER'S COMPENSATION

Dear Exact Name of Person: (or Dear Sir or Madam if answering a blind ad):

With the enclosed resume, I am writing to express my interest in exploring employment opportunities with your organization and make you aware of my background related to tax auditing, fraud investigation, and claims investigation.

As you will see from my resume, I am working as a Worker's Compensation Auditor as an independent subcontractor, and I have worked for insurers including Auto Owners, Erie Corp., The Phoenix Group, Lumberman's Insurance Company, and others. As a skilled payroll and tax auditor for compliance and assessment purposes, I am applying my expert knowledge of North Carolina laws as well as my knowledge of general liability, garage liability, and Worker's Comp.

In my previous experience with the Employment Security Commission of North Carolina, I excelled as a Fraud Investigator, Tax Auditor, and Chief Claims Investigator. When I took over the Raleigh office of ESC as Chief Claims Investigator, I inherited an inefficient operation. On my own initiative, I studied systems used in TN, VA, and FL, and I reengineered internal systems so that they became models of efficiency. While managing 18 investigators and 26 others, I made numerous changes which resulted in the investigators' caseload increasing from 15 monthly to 150 monthly while increasing detection of fraud from $235,000 a year in fraud overpayments to $6 million detected yearly.

I am skilled in working with the general public as well as organizations including the SBI, IRS, and numerous state agencies.

If you can make use of my considerable experience and skills, please contact me to suggest a time when we might meet to discuss your needs. I am available to travel and/or relocate according to your needs, and I can provide outstanding personal and professional references at the appropriate time.

Sincerely,

Winston King

WINSTON KING

1110½ Hay Street, Fayetteville, NC 28305 • preppub@aol.com • (910) 483-6611

OBJECTIVE

I want to contribute to an organization that can use an experienced professional who offers extensive experience in tax auditing, fraud investigation, and claims investigation along with expertise related to Worker's Compensation and expert knowledge of NC laws.

EDUCATION

Bachelor of Arts (B.A.), Economics with minor in Psychology, Pfeiffer University.
Extensive training in fraud investigations and auditing techniques received at the NC Justice Academy and Guilford Community College.

EXPERIENCE

WORKER'S COMPENSATION AUDITOR. 2001-present. As an independent subcontractor, am involved in auditing business, tax, and accounting records for worker's compensation and employer general liability policies to assure compliance with NC laws and insurance industry standards.
- Based on audits, assign/reassign classification codes for compliance/rating purposes.
- Inspect commercial and business properties for casualty and property coverage.
- Insurers for whom I have done work include Auto Owners, Erie Corp., The Phoenix Group, Lumberman's Insurance Company, and others.
- As a skilled payroll and tax auditor for compliance and assessment purposes, apply expert knowledge of general liability, garage liability, Worker's Comp.

Previously excelled in a track record of promotion, Employment Security Commission of NC:
TAX AUDITOR. 1991-01: Greensboro, NC. After requesting reassignment to Greensboro for family reasons, audited business accounting and tax records for payroll reporting compliance.
- Interpreted and made independent application of law, rules, and regulations relative to audit data for high- and low-volume payrolls in accordance with commonly accepted auditing standards.
- Audited businesses with multiple state operations; handled tax liability investigations, collections, judgments, delinquent tax reports, bankruptcy, estate cases, asset seizures, and auctions.
- Served tax liens, negotiated payment plans and settlements, and served as state agent for tax criminal and civil matters in a court of law.
- Specialized in detection of hidden wages and tax liability investigations; served judgments, made seizures, served tax assessments; testified as witness in court; initiated proceedings for failure to file returns; negotiated payment agreements.

CHIEF CLAIMS INVESTIGATOR. 1985-91. Raleigh, NC. Took over management of an inefficient operation, and transformed it into a respected and highly productive organization; managed 18 investigators, one assistant supervisor, one secretary, two clerical supervisors, and 22 others involved in receivables and payables activities.
- Upon taking over operation, studied similar organizations in TN, VA, and FL; then reengineered internal systems to eliminate duplicate tasks.
- Moved the operation from $235,000 a year in fraud overpayments discovered to the detection of $6 million yearly.
- Implemented a computer cross match program utilizing probability techniques which was sent to employers and which emphasized self-reporting; this boosted taxpayer satisfaction with the system while freeing up investigators' time.
- Through efficiencies which I created and implemented, the average caseload of investigators went from 15 per month to 150 per month; provided more support for investigators.

PERSONAL

Member of Civitan Club, Jaycees, Moose Lodge. President of homeowners association.

Exact Name of Person
Title or Position
Name of Company
Address (number and street)
Address (city, state, and zip)

BANKING REPRESENTATIVE

Dear Exact Name of Person: (or Sir or Madam if answering a blind ad.)

With the enclosed resume, I would like to acquaint you with my background as an office manager, administrative assistant, and banking professional as well as with the strong financial, interpersonal, and communication skills that I could offer your organization.

As you will see from my resume, I have recently excelled in a track record of advancement culminating in a position as a Personal Banking Representative for a large national bank headquartered in Pennsylvania. Throughout my career in this industry, I have provided the highest levels of customer service while effectively identifying and capitalizing on opportunities to sell the organization's products and services to the bank's customers.

In earlier positions in the administrative field, I excelled as the Administrative Assistant to the Comptroller of a large international cosmetics company, where I composed, edited, and prepared correspondence for the office as well as handling time-sensitive materials under tight deadlines. Earlier as Office Manager in a busy orthodontic office, I handled all financial transactions for the business, managed the scheduling of patient appointments, and oversaw inventory control and purchasing.

Fluent in Spanish, I have earned a reputation as a skilled communicator with a talent for dealing effectively with people. I believe my hardworking nature and ability to work with little or no supervision have been the keys to my success.

If you can use a motivated professional with strong financial, office management, and computer operations skills, I hope you will contact me to suggest a time when we can discuss your present and future needs, and how I might meet them. I can provide outstanding personal and professional references, and I thank you in advance for your time and consideration.

Sincerely,

Robert Colt

ROBERT COLT

1110½ Hay Street, Fayetteville, NC 28305 • preppub@aol.com • (910) 483-6611

OBJECTIVE	To benefit an organization that can use an experienced administrative professional who offers exceptional organizational, communication and interpersonal skills.
EXPERIENCE	***With PNC Bank, a large national bank headquartered in Pennsylvania, advanced in the following "track record" of increasing responsibilities:***

PERSONAL BANKING REPRESENTATIVE. Camp Hill, PA (2001-present). Advanced to this position after excelling as a Teller Banking Representative; provided exceptional customer service while presenting the bank's products to customers.
- Presented, sold, and provided sales referrals for various bank products and services, such as credit cards, special checking plans, etc.
- Exercised sound judgment while tactfully and effectively resolving problems related to financial transactions and account information.
- Responded to a heavy volume of customer inquiries, both over the phone and in person; answered a multi-line phone system.

TELLER BANKING REPRESENTATIVE. Camp Hill, PA (2000). Processed a high number of customer transactions daily, exhibiting attention to detail to ensure accuracy and following established policies and procedures to maintain accountability.
- Processed customer deposits and withdrawals within assigned limits, cashing checks and transferring funds between checking and savings accounts.
- Quickly built a rapport with my customers that allowed me to recognize referral and sales opportunities, generating additional revenue for the company.

ADMINISTRATIVE ASSISTANT to the COMPTROLLER. Elizabeth Arden (a division of Unilever), Puerto Rico (1996-00). Managed all administrative aspects of the office's operation, including composition, editing, typing, and proofreading of letters, memos, and other correspondence, filing, and other clerical duties.
- Read, responded to, processed, and filed a variety of time-sensitive materials, working within tight deadlines to ensure that necessary actions were completed on time.
- Acted as liaison between the Comptroller and the Customs Broker's office.
- Coordinated employee holiday and vacation schedules, as well as monitoring and arranging service visits for the maintenance and repair of office equipment.
- Received and sorted incoming mail, distributing it to the appropriate person or department within the company.

OFFICE MANAGER. Dr. Julio Gracano, Orthodontist, Puerto Rico (1993-95). Provided a full range of administrative, financial management, clerical and receptionist duties for the office of this busy orthodontist.
- Oversaw all financial functions for the office, to include processing weekly payroll, bank deposits and reconciliation, balancing the office's checkbook, and acting as liaison to Dr. Gracano's Certified Public Accountant, delivering financial documents.
- Answered a large number of incoming calls, scheduling patients; updated and maintained the appointment book for the office, noting cancellations and changes.

EDUCATION	Completed the Administrative Specialist Course, Pennsylvania Tech, Camp Hill, PA, 2000. Earned High School diploma from Colegio Ergos de Ponce, Puerto Rico, 1993.
COMPUTERS	Familiar with various popular computer operating systems and software, including Windows 95 and 97, Microsoft Word, and WordPerfect.

Date

Mr. George Brown
Senior Vice President
First Union National Bank
2391 Augusta Street SW
Atlanta, Georgia 89012

BANKING SERVICES MANAGER

This young manager is using his cover letter and resume to formally apply for a public relations position within his own bank. He realizes he must formally remind his employer of his track record of results while also emphasizing his strong qualifications for and interest in the public relations job. It's easy to get overlooked for a promotion within your own company if you don't "toot your horn."

Dear Mr. Brown:

I would appreciate an opportunity to talk with you soon about my strong interest in receiving consideration for the position of Public Relations Manager. I believe I offer the enthusiasm, talent, and knowledge that make me a professional who can make important contributions to First Union National Bank in this area.

As you will see from my enclosed resume, I am presently a Client Services Manager who consistently places at the top of my peer group in internal performance evaluations. I rapidly advanced from Administrative Assistant in the consumer banking department, gained experience as a Teller, and then advanced to this position where I represent the bank while opening new accounts and selling bank products to our clients. While excelling in my full-time positions, I have worked hard in my spare time to complete my college degree.

My ability to develop interesting and informative written materials was discovered in high school when I edited the yearbook. While attending Peace College in Raleigh for my first two years of studies, I was selected to edit the college yearbook and was credited with producing an attractive and well-organized publication. I went on to earn a degree in Mass Communications from the University of North Carolina at Charlotte where I wrote for the college newspaper. I have become involved in the Junior League and am now serving this organization as the Public Relations chairman in a role which includes preparing all newspaper releases about the organization and its civic activities.

I believe that through my enthusiasm, experience, and talent I can make valuable contributions in preparing products which will enhance the bank's ability to sell services to the public and gain new clients through informative and interesting written materials.

I hope you will call or write me soon to suggest a time convenient for us to discuss how I would fit into the bank's public relations efforts and how I might continue to serve most effectively. Thank you in advance for your time.

Sincerely,

Kerry Zaeske

KERRY ZAESKE

1110½ Hay Street, Fayetteville, NC 28305 • preppub@aol.com • (910) 483-6611

OBJECTIVE   To benefit an organization through my dynamic personality and strong communication skills, my sophisticated understanding of banking services, my background in mass communications and public relations, as well as my ability to effectively market ideas, services, and products.

EDUCATION   **B.S. in Mass Communications,** University of North Carolina at Charlotte, NC, 2000.
- Completed this degree in my spare time while excelling in my full-time job.
- Maintained a cumulative GPA of above 3.5.
- Wrote interesting and informative articles for the college newspaper.

Attended Peace College, Raleigh, NC, for my first two years of basic studies in the Liberal Arts.
- Selected by faculty advisors to edit the college yearbook during my sophomore year, applied my communication skills and creativity to write copy for and produce a well-organized and attractive publication.

EXPERIENCE   **CLIENT SERVICES MANAGER.** First Union National Bank, Charlotte, NC (2000-present). After a short time as an Administrative Assistant in the consumer banking department, received training as a Teller and was then selected for the bank's Financial Management Development Training Program; subsequently advanced to this key role which involves extensive public relations as I communicate the bank's products and services.
- Have become skilled at understanding people's financial needs and requirements in order to recommend products such as Certificates of Deposit, MasterCard and VISA credit cards, savings accounts, equity lines, and investment instruments.
- Consistently place at the top of my peer group within the region according to the bank's system of internal performance ratings.

SALES REPRESENTATIVE. Carlyle & Co., Charlotte, NC (1997-99). Consistently met aggressive sales goals through both my patience and persistence in public relations and customer service; became known as a goal-driven, skilled professional who could be counted on to always deliver customer satisfaction.

ADMINISTRATIVE ASSISTANT. First Union National Bank, Charlotte, NC (1995-97). Gained valuable experience in banking procedures and all phases of the loan process while providing clerical and administrative support to two regional vice presidents specializing in the area of consumer credit.
- Used my talent for organization and attention to detail while creating spreadsheets, coordinating word processing support, and maintaining files for two busy executives.
- Improved the filing system for increased efficiency.
- Refined my communication skills dealing with banking professionals on a regular basis.
- Advanced my knowledge of computer operations using Word, WordPerfect, Lotus, and Excel software while preparing correspondence and handling financial record keeping.

LEGAL OFFICE INTERN. Office of the District Attorney, Charlotte, NC (1992-94). Gained valuable exposure to the legal system while aiding assistant district attorneys in activities which included contacting witnesses to remind them of court appearances; became familiar with legal procedures while working with a wide range of elected officials.
- Wrote guilty pleas; advised people pleading "guilty" about how to respond to questioning.
- Earned a reputation for the maturity and judgment I displayed while relating to a variety of people from all socioeconomic and age groups.

PERSONAL   Single; will cheerfully relocate. Am an articulate speaker and skilled writer. Offer a creative and enthusiastic approach to project development and the organizational skills to see them to completion. Enjoy dealing with the public and making contributions to my community.

Date

Exact Name of Person
Exact Title
Exact Name of Company
Address
City, State, Zip

**BILLING AND
COLLECTIONS MANAGER**

Dear Exact Name of Person (or Dear Sir or Madam if answering a blind ad):

With the enclosed resume, I would like to express my interest in exploring employment opportunities with your organization.

As you will see from my resume, I offer a versatile management background and a history of advancement based on expertise in collecting multimillion-dollar accounts receivable, analyzing complex financial situations, resourcefully solving problems, and effectively dealing with people. In 1996, the California-based company named Medical Plus Services purchased the company for which I was working and recruited me to take over the management of their billing and collections department. Highly respected by my present employer, I was approached in late 2000 about a position at the corporate office in San Diego because of the company's decision to close the Richmond office in 2001. However, I made the decision not to transfer to California.

As Manager of the Billing and Collections Department, I directed efforts resulting in an average of approximately $8 million in collections monthly. Those accounts receivable collections came from insurance companies as well as 425 hospitals in 31 states.

In previous experience, I enjoyed rapid advancement to Vice President with Pennsylvania Citizens Bank in Philadelphia. Initially hired after college graduation as a Teller and selected for the management trainee program, I quickly moved up to Commercial Branch Manager, to Manager of Branch Operations, and to Vice President. I supervised numerous employees, oversaw operation of nine branches and the main office, and gained vast experience in finance and banking.

Respected for my analytical skills and sound judgment, I am known for strong negotiating skills as well as the ability to deal with people in a persuasive manner. If you can use a resourceful and mature management professional, I hope you will contact me soon to suggest a time we might meet to discuss how I could contribute to your organization. I can provide excellent professional and personal references. Thank you in advance for your courtesies.

Sincerely,

Casey Jones

CASEY JONES

1110½ Hay Street, Fayetteville, NC 28305   •   preppub@aol.com   •   (910) 483-6611

OBJECTIVE

To contribute to an organization that can use my versatile management experience and extensive financial expertise, including vast knowledge of billing and collections, as well as my strong negotiating skills and my talent for applying strong analytical abilities in order to develop practical business solutions which profitably impact the bottom line.

EDUCATION

B.A. degree in History and Economics, Emory and Henry College, Emory, VA.
Extensive executive training in financial management, collections, and billing.

EXPERIENCE

BILLING AND COLLECTIONS DEPARTMENT MANAGER. Medical Plus Services, Richmond, VA (1990-2001). Recruited to manage this department which grew to 15 employees, directed efforts which led to an average of approximately $8 million monthly in accounts receivable collections from insurance companies and hospitals throughout a period of rapid growth, changes in corporate ownership, and functional reorganizations.

- Highly respected by executives at the headquarters of Medical Plus Services, I was approached about a transfer to San Diego after management decided to close the Richmond office in 2001. I did not pursue the opportunity to relocate to California.
- Took over the billing and collections support functions for company locations throughout the country.
- Directed successful efforts which resulted in the timely collection of accounts receivable through my knowledge of the terms of contracts established with approximately 425 hospitals in 31 states.
- Supported corporate operations which provided services for more than 245,000 procedures annually utilizing 65 mobile units in the 31 states it services.
- Played a vital role in ensuring the financial well being of a company which is the largest operator of mobile medical services in the country.

Highlights of other experience: Advanced in a track record of rapid promotion as an officer and manager with Pennsylvania Citizens Bank, Philadelphia, PA:
VICE PRESIDENT and **MANAGER OF BRANCH OPERATIONS.** (1982-90). Earned rapid promotions while holding increasingly higher managerial level jobs culminating in promotion to Vice President in 1987.

- As Manager of Branch Operations II, oversaw customer service, the bookkeeping department, and teller operations for the main and nine branch offices and administered company personnel policies and procedures.
- As Manager of Branch Operations I and Assistant Vice President, was the "number two man" in the main office with responsibility for teller and vault operations as well as customer service.
- In two consecutive assignments as a Commercial Branch Manager, supervised as many as eight employees while overseeing commercial and installment lending, new customer development, customer service, and teller operations.
- Originally hired after college graduation as a Teller and selected for the management trainee program, was quickly selected for promotion to Commercial Branch Manager I and then II for branches with as many as eight employees.

PERSONAL

Excel in analyzing situations and developing well-reasoned and workable solutions.

Exact Name of Person
Exact Title
Exact Name of Company
Address
City, State, Zip

BOOKKEEPER   Dear Exact Name of Person: (or Dear Sir or Madam if answering a blind ad):

With the enclosed resume, I would like to make you aware of my interest in exploring employment opportunities with your organization and make you aware of my strong skills related to office administration, bookkeeping, and computer operations.

I have recently relocated to Farmington, my hometown, in order to live near my aging parents. You will see from my resume that I have relocated from Ashland, VA, where I excelled in a track record of promotion with one organization. I began as a Receptionist and was quickly noticed for my productivity as well as my initiative in finding new efficiencies.

After my promotion to Bookkeeper, I was involved in a variety of customer service, public relations, bookkeeping, and computer activities. Skilled with Word and Excel, and familiar with CorelDraw, I have become proficient in creating spreadsheets and charts to analyze receipts, expenditures, and trends. I also became the resident expert on all computer problems, as I learned to fix a wide variety of hardware and software malfunctions. I have used CorelDraw to create brochures, and I have also functioned as a project manager in coordinating housing and transportation arrangements for up to 700 people at conventions.

If you can use a smart and dedicated young professional to enhance your organization's efficiency, I hope you will contact me to suggest a time when we might meet to discuss your needs. I can provide outstanding references.

Sincerely,

June Chan

JUNE CHAN

1110½ Hay Street, Fayetteville, NC 28305   •   preppub@aol.com   •   (910) 483-6611

OBJECTIVE   I want to contribute to an organization that can use an experienced office professional who offers strong computer skills, including the ability to troubleshoot hardware and software problems, as well as an ability to handle multiple simultaneous priorities.

EDUCATION   **Office administration and computer operations:** Extensive on-the-job training in all aspects of office administration, computer operations, and bookkeeping; skilled in utilizing Word and Excel, and have used CorelDraw to create brochures and other materials.
Have used customized software including Membership Plus for bookkeeping.
Security and First Aid: Completed Basic Law Enforcement Training and N.C. First Responder Training, Farmington Technical Community College, Farmington, ME, 1993.
- Excelled academically; graduated in top 10% of class.
- Also completed Armed Guard/Responder training through Burns International Security Services, 1992; graduated in top 10% of class.

EXPERIENCE   **Was promoted in the following track record of promotion, 1995-2002; resigned my position in order to relocate to Farmington to live near my aging parents:**
BOOKKEEPER. Calvary Pentecostal Camp, Ashland, VA (1999-2002). At this camp environment which could house 250 people as a convention center, handled responsibilities related to bookkeeping, public relations, and administration.
- As a bookkeeper, recorded all contributions using a computer; created spreadsheets and charts to analyze receipts, expenditures, and trends.
- Became proficient in Microsoft Word and Excel.
- Worked with a team of people utilizing CorelDraw to create brochures for conventions.
- In an office with five computers, became the office expert on computer problems; learned to fix a wide range of hardware and software problems.
- Processed credit card transactions.
- Acted as Convention Coordinator and project manager during ladies conventions; handled registrations and hotel placements for up to 700 people.
- On my own initiative, streamlined office procedures to increase efficiency.
- Was commended on my cheerful disposition and ability to handle the public in a gracious manner on the telephone and in person.

RECEPTIONIST. Calvary Pentecostal Camp, Ashland, VA (1995-99). Answered five phone lines and directed calls to appropriate departments; sorted mail and filed in appropriate mail slots.
- For this organization which could sleep 250 people on the campground, was involved in handling room placement of residents; answered their questions and directed them to proper facilities.
- Organized the office by setting up a new filing system which increased productivity.
- Created new timesaving forms which took less time to complete than previous ones.

Other experience:
SENIOR ARMED CONTROL ALARM STATION OPERATOR. Burns International Security Services, Farmington, ME (1992-95). Worked at the Shearon Harris Nuclear Power Plant in New Hill, NC; was hired as Watch Officer and was promoted rapidly.

POLICE OFFICER. Farmington Police Department, Farmington, ME (1991-92). Graduated from the Police Academy in the top 10% of class; enforced city and state laws.

Exact Name of Person
Exact Title
Exact Name of Company
Address
City, State, Zip

BOOKKEEPER   Dear Exact Name of Person: (or Dear Sir or Madam if answering a blind ad):

With the enclosed resume, I would like to acquaint you with the exceptional organizational, financial planning, and problem-solving skills as well as the educational background and experience in accounting, tax preparation, supervision, and training which I could offer to your organization.

As you will see from my resume, I have both a Bachelor of Science degree and an Associate of Applied Science degree in Accounting. I excelled throughout my academic career, graduating **summa cum laude** from Virginia Tech with a **3.82 cumulative GPA**. My dedication to the accounting field resulted in numerous honors; in addition to being named to the Chancellor's List, the Dean's List, and the National Dean's List, I was also elected Vice President of the Virginia Tech Accounting Society and Secretary of the Institute of Management Accountants.

I have excelled in previous accounting positions ranging from data entry of tax returns, to preparation of payroll and tax data for local businesses for an accounting firm, to taking over and turning around the troubled financial operations of a local small business. In that position, I handled all financial transactions, quickly reining in expenses, bringing collections on delinquent accounts receivable up-to-date, and establishing proper reporting procedures for the business.

Although I am highly regarded by my present employer and can provide exceptional personal and professional references at the appropriate time, I am interested in returning to my chosen field: accounting. I feel that there is a good "fit" between my versatile accounting, management, training, and customer services skills and your company's needs.

If you can use a versatile accounting professional whose skills have been tested in a number of challenging environments, I hope you will write or call me soon to suggest a time when we might meet to discuss your needs and goals and how my background might serve them.

Sincerely,

Helen Read

HELEN READ

1110½ Hay Street, Fayetteville, NC 28305 • preppub@aol.com • (910) 483-6611

OBJECTIVE

To benefit an organization that can use an accounting professional with exceptional organizational, financial planning, and training skills who offers a strong educational background and work experience in bookkeeping and accounting.

EDUCATION

Bachelor of Science in **Accounting**, Virginia Tech, Blacksburg, VA, 1998.
- Graduated **summa cum laude**, with a **3.82 cumulative GPA**.
- Named to the **Chancellor's List** (4.0 GPA) three semesters, the **Dean's List** (3.75 GPA) three semesters, and the **National Dean's List** (4.0) three semesters.
- Inducted into Phi Theta Kappa national honor society.

Associate of Applied Science in **Accounting**, Virginia Tech, Blacksburg, VA, 1996; **honors graduate, 3.75 GPA**.

AFFILIATIONS

Was elected Vice President of the Virginia Tech Accounting Society and Secretary of the Institute of Management Accountants.

EXPERIENCE

LEAD TRAINER. Cracker Barrel, Blacksburg, VA (2001-present). Provide essential skills training and orientation to all new personnel for this busy local restaurant with more than 110 employees; ensure that all new hires comply with corporate policies and procedures.
- Assist the management in controlling labor costs through careful preparation of weekly schedules based on business forecasts and established traffic patterns.
- Direct the work of up to 20 servers, prioritizing and assigning daily tasks to maintain adequate floor coverage while providing exceptional customer service.
- Travel to new stores opening throughout the region to provide training and ensure that all internal operations of the wait staff are running smoothly.
- Perform liaison between the wait staff and the six members of the management team, reporting to supervisors daily to keep them informed of internal issues.

FULL-CHARGE BOOKKEEPER. Foster Plumbing, Blacksburg, VA (1996-2001). Took over the troubled financial operations of this local business and quickly established proper reporting procedures, eliminated delinquencies in federal tax payments, and increased positive cash flow by collecting on a large number of outstanding accounts receivable.
- Entered and posted all daily totals and bank deposits, as well as reconciling monthly bank statements and performing profit analysis for the business.
- Printed out monthly billing statements and processed payments for accounts receivable; processed invoices and purchase orders, cutting checks to satisfy accounts payable.
- Prepared financial statements and tax returns, as well as filing state withholding and unemployment, quarterly reports (941), end-of year FUTA report, and end-of-year information returns (W-2s and 1099s).
- Processed weekly payroll, handling wage garnishments and reporting employee wages in accordance with IRS regulations.
- Prepared delinquent tax returns for the previous four years, communicating with the IRS on behalf of the owner and resolving the delinquency.
- In my first six months, collected on more than $9,000 in delinquent accounts; reduced the percentage of delinquent accounts to less than five percent within two years.

ACCOUNTING CLERK. Green Accounting, Blacksburg, VA (1995-1996). Performed a number of accounting and clerical functions including payroll and tax preparation.

PERSONAL

Familiar with Lotus 1-2-3 and Peachtree accounting software. Excellent references.

Date

Exact Name of Person
Exact Title
Exact Name of Company
Address
City, State, Zip

BUSINESS MANAGER

Sometimes a detour in our career makes us realize what we really like to do! This "middle manager" on the fast track was recruited for a business management position in the automobile industry. Although he excelled in the work, he didn't find it as satisfying and stimulating as the work he'd done in banking and financial institutions. Hence, this resume and cover letter are designed to help him change industries.

Dear Exact Name of Person (or Dear Sir or Madam if answering a blind ad):

With the enclosed resume, I would like to make you aware of my background as an experienced professional with exceptional supervisory, communication, and analytical skills as well as a strong bottom-line orientation and a proven ability to maximize profits and sales.

I was recruited by AutoMax for my present position as Business Manager, and my rapid success in that position resulted in my being entrusted with the responsibility for overseeing the finance departments at both of their locations. I supervise three finance managers as well as a sales force of 15 automotive sales representatives. Through my efforts in promoting finance and warranty products, the dealership's average aftermarket profit has increased from $300 per vehicle to $500 per vehicle.

In my previous position with Virginia Bank & Trust, I was promoted rapidly, achieving a position as Assistant Vice President after only 33 months. I began with the company as a Credit Analyst and was promoted to Commercial Relationship Manager at the end of seven months of service. In this position, I actively recruited new commercial accounts and serviced existing accounts. During my tenure, my commercial accounts portfolio grew from $15 million to $25 million, and I doubled non-interest (fee-based) income from $20,000 per year to $40,000 per year.

I have earned Master of Business Administration and Bachelor of Science in Business Administration degrees from Virginia University.

If you can use a hardworking young manager with proven business savvy, I would enjoy an opportunity to meet with you in person to discuss your needs. Although I can provide outstanding references at the appropriate time, I would appreciate your holding my interest in your company in confidence at this point. I can assure you in advance that I have an exceptional reputation and could become a valuable asset to your company.

Sincerely,

William Wright

WILLIAM WRIGHT

1110½ Hay Street, Fayetteville, NC 28305 • preppub@aol.com • (910) 483-6611

OBJECTIVE To benefit an organization that can use an enthusiastic, experienced manager with exceptional supervisory, communication, and analytical skills who offers a track record of success in maximizing profitability and increasing sales.

EDUCATION **Master of Business Administration**, Virginia University, Greenville, VA, 1993 — GPA 3.6. **Bachelor of Science in Business Administration** concentration in Finance, Virginia University, 1992.

EXPERIENCE **BUSINESS MANAGER.** Somerville AutoMax, Somerville, VA (1997-present). Was recruited for this position by this automotive dealership; oversee sales force of 15 employees.
- After excelling as Business Manager at one of AutoMax's locations, was entrusted with the additional responsibility of managing the finance departments at both locations.
- Supervise three finance managers, ensuring accurate and efficient preparation, processing, and completion of loan documentation.
- Communicate directly with lenders by phone and fax to obtain financing for customers; process loan applications for nearly 200 customers per month.
- Maximize the dealership's profit by selling and promoting the sale of aftermarket products such as extended warranties and credit life insurance.
- Established a secondary finance program for customers with past credit problems.
- Increased the dealership's average profit on aftermarket sales from $300 per vehicle to more than $500 per vehicle.

At Virginia Bank & Trust, was promoted in the following "track record" of increasing responsibility by this large national bank:
1994-1997: **COMMERCIAL RELATIONSHIP MANAGER.** Greenville, VA. Was rapidly promoted within the organization; advanced to Commercial Relationship Manager after seven months with Virginia Bank & Trust, and to Assistant Vice President after only 33 months.
- Actively recruited new commercial accounts while providing the highest level of customer service to established accounts.
- Communicated the advantages of Virginia Bank & Trust and promoted our products and services to new and existing customers.
- Through my efforts, my commercial accounts portfolio grew from $15 million to $25 million during my tenure.
- Doubled fee-based (non-interest) income from $20,000 per year to $40,000 per year for accounts that I managed.

1994: **CREDIT ANALYST.** Various locations in VA. Started with Virginia Bank & Trust upon completion of my MBA program; quickly mastered skills related to loan pricing and the making of credit decisions.
- Underwrote loan requests for Relationship Managers throughout VA.
- Analyzed financial statements including balance sheets and income statements; gained valuable knowledge related to cash flow management.
- Completed Relationship Manager Development Course, November, 1994.

AFFILIATIONS Rotary International — Finance Committee Chairperson
Member, Chamber of Commerce

PERSONAL Excellent personal and professional references are available upon request.

Date

Exact Name of Person
Title or Position
Name of Company
Address (number and street)
Address (city, state, and zip)

BUYER   Dear Exact Name of Person: (or Sir or Madam if answering a blind ad.)

With the enclosed resume, I would like to initiate the process of being considered for employment within your organization. Because of family ties, I am in the process of relocating to the Dallas area by a target date of February 28, 2002. Although I already have a Dallas address which is shown on my resume, it is my sister's home and I would prefer your contacting me at the e-mail address shown on my resume or at my current telephone number if you wish to talk with me prior to February 28th.

Since graduating from the University of Puget Sound in 1998, I have enjoyed a track record of rapid promotion with a corporation headquartered in San Diego, CA. I began as an Assistant Branch Manager and Head Buyer, was cross-trained as a Sales Representative, and have been promoted to my current position in which I manage the selling process related to 3,500 different products. In that capacity, I am entrusted with the responsibility for nearly $15 million in annual expenditures, and I maintain excellent working relationships with more than 150 vendors of name-brand consumer products sold through chain and convenience stores.

In my job, rapid change is a daily reality, and I have become accustomed to working in an environment in which I must make rapid decisions while weighing factors including forecasted consumer demand, distribution patterns, inventory turnover patterns, and vendor capacity and character. I have earned a reputation as a persuasive communicator and savvy negotiator with an aggressive bottom-line orientation.

If you can use my versatile experience in sales, purchasing, distribution, and operations management, I hope you will contact me to suggest a time when we might meet to discuss your needs and how I might serve them. I can provide excellent personal and professional references, and I assure you in advance that I am a hard worker accustomed to being measured according to ambitious goals for profitability in a highly competitive marketplace.

Yours sincerely,

Charles Jefferson

CHARLES JEFFERSON

1110½ Hay Street, Fayetteville, NC 28305   •   preppub@aol.com   •   (910) 483-6611

OBJECTIVE   To contribute to an organization that can use a resourceful manager with proven skills in managing the selling process while prudently overseeing inventory carrying costs, maintaining excellent working relationships with vendors, and preparing strategic plans.

EDUCATION   **B.S. in Business Administration,** University of Puget Sound, Tacoma, WA, 1998.
- Dr. Philip and Betsey Davis Scholarship award recipient.

EXPERIENCE   *ATLANTIC DOMINION DISTRIBUTORS (1998-present):* Since graduating from the University of Puget Sound, have enjoyed a track record of success and rapid promotion with Atlantic Dominion Distributors, a company with seven locations on the West Coast, headquartered in San Diego, CA:

HEAD BUYER. Tacoma, WA (2001-present). Personally handle more than half of the buying for a company which purchases up to $25 million annually in consumer products which are then distributed to the consumer through chain and convenience stores.
- Develop and sustain effective working relationships with more than 150 vendors including Hershey, Nabisco Foods, Quaker, and other vendors of name-brand juices, candy, health and beauty aids, and groceries.
- Maintain extensive liaison with sales representatives; coordinate contests and promotions for sales representatives and customers.
- Attend national trade shows and buying conventions.
- Was commended for playing a key role in my branch's being "Branch of the Year" in 2002.
- Am responsible for prudently managing the selling process and making astute buying decisions related to 3500 products in a highly competitive market in which rapid turnover is critical.

HEAD BUYER. Tacoma, WA (2000-01). Reported directly to the Vice President while handling the buying of more than $10 million worth of merchandise annually; purchased products supplied to five locations in WA and OR from the Tacoma location.
- Established and maintained excellent working relationships with 50 vendors while purchasing juices, candy, health and beauty aids, and other consumer products.
- Was commended for my excellent decision-making ability in forecasting inventory needs and purchasing products on a timely basis at lowest cost; made weekly buying decisions.
- Maintained a close working relationship with warehouse managers to ensure inventory accuracy.
- Organized deliveries of products to locations served by the Tacoma branch.
- Conducted semiannual inventory of the Tacoma location.
- Maintained strict accountability; entered receiving documents into computer to update inventory status daily and reconciled all invoices monthly. Monitored inventory turnover.
- Learned to resourcefully troubleshoot a wide variety of inventory problems.

BUYER & ASSISTANT BRANCH MANAGER. Tacoma, WA (1998-00).
Became skilled in buying groceries and tobacco products while also functioning in the role of **Sales Representative**; was cross-trained as a Route Sales Representative.
- Learned to accurately handle all the paperwork involved in sales which included approving vendor invoices for payment by home office; preparing OR and WA excise tax reports.

COMPUTERS   Lotus, Microsoft Excel, Microsoft Word, Harvard Graphics, and WordPerfect for Windows

PERSONAL   Outstanding references available upon request. Known for reliability and integrity.

To: Melissa Marlow
Acoustics, Inc.

From: Claire Stevens

CASH AUDIT SPECIALIST   Dear Melissa:

With this letter and the enclosed resume, I would like to thank you for contacting me about employment with Acoustics, and I wish to formally express my interest in further discussing the position you have in mind.

As you will see from my resume, I offer an unusually strong combination of an outgoing personality and strong customer service skills combined with excellent accounting knowledge and an attitude of attention to detail. You will see from my resume that I earned my Bachelor's degree in Fine Arts-Theatre Arts, and I was able to express my extroverted nature and refine my public relations skills while excelling academically.

In my current position as a Cash Audit Specialist with the nation's largest Jiffy Lube franchise, which is comprised of 228 stores, I am responsible for cash auditing for 120 stores in five states. While preparing bank reports and reconciling store deposits using a spreadsheet, I am continuously providing outstanding customer service along with aggressive problem-solving related to cash discrepancies and credit card problems.

In my previous job as Office Manager for a construction company which had to downsize, I gained vast experience in construction industry accounting practices and procedures while preparing payroll, handling accounts payable/receivable, and preparing tax reports and statements. I have worked with Access, Excel, Word, Peachtree, and various other software programs. My strong customer service and public relations skills have been refined in prior jobs in fashion retailing and the hospitality industry. I have trained numerous individuals in cashiering, customer service, and sales.

Although I can provide excellent references from my current employer as well as previous employers, I would appreciate your not contacting my employer until after we discuss the position at Acoustics in more detail. I am confident that I would be well suited to any position which requires strict attention to detail, strong accounting skills, as well as an aggressive problem-solving orientation.

I will look forward to hearing from you again soon, and I thank you again for contacting me and expressing your interest in my background. Have a nice weekend!

Yours sincerely,

Claire Stevens

CLAIRE STEVENS

1110½ Hay Street, Fayetteville, NC 28305 • preppub@aol.com • (910) 483-6611

OBJECTIVE
To contribute to the growth and profitability of a company that can use a dedicated and hardworking young professional with strong accounting and computer skills.

EDUCATION
Bachelor of Fine Arts-Theatre Arts, Tulsa University, Tulsa, OK, 2000; 3.3 GPA.

COMPUTERS
Experienced with Excel, Access, Word, Peachtree, and various other software programs.
- Proven ability to rapidly master new programs, applications, and operating systems.

EXPERIENCE
CASH AUDIT SPECIALIST. Lucor, Inc., Tulsa, OK (2001-present). As a key member of the accounting team at the nation's largest Jiffy Lube franchise, which is comprised of 228 stores, am responsible for cash auditing for 120 stores in OK, NE, NM, WA, and IL.
- On a daily basis, prepare bank reports through external modems, enter data onto a cash spreadsheet, and perform reconciliation based on Jiffy Lube store deposits.
- Am continuously resolving problems and "finding money" as part of on ongoing effort to assure that 120 stores remain in strict compliance with corporate cash reporting and deposit guidelines.
- Routinely utilize an Access database and Excel spreadsheets.
- Provide outstanding service while dealing with customers disputing credit card charges.

OFFICE MANAGER. Pyramid Construction Co., Inc., Tulsa, OK (2000-01). Gained vast experience in construction industry accounting practices and procedures while preparing payroll for up to 35 people in addition to handling accounts payable, accounts receivable, general ledger posting, bank reconciliations, as well as quarterly and year-end statements.
- Prepared a variety of reports used for tax reporting while routinely utilizing Peachtree accounting, Excel, and Microsoft Word.

SALES ASSOCIATE & TRAINING MANAGER. Gap, Inc., Myrtle Beach, SC (1996-99). For this popular fashion retailer, excelled in sales and in expertly operating a cash register while also orienting and training new employees in sales, customer service, and cash register operation.
- Through my aggressive sales orientation and outgoing personality, motivated other sales associates and promoted a positive work environment which influenced customer buying behavior.
- Trained numerous sales associates in techniques which improved their sales performance and customer relations skills.

OFFICE CASHIER & TRAINING MANAGER. Planet Hollywood/Official All Star Café, Myrtle Beach, SC (1999-01). For one of the largest restaurants on the east coast, trained new servers in presentation, customer service, and teamwork while also working as the cashier; accepted all bank deposits from servers, prepared the cash drop, made credit card deposits, and prepared reports that the manager needed in order to close out the night's receipts.
- Graciously handled incoming phone lines, and took messages for the managers.

HOSTESS, SERVER, BARTENDER, & INHOUSE CATERING SPECIALIST. Doubletree Guest Suites, New York, NY (1998-99). Handled cash register responsibilities and promoted excellence in customer service while excelling in numerous duties; acted as Hostess, Server, and Bartender, and was also involved in inhouse catering.

PERSONAL
Highly motivated individual with extremely outgoing personality and excellent social skills.

Date

Exact Name of Person
Exact Title
Exact Name of Company
Address
City, State, Zip

Dear Exact Name of Person: (or Dear Sir or Madam if answering a blind ad):

I would appreciate an opportunity to talk with you soon about how I could contribute to your organization through my versatile experience and education which has emphasized the management and administration of financial and accounting operations.

As you will see from my enclosed resume, I am presently pursuing my Ph.D. in Management which I expect to receive in December of 2003 and have previously earned master's degrees in Management, and Educational Administration and Supervision. My bachelor's degrees are in Business Administration and Accounting.

I have worked for the Defense Finance and Accounting Service since 1990 and advanced from Staff Accountant positions in different divisions of the agency to my most recent job as the Reconciliation Division Chief in Kansas City, MO. In this capacity I supervised 15 top-level accountants and financial specialists while handling the planning, coordination, control, and evaluation of debt programs for government agencies and military services. Earlier with the Defense Logistics Agency as a Supervisory Operating Accountant and Systems Accountant, I supervised as many as nine accounting technicians in the Defense Contract Reconciliation, Accounts Receivable, and Special Analysis and Review divisions.

Throughout my career, I have been heavily involved in training and guiding the development and performance of others. I believe I have a talent for providing easily understood instruction and for passing on even highly technical knowledge to others in a positive and effective manner.

If you can use an articulate, intelligent, and well-educated professional who offers a reputation for versatility and adaptability, I can assure you in advance that I could rapidly become an asset to your organization. Please call or write soon to suggest a time when we might meet and discuss your current and future needs and how I might serve them.

Sincerely,

Douglas Simmons

DOUGLAS SIMMONS

1110½ Hay Street, Fayetteville, NC 28305   •   preppub@aol.com   •   (910) 483-6611

OBJECTIVE   To offer an extensive background in such diverse fields as accounting and finance, education, and management to an organization in need of a mature professional with experience in both the private and public sectors.

EDUCATION   **Ph.D. in Management** from California Coast University, Santa Ana, CA, to be awarded December 2003

B.P.A., Accounting, Mississippi State University, Starksville, MS, 2001.

M.B.A., Management, Mississippi College, Clinton, MS, 1998.

M.S., Educational Administration and Supervision, University of West Alabama, Livingston, AL, 1992.

B.S., Business Administration, University of West Alabama, Livingston, AL, 1987.

CERTIFICATION   Became a Certified Government Financial Manager (certification number 11065), 2001.

CPA, Arkansas, expected May 2003.

EXPERIENCE   *Advanced in managerial roles with the Defense Finance and Accounting Service:*

RECONCILIATION DIVISION CHIEF. Kansas City, MO (2000-present). Supervised 13 top-level staff accountants and two financial specialists while planning, organizing, coordinating, controlling, and evaluating debt programs for a wide range of government agencies.

- Selected as Acting Director of Accounting Operations, supervised three division chiefs and a secretary during his frequent absences.
- Provided support for agencies and activities such as the General Services Administration and Office of Personnel Management as well as for Department of Defense (DoD) components (the Army, Air Force, Navy, and Marine Corps).
- Trained, guided, and provided technical assistance to staff members along with making periodic performance evaluations.
- Developed and revised the job descriptions and expected performance standards for division personnel.
- Applied written and verbal communication skills while preparing reports and presenting briefings to top management officials.

STAFF ACCOUNTANT. Kansas City, MO (1998-00). As the senior staff accountant and acting division chief of the Intra-Government Accounts division, supervised eight top-level accountants and five accounting technicians while providing support for U.S. Marine Corps finance services.

- Oversaw the disbursal and reporting of payroll accounts for active duty and reserve personnel to include payments for dental, educational, Worker's Compensation and unemployment compensation claims, and life insurance.
- Managed and gave approval for signing and issuing checks from disbursement offices.
- Interpreted, administered, coordinated, and reported expenses and disbursements to the Marine Corps headquarters for unfunded reimbursable activities such as flight operations, forestry, agriculture outleasing, and recycling.
- Reviewed accounting and financial records in order to ensure their compliance with applicable government regulations and policies.

STAFF ACCOUNTANT. Columbus, OH (1987-98). For the Debt Management Division, initiated debt collection actions against defense contractors.

PERSONAL   Can provide excellent personal and professional references on request. Will relocate.

Date

Exact Name of Person
Title or Position
Name of Company
Address (number and street)
Address (city, state, and zip)

Dear Exact Name of Person: (or Dear Sir or Madam if answering a blind ad.)

I would appreciate an opportunity to talk with you soon about how I could contribute to your organization through my experience in financial management as well as through my skills in the areas of financial and operations management along with my strong customer service orientation. I have recently relocated to the Seattle area and am exploring employment opportunities with companies that can make use of my management background and financial skills.

You will see from my enclosed resume that I offer an in-depth knowledge of finance and business. My most recent job was as Controller and General Manager of a real estate rental company for approximately eight years. During this time I substantially reduced the company's debt load, virtually eliminated the amount of uncollectibles, and increased occupancy rates to a consistently high 95%. Through my diplomatic but assertive managerial style, I brought this business out of debt and transformed it into a viable operation.

During a successful career in the U.S. Army, I advanced to hold increasingly more responsible managerial positions in the fields of finance, budgeting, and pay administration as well as in personnel administration. I gained skills and refined a natural aptitude for analyzing, controlling, and resolving problems while earning a reputation as a versatile and adaptable professional.

With an associate's degree in Banking and Finance, I could be a valuable asset to an organization that can use a mature individual with the ability to get along with others in supervisory roles.

I hope you will welcome my call soon to arrange a brief meeting at your convenience to discuss your current and future needs and how I might serve them. Thank you in advance for your time.

Sincerely yours.

Roger Rose

Optional sentence that can go as the second sentence in last paragraph:
I would be happy to discuss the details of my salary history with you in person.

ROGER ROSE

Until 12/15/01: 1110½ Hay Street, Fayetteville, NC 28305   (910) 483-6611
After 12/16/01: 538 Pittsfield Avenue, Seattle, WA 95401   (405) 483-6611

OBJECTIVE

To offer a track record of success in managerial roles with organizations requiring knowledge of finance, personnel, and administrative functions along with a reputation for analytical skills and attention to detail as well as a strong customer service orientation.

EXPERIENCE

CONTROLLER & FINANCE MANAGER. Rentals Incorporated, Raleigh, NC (1995-02). Brought about major improvements in several important functional areas while handling multiple roles as a financial manager, partner, and operations manager for a company with 160 rental units; manage two accounting specialists.
- Reduced the organization's debts more than $20,000 in less than a year through the application of my knowledge and experience in business management and finance.
- Almost totally eliminated uncollectibles – reduced them to under 1%.
- Prepared advertising materials which resulted in improved occupancy levels and consistently maintained 95% fill rates on leased units.
- Took charge of all aspects of finance and business administration ranging from maintaining books, to processing all accounting data, to accounts receivable and payable.
- Prepared and managed the budget; reconciled bank accounts.
- Represented the company through heavy contact with the public while showing prospective residents units available for lease or rent.
- Resolved a wide range of customer service as well as budget and fee problems.

GENERAL MANAGER. The Novelty and Games Company, Buies Creek, NC (1991-95). Applied my knowledge of business and finance to build this company from a concept into a viable organization.
- Dealt with all aspects of establishing and successfully operating a small business: prepared and managed budgets, made bank deposits, and reconciled bank accounts as well as maintaining accounts receivable and payable ledgers.
- Controlled inventory from ordering supplies and merchandise to setting prices.

Highlights of earlier experience: Gained and refined knowledge of personnel management and finance/pay activities during a career with the U.S. Army, locations worldwide.
- As the **Manager** of a program studying the need for changes to the personnel structure of the Army, processed information and resolved problems, researched possible changes to determine their impact, and contributed input used in budget preparation.
- As a **Senior Personnel Management Supervisor,** directed up to 40 specialists engaged in processing promotions, reclassifications, transfers, and performance reports.
- As a **Finance Section Manager,** updated personnel's finance records and verified information before entering it into computers; maintained ledgers, cash books, and all related accounting records.
- As the **Chief of Military Pay and Travel,** processed pay activities for personnel in 11 states and four overseas areas.
- As **Manager of a Personnel Section,** processed military personnel and their family members who were going overseas; arranged for transportation to overseas assignments; provided information and briefings on customs, laws, and conditions in overseas areas.

EDUCATION & TRAINING

A.S. degree in **Banking** and **Finance,** Whitefall Technical Community College, Whitefall, TX. Completed numerous courses in finance, management, and personnel administration sponsored by the U.S. Army.

PERSONAL

Am known for my dedication and insistence on seeing any job through to completion. Have a high level of initiative. Enjoy public relations and customer service activities.

Date

Exact Name of Person
Title or Position
Name of Company
Address (number and street)
Address (city, state, and zip)

CONTROLLER

Dear Exact Name of Person: (or Sir or Madam if answering a blind ad.)

This professional has more jobs on his resume than he wishes he had, but two of the companies he worked for went out of business. He uses the cover letter to point out this fact to potential employers so they won't feel he's a "job hopper" who will be "here today, gone tomorrow" if they hire him.

With the enclosed resume, I would like to initiate the process of being considered for employment within your organization.

As you will see from my resume, I hold a bachelor's degree in Business Administration, an associate's degree in Data Processing, and have completed more than 30 hours of Accounting course work. I offer computer programming experience using Cobol, Basic, and RPG, and I am skilled in using popular software including Excel, Lotus, DACEASY, and other programs.

With regard to accounting, I offer experience as a controller, staff accountant, and cost accountant. An extremely loyal individual with a long-term orientation in all my undertakings in life, I want to draw your attention to the fact that there are more jobs on my resume than I am comfortable with. Through no fault of my own, I have been employed by two companies who decided to liquidate their assets or cease business operations. I can provide outstanding references from all my employers, and I can assure you that they would describe me as an industrious and disciplined individual who is very creative in applying my knowledge to improve internal systems and boost profitability.

My permanent home is in Chicago where my wife is employed as a nurse. It is my desire to become a permanent asset to an organization which can benefit from my considerable skills in consulting, management, and accounting. If you can use my experience and knowledge, please contact me to suggest a time when we might meet to discuss your current and future needs and how I might serve them. Thank you in advance for your time.

Sincerely,

Avery O'Farrell

AVERY O'FARRELL

1110½ Hay Street, Fayetteville, NC 28305 • preppub@aol.com • (910) 483-6611

OBJECTIVE	To benefit an organization that can use a detail-oriented professional with a strong bottom-line orientation who offers experience in management accounting and business management.
SKILLS	**Computer programming: COBOL, BASIC,** and **RPG** languages. **Software:** Excel, Lotus, and DACEASY; familiarity with Solomen IV and GAP software. **Accounting:** Data processing, payroll, purchasing, cost estimates, tax return preparation, preparation of P&L Statements.
EDUCATION	B.A. degree, **Business Administration,** 1987; and A.A.S., **Data Processing,** 1985; Providence University, Providence, RI. • Completed 30 hours of course work in **Accounting** at Providence University.
EXPERIENCE	**CONTROLLER.** IPG Energy, Chicago, IL (2000-present). Was recruited to supervise accounting functions for a $97 million project which involved maintaining general ledger, accounts receivable, and accounts payable; this firm is now liquidating its assets. • Reported directly to project manager and CEO. • Coordinated with the four partners, representatives from lead bank and associate banks, and officials from counties involved in the waste-energy recycling project. **CONTROLLER.** Baytree Developers, Chicago, IL (1995-00). Handled all accounting functions associated with operating this two-location, 60-employee business that processed soil and bark products sold primarily to large chain stores, including Lowe's, Food Lion, etc. • Coordinated and supervised two clerks in the home office and assisted in the day-to-day managing of both processing plants. • Supervised a variety of accounting procedures including monthly financial statements, bank statement reconciliations, and quarterly payroll tax reports. **STAFF ACCOUNTANT.** Sycamore Industries, Chicago, IL (1992-94). Supervised four clerks while preparing monthly financial statements, maintaining general ledger and fixed assets, and working as liaison with corporate accounting office. • Managed accounts payable and payroll; prepared all monthly, quarterly, and annual sales, fuel, and regulatory tax returns. • For this construction materials firm with annual revenues in excess of $15 million, prepared various analyses used as management decision-making tools. **BUSINESS MANAGER.** Providence Junior College, Providence, RI (1990-91). Prepared reports pertaining to accounts payable and cash disbursements while also maintaining data concerning student accounts receivable. • Maintained bookstore inventories; made deposits and reconciled bank statements; provided counseling for students regarding financial aid and student loans. **STAFF ACCOUNTANT.** Bryson Associates, CPA, Providence, RI (1988-90). Analyzed corporate books for compilations and preparation of financial statements. Prepared individual and corporate tax returns. Participated in field audits. **COST ACCOUNTANT.** Anderson Constructors, Providence, RI (1986-88). Prepared job cost reports and assisted with administration of subcontracts.
PERSONAL	Can provide outstanding personal and professional references upon request.

Date

Exact Name of Person
Exact Title
Exact Name of Company
Address
City, State, Zip

CONTROLLER

His employer of more than 26 years has restructured and, to keep his job with the company, he must move to Richmond. He has decided to resign from the company and seek employment elsewhere.

Dear Exact Name of Person (or Dear Sir or Madam if answering a blind ad):

With the enclosed resume, I would like to make you aware of my considerable experience in the area of accounting, finance, budgeting, and controlling.

As you will see from my resume, I have a rather unusual work history, since I have worked for only one company. I began with Quality Truck Rental, Inc. in 1984 and was promoted through the ranks until in 1990 I became a District Controller for one of Quality's 70 districts. For a district with a fleet of 800 vehicles, I received extensive recognition for exemplary performance in accounts receivable management as well as prudent accounting management in all areas.

Since 1998, Quality has been engaged in a process of eliminating administrative services performed at the district level and moving them to Richmond. I have played a key role in helping customers and staff adapt to the new concept. Although I have been strongly encouraged to be part of the restructured organization, I do not wish to move to Richmond. I can provide outstanding references at the appropriate time.

If you can use a professional with extensive experience in managing people while managing the bottom line for maximum profitability, I hope you will contact me to suggest a time when we might meet to discuss your needs. I am confident that I could become a valuable addition to your management team.

Yours sincerely,

Owens Kober

OWENS KOBER

1110½ Hay Street, Fayetteville, NC 28305 • preppub@aol.com • (910) 483-6611

OBJECTIVE	To benefit an organization that can use an experienced manager who offers a background in accounting, finance, budgeting, and forecasting along with a proven ability to adapt to change while implementing new systems to enhance growth and profitability.
COMPUTERS	Highly proficient in utilizing computer software for financial analysis and word processing; extensive experience with software programs including Microsoft Excel, Microsoft Word, and Lotus 1-2-3.
EDUCATION	**Associate in Applied Science in Business Administration,** Sidona Technical Institute, Sidona, AZ 1984; named as class **Honor Student.**.

- Excelled in professional training programs sponsored by Quality Truck Rental, Inc. related to cost accounting, financial analysis, forecasting, and budget preparation.

EXPERIENCE

Excelled in handling a variety of special projects and multiple responsibilities while working for Quality Truck Rental, (Quality Transportation Services), locations in AZ, 1984-present:

- Quality has restructured nationally, moving central support activities from its 70 districts to Richmond; I have played a key role in helping the company restructure and, although I have spent 26 enjoyable years with the company, I have decided not to relocate to Richmond.
- Can provide outstanding references from individuals at all company levels.

REGIONAL CONTROLLER. Tempe, AZ (1998-present). Assisted the General Manager with matters pertaining to financial analysis of the business while answering customer questions, resolving billing problems, and supporting the sales staff in obtaining answers and resolving problems related to the "migration" of administrative functions from the Tempe District to the Richmond Shared Services Center.

- Demonstrated my loyalty to Quality by helping both customers and sales staff accept and develop enthusiasm for the new concept of the Shared Services Center in Richmond; was instrumental in training and developing a new General Manager.

DISTRICT CONTROLLER. Tempe, AZ (1990-98). Excelled as District Controller of one of Quality's 70 districts, and managed up to seven Accounting Clerks in activities including accounts receivable and payable, repair expense accounting, vehicle cost records, vehicle licensing and permitting, and computer system administration.

- Ensured proper control of company assets in this $25 million district; oversaw $20 million in annual revenues while supporting the District Manager and General Managers with forecasting, budgeting, financial analyses of operations, general ledger maintenance, as well as monthly profit and loss statements.
- Prepared the district's annual financial plan, and am proud of our track record in nearly always exceeding profitability and revenue goals.
- Led the district to achieve outstanding results in internal audits conducted every 12-24 months by Quality officials.
- Received recognition for exemplary performance in accounts receivable management; was recognized for my initiative in implementing accounting controls.
- Provided the leadership in implementing PCs in the district, and served unofficially in the role of System Administrator.
- For a fleet of 800 vehicles, provided oversight of licensing for interstate operations.
- Analyzed financial statements including balance sheets and income statements.

Other Quality experience: **OFFICE MANAGER.** Milestown, AZ (1984-90).

PERSONAL   Excellent reputation and can provide outstanding personal and professional references.

Exact Name
Title or Position
Name of Company
Address (number and street)
Address (city, state, and zip)

CREDIT MANAGER

Dear Exact Name of Person: (or Dear Sir or Madam if answering a blind ad.)

If you want to job hunt in industries other than the one you're in, keep the Objective on your resume all purpose and versatile. Notice the Personal Section. Sometimes you can show off an accomplishment in the Personal Section which doesn't seem to fit in anywhere else on the resume. It may still be an accomplishment which could make the prospective employer react to you in a positive fashion.

With the enclosed resume, I would like to indicate my interest in your organization and my desire to explore employment opportunities.

As you will see from my enclosed resume, as Credit Manager of a large building supply company, I have played a key role in the growth of the company from two stores with sales of less than $15 million to five stores with more than $40 million in sales. I have been in charge of approving all new accounts for all stores, and I have implemented internal controls which have reduced the number of days of sales outstanding by more than 20 days. Although I am held in high regard by my current employer, the business is in the process of merging with a larger regional company, so I am taking this opportunity to explore opportunities with other area firms.

I hope you will welcome my call soon to arrange a brief meeting at your convenience to discuss your current and future needs and how I might serve them. Thank you in advance for your time.

Sincerely yours.

Phillip Harris

Alternate last paragraph:
I hope you will call or write me soon to suggest a time convenient for us to meet and discuss your current and future needs and how I might serve them. Thank you in advance for your time.

PHILLIP HARRIS

1110½ Hay Street, Fayetteville, NC 28305 • preppub@aol.com • (910) 483-6611

OBJECTIVE	To add value to an organization that can use a well-organized manager who is skilled in developing new systems and procedures for profitability enhancement, establishing new accounts and managing existing ones, and administering finances at all levels.
EDUCATION	**Bachelor of Science in Business Administration (B.S.B.A.) degree**, concentration in Finance, Western Tennessee University, 1991.

- Member, Beta Kappa Alpha Banking and Finance Fraternity.
- Was active in intramural softball, basketball, and arm wrestling.
- Worked throughout college in order to finance my college education.

Completed **A.I.B. in Consumer Lending,** Pitt Community College, 1996.

EXPERIENCE

CREDIT MANAGER. All Purpose Building Supply, Raleigh, NC (2000-present). Was specially recruited by the company to assume this position which involved establishing a credit department with three employees.

- Played a key role in the growth of the company from two stores with sales of less than $15 million, to five stores with sales of more than $40 million.
- Reduced the number of days of sales outstanding by 20+ days.
- Was in charge of approving all new accounts for five stores.
- Developed and maintained an excellent working relationship with all customers.
- Formulated and implemented key areas of company policy by authoring credit policies; directed activities including account adjustments, skip tracing, liening, and billing.
- Coordinated with the corporate attorney; prepared cash flow projections and provided the controller with financial information for profit-and-loss statements and balance sheets for the company owners.
- Implemented procedures that lowered chargeoffs and increased collection activity while accounts receivables grew from $2 million to $7.5 million.

CONSUMER LOAN OFFICER. East Coast Federal Savings & Loan, Raleigh, NC (1996-00). Was promoted to responsibilities for handling activities in these areas:

commercial lending	consumer lending
collections	credit card approval
credit investigations	marketing of consumer loans

LOAN OFFICER & COLLECTION REPRESENTATIVE. NCNB National Bank of North Carolina, Raleigh, NC (1991-95). After excelling as a Collection Representative, was promoted to Loan Officer, in charge of lending money for consumer purchases and performing credit investigations.

- As a Collection Representative, collected past due accounts, cross-referenced bank records versus automobile dealerships' records, and investigated consumer account payment records while also handling foreclosures, repossessions, insurance claims, and skip tracing of delinquent accounts.
- Performed liaison with banking auditors and legal personnel.
- Gained expertise in all aspects of banking and lending.

SALESMAN/ACCOUNT REPRESENTATIVE. Premier Building Supply, Oakland, TN (1988-91). Worked at this construction industry supply company in the summers and breaks during the years when I was earning my college degree.

- Learned to deal with people while selling building materials, light fixtures, garden supplies, and hardware; graduated into responsibilities for handling major accounts.

PERSONAL In high school was a member of the National Math Honor Society and the Science Club and set my school's record in the shot put while also excelling in football and wrestling.

Exact Name of Person
Exact Title
Exact Name of Company
Address
City, State, Zip

**CREDIT UNION BRANCH
MANAGER**

Dear Exact Name of Person (or Dear Sir or Madam if answering a blind ad):

With the enclosed resume, I would like to make you aware of an experienced financial industry professional with exceptional communication, motivational, and supervisory skills and a background in branch management, consumer lending, and account management in credit union environments.

As you will see, I have been excelling with Pentagon Federal Credit Union, advancing in a track record of increasing responsibility. In my most recent position as branch manager of the busy Silver Springs location, I supervised a staff of 18 employees, including two loan officers. I developed and implemented an annual operating budget of $700,00 and oversaw the administration of a $2 million change fund. By developing innovative and effective business and marketing plans, I have increased membership by 67%, loan dollars by 271%, and number of product sales per visit by 151%.

Previously as assistant manager of the telephone call center in Baltimore, MD, I supervised 25 employees handling 1,500 calls per day to provide members with banking services by phone. I acted as manager in my supervisor's absence, and also served as a loan officer, with authority over $40,000 in aggregate indebtedness. In addition, I organized and conducted morale focus groups for four telephone branches. Earlier, as an account researcher, I reorganized the work flow to increase the effectiveness of the accounts research staff, and created computerized versions of account reports and other documents.

Although I was highly regarded by this employer and can provide outstanding personal and professional references at the appropriate time, I have resigned my most recent position and am permanently relocating to Florida, in order to be closer to my family.

I have earned a Bachelor of Science in Business from the University of Maryland, and supplemented my degree program with numerous courses to enhance my knowledge and effectiveness within the finance industry. My strong combination of education and experience would be of great benefit to your organization.

If you can use a self-motivated and experienced financial professional with exceptional communication, motivational, and supervisory skills, I hope you will contact me to suggest a time when we might meet.

Sincerely,

Suzanne Newton

SUZANNE NEWTON

1110½ Hay Street, Fayetteville, NC 28305 • preppub@aol.com • (910) 483-6611

OBJECTIVE

To benefit an organization that can use an experienced banking and finance professional with exceptional communication, motivational, and supervisory skills who offers a background in branch management, consumer lending, and account management.

EDUCATION

Bachelor of Science degree in Business, University of Maryland, Silver Springs, MD, 1991.
Completed a number of courses supplemental to my business degree, including:
- Fair Credit Reporting Act compliance course, MD Credit Union Network, 2002.
- Supervisory Excellence course, Pentagon Federal Credit Union, 1992.
- Resource Management course, University of Maryland, 1991.
- Contract Negotiation course, University of Maryland, 1990.

EXPERIENCE

With Pentagon Federal Credit Union, have been promoted to positions of increasing **responsibility in this busy financial environment:**
BRANCH MANAGER. Silver Springs, MD (2000-02). Promoted to this position from Assistant Manager of the Baltimore call center; managed the busy Silver Springs branch of this large federal credit union.
- Supervised a staff of 18 employees, including two loan officers.
- Developed and implemented an annual operating budget of $700,000 and oversaw the administration of a $2 million change fund.
- Devised innovative business and marketing plans; have increased membership by 67%, loan dollars by 271%, and product sales per visit by 151%.
- Acted in the capacity of a loan officer, with a lending authority of $130,000 in aggregate indebtedness.
- Interviewed, hired, and trained all new employees; counseled marginal employees to improve performance and administered incentives to reward excellence.
- Provided verbal feedback to each employee on a quarterly basis and wrote periodic employee evaluations.
- Maintained prescribed security controls; ensured that routine maintenance was performed and all security equipment was functioning properly.

ASSISTANT MANAGER. Baltimore, MD (1995-00). Supervised a branch providing financial services by telephone for Pentagon Federal Credit Union members; provided members with all financial services with the exception of the direct disbursement of cash.
- Supervised 25 employees handling 1,500 calls per day; performed the duties of manager.
- Coordinated training of Member Service Representatives and Loan Officers, ensuring that all staff members were informed of current policies, products, and services.
- Consulted with members on loan products; reviewed and evaluated loan applications.
- Developed and implemented procedures for streamlining the execution of on-line transactions by call center representatives.
- Organized and conducted morale focus groups for four telephone branches.

ACCOUNT RESEARCHER. Baltimore, MD (1991-1995). Promoted to this position after a year as a Member Services Representative; performed in-depth research into account problems, analyzing and verifying the accuracy of data in order to resolve the problem.
- Reorganized work flow to increase effectiveness of account research staff.
- Generated statistical reports, analyzed the types of problems found, and recommended procedural changes to resolve existing problems and prevent future problems.
- Created computerized versions of account reports and other documents.

PERSONAL

Excellent personal and professional references are available upon request.

CREDIT UNION SALES REPRESENTATIVE

Dear Sir or Madam:

With the enclosed resume, I would like to make you aware of my considerable background and track record of accomplishment in financial services, sales, customer service, and collections.

As you can see from my enclosed resume, I have over seven years of professional experience. I have held positions as a Member Specialist, Account Manager, Full Service Banker, Front Desk and Accounting Clerk, and Sales Associate. My experience has enabled me to develop good communication, management, and supervisory skills which are essential in today's business world.

My personal strengths include dependability, a positive attitude, and the ability to quickly learn new procedures and techniques. I am a self-starter who enjoys becoming involved with new challenges, people, and situations. I deal with problems using tact and diplomacy, and I function well under stress and pressure.

If you can use an experienced banking and finance professional, I look forward to hearing from you soon to arrange a time when we might meet to discuss your needs. I can assure you in advance that I have an outstanding reputation and could quickly become a valuable asset to your company.

Sincerely,

Dawn Grass

DAWN GRASS

1110½ Hay Street, Fayetteville, NC 28305 • preppub@aol.com • (910) 483-6611

OBJECTIVE	To contribute to an organization that can use my experience in financial services, sales, customer service, banking, and collections.

QUALIFICATIONS

- Establish rapport with individuals of diverse backgrounds and experience levels.
- Timely and responsive to deadline requirements.
- Work independently and as a team member.
- Responsible, reliable, and efficient.

EDUCATION

Bachelor of Science degree in **Business and Management**, University of Maryland University College, College Park, MD, 2002.

Associate of Arts degree in **Management Studies**, University of Maryland University College, College Park, MD, 1998.

Completed two years of college level study in Accounting, Virginia State University, Petersburg, VA, 1996.

EXPERIENCE

SALES REPRESENTATIVE & MEMBER SPECIALIST. Chartway Federal Credit Union, Norfolk, VA (2002-present). Performed a wide range of customer service, sales, banking, and financial services in this busy credit union environment.

- Provided information to current and new members concerning membership eligibility, products, and services, including loan products and membership benefits.
- Processed and completed all new account transactions, payroll deductions, direct deposits, transfer forms, and share draft orders.
- Sold all of the credit union's financial products and services to members.
- Gained expert knowledge of second mortgage products.
- Set up rental safe deposit box records and assisted in gaining access to boxes.
- Balanced cash box with Teller Policy guidelines; processed loan applications.
- Recognized and capitalized on opportunities to up-sell member loan products and services; advised members of loan decisions.

ACCOUNT MANAGER. NationsBank, Norfolk, VA (2001-02). Provided a variety of credit counseling, customer service, and collections services for this large national bank.

- Demonstrated exceptional communication and customer service skills while collecting on delinquent credit card accounts by offering payment alternatives and/or payment plans.
- Documented preferred payment arrangement in customer's account file.

FULL SERVICE BANKER. Columbus Bank & Trust, Columbus, GA (2000-01). Delivered quality customer service while performing various duties as a Customer Service Representative, Teller, and Head Teller.

- Ran a cash drawer, balanced main vault, performed general bookkeeping, ordered money, opened new accounts, conducted interviews, and took loan applications.
- Assisted customers by answering questions concerning accounts and banking options.
- Acted as Branch Manager in the absence of that supervisor.
- As Branch Manager/Full Service Banker, was expected to make management decisions.

Other Experience: FRONT DESK CLERK. Directorate of Public works, Billeting Branch, Fort Benning, GA (1999-00).

SALES ASSOCIATE. Army and Air Force Exchange Service, Germany, (1997-98).

ACCOUNTING CLERK. Symbol Technologies, GMBH (MSI), Germany (1996-97).

PERSONAL

Excellent personal and professional references are available upon request.

Exact Name of Person
Title or Position
Name of Company
Address (number and street)
Address (city, state, and zip)

DATA PROCESSING   Dear Exact Name of Person: (or Sir or Madam if answering a blind ad.)

With the enclosed resume, I would like to express my interest in exploring employment opportunities with your organization.

As you will see, I offer a reputation as an articulate professional with exceptional time management and data processing skills. I am especially proud of my accomplishments in earning a bachelor's degree in Business Administration with a concentration in Healthcare Administration and an earlier associate's degree in Data Processing while simultaneously working two jobs and taking care of a home and family. I also have received Certification in Management from the AMA.

In multiple simultaneous roles with an orthopedic practice, I have acted as the Data Processing Coordinator, Supervisor of the Medical Transcription Department, Procedural Coder, Billing and Collections Manager, and Front Office Supervisor. Among my contributions has been personally automating and updating ADP systems to a level where we are recognized as one of the most sophisticated medial office systems in the country. I have also been credited with reducing a serious backlog of medical transcriptions, implementing a database which allows each terminal or PC instant access to every patient file, and making long-lasting improvements through a project which replaced manual appointment books with a computerized scheduling system.

Through my extensive and versatile experience gained in this practice, I offer exceptional knowledge of medical billing, ICD-9/CPT coding, collections and office administration. While overseeing the billing and collections functions for the practice, I contributed a firm yet fair and tactful style of communication while dealing with uncooperative customers and while handling extensive contact with personnel in insurance companies and collections agencies.

If you can use a mature and dedicated hard worker who would be committed to producing quality results while offering a combination of skills, experience, and knowledge, I hope you will contact me to suggest a time when we might meet to discuss your needs. I can provide outstanding references at the appropriate time.

Sincerely,

Marissa Stone

MARISSA STONE

1110½ Hay Street, Fayetteville, NC 28305 • preppub@aol.com • (910) 483-6611

OBJECTIVE   To contribute to an organization that can benefit from an articulate professional with a reputation for initiative and insight into the future of information management as well as exceptional knowledge of medical billing, ICD-9/CPT coding, collections, and office administration.

EDUCATION   Bachelor's degree, **Business Administration,** Park College, Parkville, MO, 2001.
- A Dean's List student, I attended specialized coursework in **Healthcare Administration.**
- Refined time management skills and attention to detail while simultaneously completing degree requirements, working two jobs, and taking care of a home and family.

Associate's degree, **Data Processing,** Park College, Parkville, MO.

CERTIFICATION   Received Certification in Management, AMA, 1999.

EXPERIENCE   *Have been credited with highly effective managerial and communication skills while excelling in multiple simultaneous roles with Cape Fear Orthopaedic Clinic, Parkville, MO:*

DATA PROCESSING COORDINATOR. (2000-present). Personally automated and upgraded ADP systems while maintaining hardware and software to include actions ranging from training employees to use software, to loading revisions, to maintaining the security and integrity of both the billing and medical records databases.
- Since January, have assumed additional responsibilities as **SUPERVISOR** for the Medical Transcription Department; reduced a serious backlog in only four months while overseeing the activities of six transcriptionists
- Upgraded a computer system which is now recognized as one of the most sophisticated medical office systems in the entire country.
- Ensure every surgical procedure or type of treatment done outside the office or internally is properly coded and every claim correctly billed to the appropriate insurance carrier.
- Implemented a medical records database which allows each terminal or PC in the office instant access to every patient file (2000).
- Made significant, long-lasting improvements to office procedures through a 1996 project replacing manual appointment books with a computerized scheduling system.

PROCEDURAL CODER. (1999-00). Learned extensive orthopaedic procedural codes and built a strong background in orthopaedic surgery procedures while assigning codes for inpatient and outpatient procedures, consultations, and emergency room visits.

BILLING AND COLLECTIONS MANAGER. (1990-98). Provided oversight for all aspects of the accounts receivable process including following up on claims, sending uncollectible accounts to collection agencies, and making collection calls.
- Maintained regular dealings with personnel in insurance companies and collection agencies.
- Contributed a firm, fair, and tactful manner of dealing with uncooperative customers and learned the importance of collecting on accounts at the time of the appointment in order to reduce the number of late payments and necessity for initiating collection actions.

MEDICAL TRANSCRIPTIONIST. (1999-present). In a part-time position, increased my typing speed to more than 65 wpm and polished my writing skills while editing reports from doctors and therapists at a psychiatric hospital.

PERSONAL   Can handle tough jobs which require overcoming obstacles and finding more efficient methods of operation. Enjoy meeting challenges, deadlines, and pressure head on.

Date

Exact Name of Person
Title or Position
Name of Company
Address (number and street)
Address (city, state, and zip)

DISTRICT MANAGER   Dear Exact Name of Person: (or Sir or Madam if answering a blind ad.)

With the enclosed resume, I would like to express my interest in exploring employment opportunities with your organization.

As you will see, I am an experienced and well-rounded executive who offers extensive financial management knowledge along with a reputation for achieving results through dynamic sales abilities. In a track record of accomplishments with American General Finance, I have been recognized with a prestigious award for managing the district with the top insurance sales records in the entire eastern U.S area of operations of the dominant finance company in the area.

Also recognized as "Best Operator" within the division during two recent fiscal years, I excel in such activities as analyzing branch operations as well as business and market trends. I actively identify opportunities for improving profitability, develop and implement corrective actions to solve operational problems, and provide advice and guidance for branch managers and employees in eight units serving six counties.

I was handpicked for his position based on my performance as Branch Manager for a $10 million branch with nine employees servicing 3,000 accounts after quickly receiving two earlier promotions to this level. During this period I earned recognition as one of the top 25 agents in the company and became a member of the "Solid Gold Producers Club" for insurance sales professionals. Other accomplishments included recognition as the top producer in credit insurance for the entire eastern U.S. area of operations.

If you can use a dynamic and results-oriented professional with extensive experience in financial management operations, I hope you will contact me to suggest a time when we might meet to discuss your needs. I can provide outstanding references at the appropriate time.

Sincerely,

William Henry

WILLIAM HENRY

1110½ Hay Street, Fayetteville, NC 28305 • preppub@aol.com • (910) 483-6611

OBJECTIVE	To contribute extensive financial management knowledge to an organization that can use an experienced, well-rounded executive offering a background as a results-oriented and dynamic sales professional.
EDUCATION	**B.S. in Accounting,** The University of North Carolina at Pembroke, 1993.
EXPERIENCE	*Have built a track record of accomplishments with American General Finance,* **Evansville, IN (1993-present):**

DISTRICT MANAGER. Pembroke, NC (2000-present). Am excelling in leading the way to enhanced branch profitability, control, and growth for a district which includes eight units in six counties of southeastern North Carolina.

- Was honored as **"Best Operator"** within my division in 2001 and earlier in 2000.
- Won the **"Chairman's Award"** for managing the district with the top insurance sales records in the entire eastern U.S. area of operations.
- Ensure strategic plans made by the Director of Operations are carried out in order to achieve the highest market penetration as the area's dominant finance company.
- Maintain a highly visible and active presence while providing guidance, control, and leadership for branch managers and employees.
- Interview and approve candidates for internal promotions as well as new hires for management and management training positions.
- Oversee the administration, review, and control of training activities.
- Develop and implement effective solutions to salary administration, employee relations, and performance problems.
- Closely monitor and report on competitor activities, marketplace concerns, legislative issues, branch problems, and other issues which could impact the company's profitability; vigilantly monitor bottom-line results.
- Develop and implement corrective action plans to minimize operational problems.
- Provide leadership while developing and administering effective sales and solicitation programs and promoting the company to employees, dealers, and merchants.
- Analyze branch operations, business and market trends, and other factors in order to identify opportunities for improving profitability and performance.

BRANCH MANAGER. Lumberton, NC (1993-00). Quickly earned two promotions and became the manager of a $10 million branch whose nine employees serviced 3,000 accounts.

- Was recognized as the **top producer in credit insurance** for the entire eastern U.S.
- Earned recognition as the **"Best Operator"** in the district for 1997.
- Became a member of the **"Solid Gold Producers Club"** for insurance sales professionals.

Highlights of earlier experience:

ASSISTANT MANAGER. Associates Financial Services, Pembroke, NC. Assisted in the management of a $12 million mortgage office.

LOAN ORIGINATOR. Sears Mortgage Co., Raleigh, NC. Originated, processed, and packaged purchase money and refinanced first mortgages including FHA and VA as well as conventional Fannie Mae and Freddie Mac mortgages.

BRANCH MANAGER. Freedlander Mortgage Corporation, Raleigh, NC. Handled all aspects of the loan, from origination to processing, packaging, and closing; serviced conventional purchase and refinanced first and second mortgages.

PERSONAL	Was a scholar-athlete in college and high school: high school Beta Club, Dean's List in college.

Exact Name of Person
Title or Position
Name of Company
Address (number and street)
Address (city, state, and zip)

FINANCIAL ADVISOR

Dear Exact Name of Person: (or Sir or Madam if answering a blind ad.)

With the enclosed resume, I would like to initiate the process of being considered for employment within your organization in some capacity in which you can use my extensive knowledge of finance and investing combined with my leadership skills, management experience, and resourceful problem-solving style.

In my most recent position I have come to be regarded as an astute manager of financial resources while analyzing and preparing financial plans and investment programs for individuals and families. On my own initiative, I have also founded and serve as President of a popular investment club with members from four states, and I have provided the leadership and financial expertise needed to keep the club's bank and investment portfolio and accounts active and profitable. I offer highly refined sales and marketing skills.

Prior to my current job in the financial services industry, I earned a Master's degree in Human Resources in addition to a B.A. in Economics, and I served as Director of Training and Human Resources for a crisis-oriented medical evacuation company which had to be ready to relocate on little notice for worldwide emergencies. In that job I worked with international officials and humanitarian relief organizations as I also resourcefully streamlined numerous internal operating procedures to ensure greater productivity and efficiency.

In prior positions as a military officer, I excelled as a Pilot, College Instructor, Logistics Coordinator & Purchasing Agent, and Administrator. During the war in the Middle East, I provided logistical support to a 3,000-person organization while representing the U.S. Government as a Purchasing Agent and buyer of supplies from Saudi Arabian businesses and agencies.

If you can use a sharp and experienced young manager with an aggressive bottom-line orientation, I feel certain that my versatile background could be valuable to you. I am accustomed to working in environments where creative opportunity finding and resourceful problem solving are the keys to success. I can provide outstanding personal and professional references at the appropriate time.

Sincerely,

Michael Kehoe

MICHAEL KEHOE

1110½ Hay Street, Fayetteville, NC 28305   •   preppub@aol.com   •   (910) 483-6611

OBJECTIVE   To contribute to an organization that can benefit from my management abilities and problem-solving skills as well as my experience in finance and investing, training management and personnel administration, and computer operations.

COMPUTERS   Fluent in using Windows 3.1 through Windows 95 and 97, Microsoft Office, WordPerfect 6.0, Quicken 3 and 6.0 Deluxe, Delrina Form Flow, and the Standard Army Training System 3.1 and 4.0 software.

EDUCATION   **M.A., Human Resources,** Webster University, El Paso, TX campus, 1992, 3.94 GPA.
B.A., Economics, Northeastern University, Boston, MA, 1988.
Excelled in advanced military training including a program for medical managers.

LICENSES   Have earned my Series 6 & 63 licenses.
Am a licensed Life & Health agent for the state of North Carolina.

EXPERIENCE   **FINANCIAL ADVISOR.** USPA & IRA, Boston, MA (2001-present). Analyze and prepare financial plans and investment programs for military families.
- Assists clients in debt management through the use of loans and liquidation schedules.
- Sole proprietor responsible for the hiring, management, and payroll of three employees.

FOUNDER & PRESIDENT. The Forty Below Investment Club, Boston, MA (1998-present). Founded and continue to serve as President of a club with members from four states.
- Provided the leadership and financial expertise needed to keep the club's bank and investment portfolio and accounts active and profitable.
- Have guided investors toward new investments while keeping participation high.

DIRECTOR OF TRAINING & HUMAN RESOURCES and **PILOT.** U.S. Army, Fort Bragg, NC, (1998-2001). Initiated and implemented improvements which increased the productivity of an office providing training and administrative support for 140 people; supervised 15 employees and controlled $18 million in equipment and supplies for a medical support company.
- Managed a 17-person MEDEVAC team with an extensive fleet of medical evacuation assets; established and maintained cordial working relationships with military officials and with humanitarian relief organizations.
- Directed all phases of a comprehensive training program; scheduled personnel for professional development schools and classes, tracked and analyzed personnel statistics, and administered the awards and promotions program.

Military experience: Excelled as a military officer known for exceptional executive abilities.
TRAINING, SUPPLY, AND ADMINISTRATIVE MANAGER and **PILOT.** U.S. Army, Ft. Wainwright, AK (1995-98). Integrated automated systems, training policies, and personnel systems and procedures into a comprehensive support system for a medical organization.
- Utilized the Windows operating system in personnel administration.

LOGISTICS COORDINATOR & PURCHASING AGENT. U.S. Army, Ft. Bliss, TX (1992-95). Played a key role in scheduling, planning, and providing logistical support to a 3,000-person organization involved in frequent worldwide projects.

PERSONAL   Excellent references are available upon request. Outstanding reputation.

Date

Personnel Office
The City of Raleigh
City Hall
433 Beacon Street
Raleigh, NC 28708

**FINANCIAL ADVISOR
AND BRANCH MANAGER**

Dear Sir or Madam:

With the enclosed resume, I would like to make you aware of my strong interest in receiving consideration for the position of Analyst which you recently advertised in the *Raleigh Observer-Times*.

As you will see, I am presently a Financial Advisor and Branch Manager for IFG Network Securities at the Charlotte branch office. When I stepped into this position in 2000, I took over a client base of approximately 100 people and in just over a year, had doubled it to 220 clients. With Life & Health and Long-term Care Insurance Licenses in addition to my Series 6, 22, 63, and 65 Securities Licenses, I manage assets which include stocks, bonds, mutual funds, and partnerships for clients throughout the southeastern region of the country. One of the changes which has allowed me to double my client base so quickly was the development of a new marketing system which has been highly effective.

I am pursuing my M.B.A. at the University of North Carolina and have completed more than half of the degree requirements. I received my B.S. in Business Administration from Seattle University in 1996 with a minor in Economics.

Prior experience includes working as a Travel Consultant and Bookstore Manager as well as completing H&R Block training leading to certification as a Tax Preparer/ Consultant. You will see that most of my experience has required an individual who can work well independently while displaying strong analytical and problem-solving skills.

I am confident that I possess the skills, experience, and knowledge the City of Raleigh is seeking in candidates for this job. I hope to hear from you soon to arrange a time when we could meet to discuss your current and future needs and how I might help meet them. I can assure you in advance that I have an excellent reputation as a mature and reliable professional and could rapidly become an asset to your organization.

Sincerely,

Henry Wadell

HENRY WADELL

1110½ Hay Street, Fayetteville, NC 28305 • preppub@aol.com • (910) 483-6611

OBJECTIVE	To offer a background of experience in consulting and management along with excellent communication skills and knowledge of computer and office operations to an organization that can benefit from my excellent analytical, quantitative, and problem-solving skills.
EDUCATION & TRAINING	Pursuing an **M.B.A.**, University of North Carolina at Charlotte, Charlotte, NC. **B.S., Business Administration** with a minor in Economics, Seattle University, Seattle, WA May 1996. Have completed extensive professional training which culminated in acquiring my Series 7, 6, 22, 63, and 65 Securities Licenses and Life & Health and Long-term Care Insurance Licenses, as well as a certificate in Tax Preparation from H & R Block.
EXPERIENCE	**FINANCIAL ADVISOR** and **BRANCH MANAGER.** IFG Network Securities, Charlotte, NC (2000-present). Service a client base in two cities while as overseeing the daily performance of the office and supervising one assistant; have aggressively built the business from 100 clients in 2000 to 220 clients currently.

- Provide services in a variety of areas and have received my Series 7, 6, 22, 63, and 65 Securities Licenses as well as Life & Health and Long-term Care Insurance Licenses.
- Created a new marketing system which has been highly effective in bringing in new clients and developing referrals.
- Handle a wide range of activities including marketing, developing prospects, budgeting, and cost control.
- Am successful in soliciting organizations to sponsor major events including educational seminars conducted by my branch.
- Analyze client portfolios and manage assets which include mutual funds, stocks, bonds, and partnerships for clients through the southeastern U.S.
- Became a Financial Consultant after working as a **Sales Assistant.**

TRAVEL CONSULTANT. SATO Travel and Northwest Airlines/SATO-OS Program, Seattle, WA (1995-00). Researched travel information using the DATAS II and START computer systems in order to assist customers with rail, air, and cruise travel as well as with package and group tours, hotel reservations, car rentals, and car and pet shipment.

- Filed, typed, maintained records, and balanced daily sales.
- Was entrusted with handling all bookings for U.S. Government corporate accounts.

BOOKSTORE MANAGER. Stars and Stripes, Germany (1993-95). Oversaw all aspects of store operation, including supervision of personnel; daily ordering, pricing, and stocking of merchandise; handling and monitoring of all monetary transactions.

- Performed accounting procedures which included balancing daily sales reports with ship

Highlights of other experience: learned to work independently while self employed as a Beauty Consultant for Mary Kay Cosmetics and Tax Preparer/Consultant for H&R Block.

COMPUTERS	Offer computer knowledge which includes the following software applications:		
	Kettley's for estate planning	HySales for analysis	Microsoft Money
	Morningstar for financial analysis	contact management	Word and WordPerfect
PERSONAL	Am highly versatile and adaptable. Have lived and worked overseas and traveled extensively throughout Europe. Am available for relocation.		

Date

Exact Name of Person
Exact Title
Exact Name of Company
Address
City, State, Zip

FINANCIAL ANALYST   Dear Exact Name of Person: (or Dear Sir or Madam if answering a blind ad):

With the enclosed resume, I would like to take the opportunity to make you aware of my background in personal financial management and my credentials as a licensed insurance sales professional.

As you will see from my resume, I am presently a Senior District Leader and Personal Financial Analyst affiliated with Primerica Financial Services. I am a Registered Representative with this organization and am licensed in series 6 and 63 through NASD (National Association of Securities Dealers). Additionally I have completed the Secure Auto and Homeowners Certification Program and qualified as a Certified Field Trainer with Primerica. I have been licensed by the state Department of Insurance as a Life and Health Agent and a Property and Liability Agent.

An excellent manager of time as well as human and material resources, I have completed the studies leading to these certifications and licenses while simultaneously meeting the demands of a full-time career in the U.S. Army. Throughout my military career I have been singled out for leadership roles and placed in positions of responsibility for multimillion-dollar inventories of sophisticated weapons systems and ammunition. I have been highly successful in building teams and leading personnel to exceed expected standards in all operational areas.

I offer a reputation as a professional who can be counted on to meet challenges head on with enthusiasm and a positive approach. I hope you will welcome my call soon when I try to arrange a brief meeting to discuss your goals and how my background might serve your needs. I can provide outstanding references at the appropriate time.

Sincerely,

Tracy McGrady

Alternate Last Paragraph:
I hope you will write or call me soon to suggest a time when we might meet to discuss your needs and goals and how my background might serve them. I can provide outstanding references at the appropriate time.

TRACY MCGRADY

1110½ Hay Street, Fayetteville, NC 28305 • preppub@aol.com • (910) 483-6611

OBJECTIVE   To benefit an organization that can use an experienced professional with strong leadership skills who offers versatile experience in supervision and training of personnel, insurance and financial services, and operation and installation of communications systems.

**EDUCATION
& LICENSES**   Completed professional training and education leading to licenses in the following areas:
Registered Representative, licensed in series 6 and 63, NASD (investment company and variable annuity products), Primerica Financial Services, 2001
Life and Health Agent and **Property and Liability Agent,** licensed by the North Carolina Department of Insurance, 2001 and 2000
Secure Auto & Homeowners Certification Program, Primerica, 2001

EXPERIENCE   **SENIOR DISTRICT LEADER** and **PERSONAL FINANCIAL ANALYST.** Primerica Financial Services, Charlotte, NC (2000-present). Manage approximately $30,000 in assets while applying financial management knowledge and the ability to sell services.
- Ensure clients own the proper types and amounts of insurance to meet their needs and establish short and long-term investment accounts.
- Prospect for new clients, educate them on available products, and make presentations to targeted audiences; process insurance applications and records.
- Became qualified as a Certified Field Trainer.
- Demonstrate the ability to manage multiple simultaneous tasks while achieving results in financial management and meeting the demands of a military career.

Advanced to hold senior supervisory and leadership roles, U.S. Army:
SUPERVISOR. Ft. Bragg, NC (1999-2000). Quickly became known as a results-oriented leader and team builder.

SUPERVISOR FOR SPECIAL INVENTORY CONTROL. Korea (1998-99). Cited in official performance evaluations as a leader who could be counted on to share knowledge and inspire others, controlled $27 million in vehicles and ammunition; supervised 46 people.
- Created an inventory form adopted as the standard throughout the parent organization.

PERSONNEL, ADMINISTRATIVE, AND LOGISTICS SUPERVISOR. Ft. Bragg, NC (1996-98). Selected ahead of other qualified and experienced supervisors for this interim job, was praised for my sound judgment and respect for others while overseeing a wide range of technical, maintenance, supply, and administrative support for 121 people.
- Oversaw the set up, wiring, and installation of Local Area Network (LAN) lines for the organization, supervising seven personnel.
- Installed remote, mobile, and stationary SINCGARS units, providing secure communication between the organization and higher headquarters.

SUPPLY AND OPERATIONS SUPERVISOR. Germany (1994-96). Was consistently described as a team builder who met challenges head on while supervising as many as 27 people and controlling inventories valued up to $9 million.
Recognized for "unswerving dedication" during around-the-clock combat operations in the war in the Middle East, was honored with Bronze Star and Kuwait Liberation Medals.

TRAINING   Completed extensive military leadership and technical training with an emphasis on Multiple Launch Rocket Systems (MLRS) operations and training management.

PERSONAL   Entrusted with a Top Secret security clearance. Earned numerous medals and honors.

Date

Mr. Jerry Vestry
American Express Financial Services
Suite 2220
Tampa, FL 33062

FINANCIAL CONSULTANT

This resume and cover letter could also have been shown in the Junior Manager Section. Notice that this career letter has a philosophical style.

Dear Mr. Vestry:

With the enclosed resume, I am responding to your ad in the *Wall Street Journal* for a Financial Services Coordinator.

As you will see from my resume, I have most recently excelled as a Financial Consultant with one of the leading financial services companies in the nation.

Your ad mentioned that your ideal candidate "will have some understanding of commodities markets and will possess a proven ability to use technical knowledge in a creative way." Prior to becoming a Financial Consultant, I worked as a Commodities Broker, and I possess an expert understanding of commodities markets.

After years of studying different markets and many charts, I have noticed that all markets exhibit the same natural recurring tendencies. My ideas and systems revolve around these principles. My investment objectives are simple: to make as much money as the markets will yield during a given time frame. Constantly evolving and changing, markets go through lively phases and dead, illiquid phases. While some markets are best daytraded, others are good for position trades only. Other markets are good for being short option premium and nothing else. No one trading system works all the time. Conditions must be appraised before any objective, strategy, or individual trading tactic can be employed. I have devised systems and principles to be used during different market environments, and I have used them successfully in reaping huge financial rewards.

If you are seeking someone who offers extensive experience in nearly every type of financial market, I would enjoy the opportunity to meet with you in person to discuss further details of the position you advertised. I can provide excellent personal and professional references, including from my current employer, but I would prefer that you not contact my current employer until after we meet in person to discuss your needs. Thank you in advance for your time and your consideration.

Sincerely yours,

Hugh Dudley

HUGH DUDLEY

1110½ Hay Street, Fayetteville, NC 28305 • preppub@aol.com • (910) 483-6611

OBJECTIVE	To benefit an organization that can use an experienced manager with strong consulting skills along with expert knowledge of financial products including investments, savings, and protection and credit products.
LICENSES	Have the following NASD licenses:

        Series 7 — General Securities Agent
        Series 65 — Uniform Investment Adviser
        Series 63 — Uniform Securities Agent

Became a registered Commodities Broker as of February, 1993.

Became a member, Chicago Board of Trade and the Chicago Board Options Exchange, 1992; acquired seats on and received my license to trade on both exchanges.

EDUCATION   Graduated *cum laude* with a B.A. degree in Business Administration and Accounting, Tufts University, Medford, MA, 1991; member, Alpha Chi National Honorary.

- Entered college as a biology major; upon taking my first investment course, discovered my love of the investment business, and made 37 A's out of 38 courses through my senior year.

ELECTED &
ACADEMIC
HONORS

- Received *Wall Street Journal* award given to top Business Administration student.
- Elected President, Business and Economics Club.
- Was the honored recipient of the award given to the top business student.
- Won scholarships from two major corporations/institutions.

EXPERIENCE   **FINANCIAL CONSULTANT.** Smith Barney, Panama City, FL (2000-present). Developed a base of clients for whom I devised financial strategies to help them achieve the long-term financial goals which I had helped them identify.

- Established portfolios for clients and selected appropriate investments based on client age, desire for asset growth, need for diversification, risk profile, and other factors.
- Helped several clients realize very large increases in their total asset base.
- Refined my ability to assess financial needs, provide prudent advice, and close a sale.
- Excelled in building relationships and cementing trust while gaining valuable sales and customer relations experience in a financial services environment.

COMMODITIES BROKER. LaFayette Commodities, Chicago, IL (1992-00). Placed customer orders directly to trading pits and worked with customers on investment strategies; became familiar with many "do's and don'ts" of trading by observing customer trading tendencies and through my own experiences.

- As a Broker, learned what type of order to use during different market environments.
- Have been trading my own account from a home office since July, 1994; have full equipment setup, instant quotes, and direct access to the trading pits by phone.

OEX MARKET MAKER. CBC Options, Chicago Board Options Exchange, Chicago, IL (1992). Trained to become a floor trader and learned how to execute trades and manage investment/ portfolio risks; applied different strategies while managing an equity trading account and refined my ability to make sound investment decisions in a fast-paced environment; became regarded as an "expert" on the options market and its strategies.

Exact Name of Person
Title or Position
Name of Company
Address (number and street)
Address (city, state, and zip)

FINANCIAL CONSULTANT

Dear Exact Name of Person: (or Dear Sir or Madam if answering a blind ad.)

Having a wife who is interested in moving back to her hometown to be near her aging parents is what has prompted this high achiever to seek employment in a new area.

With the enclosed resume, I would like to make you aware of my interest in exploring suitable opportunities within your organization which can utilize my proven sales abilities, entrepreneurial spirit, as well as my background as a Stockbroker and Investment Counselor.

Although I am excelling in my current position with a South Carolina Bank and am being groomed for further rapid promotion, I am exploring opportunities in your area. I can provide outstanding references from my current employer at the appropriate time.

As you will see from my resume, in my current position as a Stockbroker and Investment Counselor, I am responsible for 22 branch locations in nine counties and am involved in meeting with clients and potential clients to develop investment plans and strategies. I have consistently generated $800,000 a year in revenues and have been ranked for the past four years in the top four of the top sales producers at my bank. Although I came to the bank armed with my Series 6 and 63 licenses, I have recently earned my Series 7 license while excelling in my full-time job. In my prior position, I excelled as a Securities and Insurance Broker with a securities firm where I rapidly became respected for my creativity, technical knowledge, and dynamic marketing style. I am highly computer literate and am skilled at using various software programs to create graphics, charts, illustrations, and printouts.

You would find me in person to be a congenial individual who can be counted on to produce outstanding results in the most competitive situations. If you can use a dedicated professional who can provide outstanding personal and professional references, I hope you will write or call me to suggest a time when we might meet to discuss your needs and goals and how I might meet them. I can assure you that I could rapidly become a vital and contributing member of your team.

Sincerely,

Richard David Beers

RICHARD DAVID BEERS

1110½ Hay Street, Fayetteville, NC 28305 • preppub@aol.com • (910) 483-6611

OBJECTIVE To benefit an organization that can use a hardworking and aggressive young professional with unlimited initiative and resourcefulness, strong communication and organizational skills, as well as proven sales and marketing abilities.

FINANCIAL LICENSES Hold Series 7, 6 & 63 Securities Licenses, licensed by the NASD and the SEC.
Obtained a Life & Health Insurance License.
• Studied for and obtained these licenses while excelling in full-time jobs.

EDUCATION **B.A. degree** in Sociology, New Haven University, New Haven, CT, 1987.
Excelled in Ranger School, the 72-day "stress-test" management school designed to test the mental and physical limits of the military's most talented leaders.

COMPUTERS Familiar with software including Word, WordPerfect, Microsoft Works, and Windows
Skilled in formulating different investment strategies using software programs to create graphs, charts, and printouts; adept at developing illustrations for mutual funds and annuities.

EXPERIENCE **STOCKBROKER & FINANCIAL CONSULTANT.** Nation's Bank Investment Services, Florence, SC (2000-present). Responsible for 22 branch locations in nine counties, am involved in meeting with clients and potential clients to develop investment plans and strategies; train key individuals at the 22 branches to recognize qualified customers through profiling and by helping these customers develop financial plans.
• Have consistently generated $800,000 per year in revenue through my ability to set high goals and then persistently following through with well executed plans.
• Studied for and obtained my Series 7 license while excelling in this full-time job.
• Ranked in the top four of the bank's top sales performers for four straight years.
• Have become skilled at analyzing customer needs and developing financial plans.

SECURITIES & INSURANCE BROKER. Dale Securities, Inc., Florence, SC (1993-00). Rapidly became respected for my creativity, technical knowledge, and dynamic marketing style while developing portfolios/plans for private pensions, retirement, and investments for individuals, family entities, and organizations.
• Became known for my skill in creating packages with products including tax-sheltered mutual funds and annuities, 401(k) plans, as well as variable universal life insurance.
• In the belief that "a picture is worth a thousand words," used my computer software knowledge to create printout "pictures" for investment strategy proposals.
• Acquired valuable insights into the tax advantages available for different types of investors, depending on risk aversion and overall goals in financial planning.
• Gained expert knowledge regarding laws governing mutual funds and annuities.
• Learned how to talk about financial planning and investment concepts with all types of people, from the savvy business person to the person with no technical knowledge of finance.

PRINCIPLES OF MANAGEMENT INSTRUCTOR. U.S. Army, Ft. Bragg, NC (1990-93). At the Army's largest U.S. military base, was specially selected as an instructor in the Non-Commissioned Officer's Course, a seven-week management training program.

GENERAL MANAGER. U.S. Army, Ft. Bragg, NC (1988-90). As a squad leader in the famed 82nd Airborne Division, excelled in leading a six-person Scout Squad—an organization which had to remain continuously ready to relocate worldwide in order to respond to international crises, terrorism, conflict, or disasters; controlled an inventory valued at $125,000.
• Designed and supervised the implementation of training programs.

PERSONAL Am an extremely positive and cheerful person who adapts easily to new situations.

Exact Name of Person
Title or Position
Name of Company
Address (number and street)
Address (city, state, and zip)

FINANCIAL CONSULTANT

Dear Exact Name of Person: (or Sir or Madam if answering a blind ad.)

With the enclosed resume, I would like to express my interest in exploring employment opportunities with your organization.

As you will see, I offer an extensive background of experience in lending and collections gained while building a reputation as an astute financial consultant. Currently Assistant Manager of a $6 million retail finance office, I handle activities ranging from supervising two employees, to assisting the manager in real estate and retail lending, to managing the collections department for all accounts.

Earlier as a Financial Consultant with Merrill Lynch, I completed extensive training and licensing and, within six months of joining this prestigious firm, had established 264 accounts and produced $5 million in managed money for clients in five states. Other accomplishments included placing $12 million in life and business insurance and $3 million in mortgages while soliciting high net worth clients for participation in stock and bond purchases.

Prior to joining Merrill Lynch I advanced rapidly as a Field Manager with an emphasis on all phases of both retail and commercial credit and collections after earlier managing the collections department for another finance corporation. As a Credit and Collections Specialist with one major finance corporation, I achieved the establishment of a 3,000-plus account portfolio with less than .06% delinquency within 30 days.

If you can use a dynamic and results-oriented professional with extensive experience as a financial consultant, I hope you will contact me to suggest a time when we might meet to discuss your needs. I can provide outstanding references at the appropriate time.

Sincerely,

Chris Drew

CHRIS DREW

1110½ Hay Street, Fayetteville, NC 28305 • preppub@aol.com • (910) 483-6611

OBJECTIVE

To contribute to an organization that can use an astute financial consultant with extensive experience in lending and collections.

EXPERIENCE

ASSISTANT MANAGER. AVCO Finance, Raleigh, NC (2001-present). Work as second-in-command of a $6 million dollar retail finance office; supervise two employees.
- Specialized in retail lending of small cap — $5,000 and below.
- This office was sold to Associates Financial Services Group in 2001.

SENIOR LOAN OFFICER. WDIA Financial Services, Raleigh, NC (2000-01). Serviced clients in NC and SC and maintained extensive involvement with the military.
- Interviewed clients for mortgage loans, both first and second.
- Evaluated clients for auto, mobile home, and retail credit up to $20,000.
- Collected all accounts and maintained a 1% overall status in delinquency.
- Managed the office in the absence of the branch manager for six months.
- Prepared reports on lending and collections monthly.
- Worked until office was sold to New York Credit Union.

FINANCIAL CONSULTANT. Merrill Lynch, Raleigh, NC (1995-00). With clients in NC, SC, GA, VA, and NY, completed extensive training and licensing in 1999-00 prior to May, 1999; from May-September 1999, established 264 accounts and produced $5 million in managed money in my first six-month period.
- Solicited high net worth clients for participation in stock and bond purchases.
- Developed 401(k), Daily-JK SEP, and retirement plans for small and midsize businesses.
- Completed six modules of Professional Development Program (PDP) with Princeton University in "Live from Princeton."
- Placed $12 million in Life and business insurance through Merrill Lynch Life Insurance.
- Placed $3 million in mortgages through Merrill Lynch Credit Corp. – MLCC.
- Opened 120 individual accounts and 144 retirement accounts in a six-month period.
- Am skilled at processing orders; processed 100 per day on TGA SUPER-DOT System.

FIELD MANAGER. Commercial Credit Corporation, Baltimore, MD (1991-95). Began as a Customer Service Representative, was promoted to Manager Trainee; advanced to Technical Communications Writer, and was promoted to Field Manager.
- Completed extensive training in all phases of credit and collections, both retail and commercial.
- Played a key role in developing the Technical Communications Department's Manual.

CREDIT/COLLECTION SPECIALIST. Household Finance Corporation, GA and FL Region (1988-91). Managed Collections Department for Southern Georgia and Florida District while training as a Credit Analyst.
- Established a 3000-account portfolio with less than .06% delinquency within 30 days.

EDUCATION

M.A. in Business Administration and Religious Education, University of Florida, Orlando, FL, 1991.
B.A. in Business Administration and Sociology, University of Georgia, Augusta, GA, 1988.

PERSONAL

Member, National Association of Credit and Collections Specialists. Strong references.

FINANCE MANAGER, AUTOMOTIVE INDUSTRY

Dear Ms. Wareham:

With the enclosed resume, I would like to make you aware of my background as an articulate young professional who offers a strong customer service focus as well as exceptional communication and negotiation skills that have been proven in challenging positions in the automobile industry.

Although I have applied my exceptional communication skills in automotive dealership environments for the last eight years, I think you will see that the abilities that I honed in these positions would make me a valuable addition in any customer service environment. As Finance Manager for Ned Smith's Used Cars, I oversee funding of all customer loans, conducting negotiations with representatives from various lending institutions in order to acquire loan approval at the best possible annual percentage rate. Additionally, I hold final responsibility for closing the sale and have excelled at tactfully overcoming last-minute objections and convincing the customer to sign the purchase agreement.

Earlier as Customer Service Representative and Automotive Salesperson at Cumberland Chrysler-Plymouth of Hastings, NE, I provided direct customer service for this busy dealership. In addition to tracking individual and dealership compliance with customer service goals, I recorded, investigated, and resolved customer complaints. Prior to this position, I served as a Service Advisor for Universal Ford in Richmond, VA.

As you will see, I have earned an Associate's degree in Business Management from St. Pauls College in St. Pauls, VA. I feel that my education and practical experience as well as my customer service orientation, strong communication skills, and natural sales ability would make me a worthy addition to your customer service team.

If you are in need of an articulate and experienced customer service professional whose communication skills have been proven in stressful situations requiring tact and diplomacy, I hope you will contact me to suggest a time when we might meet. I assure you in advance that I have an excellent reputation and could quickly become an asset to your organization.

Sincerely,

Karen Fox

KAREN FOX

1110½ Hay Street, Fayetteville, NC 28305   •   preppub@aol.com   •   (910) 483-6611

OBJECTIVE   To benefit an organization that can use an articulate young professional with exceptional communication and organizational skills whose customer service ability, finance knowledge, and salesmanship have been tested in high-volume new and used automotive dealerships.

EDUCATION   Earned an **Associate's degree in Business Management** from St. Pauls College, St. Pauls, VA, 1994.
Completed two years of college-level course work towards degree in Business Communications, Hastings College, Hastings, NE, 1989-1991.

EXPERIENCE   **FINANCE MANAGER.** Ned Smith's Used Cars, Inc., Hastings, NE (2001-present). Solely responsible for all finance department operations of this busy used car dealership; worked closely with the general manager and supervised up to 20 automotive sales representatives in his absence.

- An articulate communicator, I tactfully overcome last-minute customer objections to close the sale; adept at handling customers during this delicate phase in the sale process.
- Conduct negotiations with various banks, credit unions, and other lending institutions on a daily basis to obtain loan approval for customers.
- Successfully dealt with customers in a tense and sometimes hostile environment on a daily basis; was instrumental in effecting increases in sales and incentives.
- Present various warranty products to customer at closing; responsible for more than 75% of the warranty sales in the dealership.
- By maintaining a high volume of aftermarket sales and obtaining favorable terms from lending institutes, achieved an average finance income of $500 per car.
- Typed and processed contracts and loan applications; mailed completed paperwork to the lending institution that funded the deal.

CUSTOMER SERVICE REPRESENTATIVE and **AUTOMOTIVE SALESPERSON.** Cumberland Chrysler-Plymouth, Hastings, NE (1997-00). Performed customer service and receptionist duties; served as an automotive sales representative for this busy local new and used car dealership.

- Monitored the dealership's performance on monthly, quarterly, and annual customer service index (CSI) reports; made suggestions for improvement based on customer input.
- Processed follow-up surveys with new and repeat sales, service, and body shop customers to ensure they were satisfied with the service they received.
- Operated a computer to retrieve credit reports on sales customers from the Equifax system.
- Provided direct customer service in response to customer complaints; answered multi-line phones and operated the switchboard and voice mail system.
- As an automotive sales representative, I assisted customers in the selection of new and used vehicles.

SERVICE ADVISOR. Universal Ford, Richmond, VA (1994-97). Performed troubleshooting and diagnosis of customer's vehicle and provided price estimates for vehicle repairs and service.

- Dealt with customers in a tactful and diplomatic manner; developed and presented possible solutions to the customer's service issues.
- Wrote service orders for computer diagnostics, maintenance, or mechanical repairs; provided customer with a cost estimate on proposed repairs.

PERSONAL   Excellent personal and professional references are available upon request.

Date

Exact Name of Person
Exact Title
Exact Name of Company
Address
City, State, Zip

FINANCE MANAGER, AUTOMOTIVE INDUSTRY

Dear Exact Name of Person (or Dear Sir or Madam if answering a blind ad):

With the enclosed resume, I would like to make you aware of my background as an articulate professional with exceptional supervisory and training abilities who offers a track record of success in automotive leasing, management, sales, and finance.

After establishing "from scratch" the Finance Department of Leith Chrysler, I advanced to my current position as Finance Manager for Leith Mitsubishi of Rolla, where I have achieved an average per-car profit of $800 in additional finance income. I also handle a large volume of lease agreements and am familiar with all aspects of automobile leasing. Through my strong bottom-line orientation and solid relationships with local lending institutions, my department achieved the best net average among all Leith dealerships over a 21-month period.

I began my career with Leith as a Sales Representative and quickly advanced to positions of increasing responsibility, advancing to Sales Manager at Leith Isuzu before moving into the Finance Department. I supervised as many as 12 associates, maintaining an average front-end profit of $1,285 per vehicle and was recognized as the number one Isuzu dealership in Missouri. As a Team Leader, I managed and trained six associates ensuring that each person under my supervision maintained sales of 10 cars per month and an average customer service index (CSI) of 95% or better.

In earlier positions with the U.S. Air Force, I demonstrated the leadership and motivational skills while supervising as many as 30 military and civilian personnel. During the Gulf War, I supervised the loading and transportation of more than 2 million pounds of explosives from trucks onto aircraft, accomplishing this task without injury or incident.

If you can use an accomplished manager and motivated finance and sales professional who offers exceptional communication, staff development, and negotiation skills that have been proven in difficult situations requiring tact and diplomacy, I hope you will contact me soon to suggest a time convenient for you when we might discuss your needs. I can assure you in advance that I have an excellent reputation and would quickly become an asset to your organization.

Sincerely,

Oscar Pinkus

OSCAR PINKUS

1110½ Hay Street, Fayetteville, NC 28305　　•　　preppub@aol.com　　•　　(910) 483-6611

OBJECTIVE	To benefit an organization that can use an articulate professional with exceptional communication and motivational skills who offers a track record of accomplishment in finance, leasing, management, and sales.
EDUCATION	Business Administration curriculum, Community College of the Air Force, Germany, 1993-1999. Completed numerous personal leadership and development courses as part of my military training, including the Air Force Leadership Development Course and extensive training related to the storage, handling, and transportation of hazardous materials.
EXPERIENCE	*With Leith Clearance Center of Rolla, have advanced in the following "track record" of increasing responsibilities for this local operation of the large national automotive group:* *2000-present:* **FINANCE MANAGER.** Leith Chrysler & Leith Mitsubishi, Rolla, MO. Handpicked to establish and run the finance department for Leith Chrysler; **was recognized for achieving the best net average among all Leith dealerships for a 21-month period.**

- Prepare finance contracts, ensuring that all bank loan, title transfer, and other paperwork was accurately prepared according to lending institution and DMV guidelines.
- Conduct negotiations with various banks, credit unions, finance companies, and other lending institutions to obtain customer financing and negotiate interest rates.
- An articulate communicator, tactfully overcome last-minute objections to close the sale; adept at handling customers during this delicate phase in the sale process.
- Train automotive sales representatives on techniques of closing the sale.
- Familiar with all aspects of automobile leasing; coordinate with banks to arrange lease agreements for qualified customers.
- Increased finance penetration from 57% to 74% and warranty sales from 28% to approximately 48%.
- By maintaining a high volume of credit life, extended warranty, and aftermarket sales, was able to achieve an average per-car profit of $800 in finance department income.

1999: **SALES MANAGER.** Leith Isuzu, Rolla, MO. Oversaw all operational aspects of the sales department for the dealership; supervised and trained as many as 12 automotive sales representatives.
- Scheduled promotions and special events as well as coordinating weekly advertising campaigns.
- Responsible for inventory control and ordering for an inventory of 225 new and 50 used vehicles; accountable for ensuring that overage units were sold as quickly as possible.
- Ensured a customer satisfaction rating of 95% or better.
- Maintained an average front-end profit per vehicle sold of $1,285.
- Recognized as the number one Isuzu dealership in the state of North Carolina.

1993-1999: **SALES TEAM LEADER.** Leith Mitsubishi, Rolla, MO. Directed the work of six other Automotive Sales Representatives, serving as Assistant Sales Manager and maintaining a 250-car inventory for the Mitsubishi dealership.
- Supervised and trained six sales associates, ensuring that each one sold ten units per month while maintaining a customer satisfaction rating of 95% or better.

PERSONAL	Recognized with a number of prestigious honors for exemplary bottom-line results.

Exact Name of Person
Exact Title
Exact Name of Company
Address
City, State, Zip

FINANCIAL SERVICES REPRESENTATIVE

Dear Exact Name of Person (or Dear Sir or Madam if answering a blind ad):

With the enclosed resume, I would like to make you aware of my skills and experience in the financial services field as well as my proven customer service and sales abilities. I am in the process of permanently relocating to Austin where my extended family lives, and I will be there from April 7-16th to explore housing options prior to our final move in May.

As you will see from my resume, I have been promoted rapidly while excelling in jobs with credit unions and banks. I can provide outstanding personal and professional references from all previous employers. In my most recent position as a Financial Services Representative, I was honored as the Top Branch Employee in recognition of my accomplishments, and I was credited as the key factor in my location's earning "Branch of the Year" honors for the greatest level of improvement in sales and financial growth.

I am accustomed to the fast pace and aggressive bottom-line orientation of financial institutions, and I am known for my cheerful, outgoing personality as well as my extensive knowledge of financial products and services. On my own time while excelling in my full-time jobs, I have completed college courses and numerous professional development programs, and I am committed to earning my college degree in my spare time while continuing to advance in my field.

If you can use a highly motivated self-starter who could contribute to your bottom line with enthusiasm, please contact me to suggest a time when we might meet to discuss your needs and how I might serve them. Although our permanent move will be in May, I would be available to meet with you face to face during the week of April 7-16th if you wish. Thank you in advance for your time and professional courtesies.

Yours sincerely,

Linda Daum

LINDA DAUM

1110½ Hay Street, Fayetteville, NC 28305   •   preppub@aol.com   •   (910) 483-6611

OBJECTIVE	To offer my experience in financial services to an organization that can use a self-motivated and articulate young professional with talents for prioritizing, handling pressure, and building strong client relations based on an enthusiastic and dedicated personal style.
EDUCATION & TRAINING	Completed approximately 22 credit hours of general studies, Austin Community College, TX. Graduated from McCallum High School, Austin, TX, 1996. Earned certificates in the following areas of professional development: Consumer Lending, September 2001 Service Plus, August 2001 Member Services, June 2001 Completed the Notary Public course, Austin Technical Community College, TX, 2001.
SPECIAL SKILLS	*10-key calculators:* use by sight *computers:* MS Windows 95, Excel, MS Office Applications, and MS Word; type 35 wpm
EXPERIENCE	**FINANCIAL SERVICES REPRESENTATIVE.** Sharonview Federal Credit Union, Austin, TX (2001-present). Was recognized as the **"Top Branch Employee"** in recognition of my sales accomplishments which included very active and successful efforts during two credit union-wide cross selling promotions for debit and credit card products as well as for life and disability insurance sales.

- Earned recognition as an important player during team efforts which resulted in "Branch of the Year 2001" honors for the greatest level of improvement in sales and membership.
- Handled New Accounts Representative duties which included opening accounts, processing applications, and informing new account holders of benefits and services.
- Opened IRA accounts and sold CDs (certificates of deposit).
- Acted as a Cash Operations Specialist and Teller for deposits and withdrawals as well as accepting loan payments.
- Ordered cash for the branch and maintained funds in the vault.
- Interviewed applicants for consumer loans and processed their requests; administered loan closings.

MEMBERSHIP SERVICES SPECIALIST. Ft. Bragg Federal Credit Union, Austin, TX (2000-01). Provided fast, friendly service in an extremely high-volume and hectic branch with an emphasis on completing cash transactions for members.

- Cited for my willingness to contribute my time and knowledge to help others, was effective at cross selling credit union services and products.
- Balanced and settled ATM (automated teller machine) transactions.

COMMERCIAL ACCOUNT AND VAULT TRANSACTIONS TELLER. First National Bank of Temple, TX (1997-00). Processed all cash orders to and from the Federal Reserve Bank and five branch banks – an amount in excess of $2 million each week.

- Handled the cash orders and commercial account deposits for such large companies as Wal-Mart, Sam's Club, and Dillards.
- As Acting Supervisor, assisted and guided the front line staff and drive-in window tellers.

TELLER. United Heritage Federal Credit Union, Austin, TX (1997). Was cited for my ability to provide accurate and virtually error-free work while processing cash transactions, balancing a drawer daily, and processing incoming mail transactions.

PERSONAL	Offer excellent communication skills. Enjoy the challenges of a fast-paced workplace.

**FUNDS TRANSFER
SECURITIES ASSISTANT**

Dear Sir or Madam:

With the enclosed resume, I would like to introduce you to my considerable experience in banking and financial services and make you aware of my interest in utilizing my skills for the benefit of your company. After spending the past eight years in the banking community in Charlotte, I have recently married and moved to Raleigh, where my husband is a permanent resident and homeowner. I am excited about reestablishing my career in the Raleigh market, and I can provide outstanding references at the appropriate time.

As you will see from my resume, I began my banking career in New York City, where I excelled in positions with Chemical Bank and Chase Manhattan Bank. For Chase Manhattan, I worked as a Supervisor and I managed 18 tellers.

In 1995, I made the decision to leave the northeast and move south, and relocated to Charlotte where I reestablished my banking career. I excelled in a track record of advancement with First Union National Bank, and I performed with distinction as an Accounting Assistant II and then, most recently, as a Funds Transfer Securities Analyst.

In addition to my extensive banking background and understanding of financial instruments, I am known for my exceptionally strong initiative and work ethic. I have never missed a day of work in my life except in 2000, when my beloved grandmother died. Extremely hardworking, I have become highly respected for my skill in dealing with others. In every job I have held, I have always been designated to handle the most difficult customer problems because of my grace and tact in dealing with others. Out of personal pride, I always maintain the highest standards of productivity, and I am confident that I could become an asset to a banking or financial services organization.

If you can use a highly motivated hard worker to become a valuable member of your team, I would appreciate your contacting me to suggest a time when we might meet to discuss your needs and how I might serve them. Thank you in advance for your time and professional courtesies.

Sincerely,

Nora Priest

NORA PRIEST

1110½ Hay Street, Fayetteville, NC 28305   •   preppub@aol.com   •   (910) 483-6611

OBJECTIVE   I want to contribute to an organization that can use an experienced banking and financial services professional who offers exceptionally strong customer service and public relations skills in addition to specialized expertise in numerous technical areas of banking operations.

EXPERIENCE   Excelled in the following track record of advancement to increasing responsibilities with First Union National Bank, Charlotte, NC (1995-present).
2000-present: FUNDS TRANSFER SECURITIES ANALYST. Was extensively involved in training other banking professionals while playing a key role in managing department staff members; monitored productivity, allocated workload, and evaluated performance.
- Served as staff lead in the absence of the team leader; acted as liaison between core and production.
- Conducted staff training focusing on communications, customer service, procedures and policies, and research/analytical skills.
- Maintained security database for Funds Transfer Application; ensured use of proper protocol and measures.
- Became adept in handling sensitive issues; was known for my tact, grace, and professionalism.

1996-00: ACCOUNTING ASSISTANT II. Was extensively involved in training others, including new employees, in this job which involved reconciling and monitoring Bankcard ledger accounts and balancing MasterCard accounts; performed general accounting and reporting including special projects and research.
- Set up corporate accounts; updated account information; performed credit checks.
- Researched and verified customer application information for acquisitions department.
- Answered department phone lines and provided the highest level of customer service.
- Applied my expert knowledge of interest rates, customer spending habits, and the credit card application process.

1995-96: TELLER. After moving to Charlotte, reestablished in banking career in this southern city by beginning in a job as a teller; was rapidly promoted to the job above after distinguishing myself in processing transactions for commercial and personal accounts, maintaining cordial contact with customers, and issuing certified checks and money orders.
- Performed data entry, application processing, and general keyboarding functions.

Other banking experience: Excelled in the following jobs with banking giants in New York.
LEAD TELLER/SUPERVISOR. Chase Manhattan Bank, Jamaica Estates, NY (1991-95). Supervised 18 tellers while processing transactions for commercial customers including commercial checks, deposits, and payroll transactions; maintained and controlled the accuracy of each teller's cash drawer.

COMMERCIAL PAYING/RECEIVING TELLER. Chemical Bank, Jamaica, NY (1990-91). Performed cash distribution, documentation, and verification as well as accountability for the cash drawer; managed work load according to the highest standards of quality.

EDUCATION   **Associates in Liberal Arts,** Borough of Manhattan Community College, New York, NY. Extensive training related to banking and financial services including branch operations, funds transfer, and call center operations.

PERSONAL   Have never missed a day of work except for three days in 2000 when my grandmother died.

Date

Dear Sir or Madam:

   With the enclosed resume, I would like to make you aware of the considerable experience in credit, accounts payable, accounting, and collections which I could put to work for you.

   As you will see from my resume, I am currently working as Human Resource Coordinator for Tyson Farms, Inc., and I am involved in wage and salary administration, completing Worker's Compensation documentation, calculating and processing payroll for 48 people, and handling accounts payable.

   In my previous position, I excelled as an Accounts Manager and Collections Specialist with Wachovia Sales Finance, Inc. Because of my hardworking nature as well as my skills in negotiating and resolving difficult problems related to past due accounts, I was selected as Team Leader for the agency with the responsibility of training new employees. I utilized the Davox Power Dialer in making up to 150 calls daily while collecting on electrical, medical, and fitness accounts as well as others. I am skilled at obtaining credit information and in skiptracing delinquent customers. I have handled both voluntary and involuntary repossessions.

   In two previous jobs I also handled collections. I handled collections and other duties for a medical practice, and I handled credit and collections for Online Information Services. In every collections job I have held, I have always been selected to train new employees.

   If you can use my excellent communication skills and accounting knowledge, I hope you will contact me to suggest a time when we might meet in person to discuss your needs and how I might serve them. I can provide outstanding personal and professional references at the appropriate time. Thank you in advance for your time.

                                        Yours sincerely,

                                        Cynthia Hickman

CYNTHIA HICKMAN

1110½ Hay Street, Fayetteville, NC 28305 • preppub@aol.com • (910) 483-6611

OBJECTIVE

I want to contribute to an organization that can use an experienced young professional who offers an extensive background in collections along with knowledge of banking and credit.

EDUCATION

A.A.S., **Human Resources Technology**, Wayne Community College, Goldsboro, NC, 1999.
Bookkeeping, credit, and accounting: Completed extensive training in all aspects of collections and credit through courses and training programs sponsored by Wachovia Sales Finance and Online Information Service.
Technical: Completed training in Administering Breath, Alcohol, and Drug Analysis

COMPUTERS

Skilled in utilizing a variety of software including Microsoft Word, WordPerfect, Excel, Windows NT; proficient with Computer Imaging

EXPERIENCE

HUMAN RESOURCE COORDINATOR. Tyson Farms, Inc., Goldsboro, NC (2001-present). Am involved in the employment process while coordinating various aspects of wage and salary administration; assure compliance with legal requirements and government regulations.
- Gather production floor data; maintain purchase orders.
- Administer/facilitate placement of associates; coordinate/administer associate benefits.
- Maintain MSDS, OHSA log, and complete Worker's Compensation documentation.
- Calculate and process payroll for 48 people; utilize PeopleSoft software for maintaining payroll data; handle wage verifications for associates.
- Handle accounts payable; input purchase orders into accounts payable menu, then assure checks and balances and process payments.

ACCOUNTS MANAGER & COLLECTIONS SPECIALIST. Wachovia Sales Finance, Inc., Greenville, NC (2000-01). Excelled in this job which involved collecting past due accounts, most of which were 15 to 29 days past due; was selected as Team Leader for this agency with the responsibility for training new employees.
- Utilized the Davox Power Dialer; personally made up to 150 calls daily.
- Was commended by management for negotiating skills and collections skills.
- Trained new hires on all aspects of inside collections and the computer system we used.
- Handled voluntary and involuntary repossessions.

CREDIT COLLECTIONS REPRESENTATIVE. Online Information Services, Greenville, NC (1996-99). Was promoted to Team Leader and trainer for all new hires because of my unusually strong collections, customer service, and problem-solving skills.
- Was responsible for all accounts rated delinquent as well as those already in collections.
- Collected on medical, electrical, and fitness accounts; obtained credit report on problem accounts; skiptraced delinquent customers.

DENTAL ASSISTANT II. Elbert L. Johnson D.D.S., Goldsboro, NC (1994-95). Was responsible for billing and collections while performing office work which included scheduling, filing, and telephone interaction; was commended on my gracious public relations skills.

SECRETARY. Wayne Community College, Continuing Education Department and Radiology Department, Goldsboro, NC (1991-93). For the Continuing Education Department, prepared correspondence and processed student registrations for Continuing Education classes.

PERSONAL

Am a well organized individual with excellent communication and decision-making skills.

Date

Exact Name of Person
Exact Title
Exact Name of Company
Address
City, State, Zip

INSURANCE AGENT   Dear Exact Name of Person (or Dear Sir or Madam if answering a blind ad):

With the enclosed resume, I would like to make you aware of my interest in exploring employment opportunities with your organization. As you will see from my resume, I recently completed my B.S. degree in Business Administration from Boston College, and I am in the process of relocating permanently to the Washington, D.C./ Maryland area.

I began working at the age of 14 in hospitality industry jobs, and I financed my college education in jobs as a waitress and wait staff manager. Prior to college graduation, I was recruited for my current position as an Insurance Agent by a company founded in 1874, and I have obtained my Life and Health License. I am excelling in all aspects of my job and have especially enjoyed the sales and customer service aspects of my job as well as the community involvement. While earning my college degree, I excelled in an internship and part-time job in the medical community, and I received letters commending my strong public relations and problem-solving skills. Throughout my life, I have always gravitated toward jobs which involved helping others. As a waitress and waitstaff manager, I was always the individual selected to handle the most difficult customer problems.

Since my husband and I are in the process of relocating permanently to the Washington, DC/Maryland area, I am seeking an organization which can make use of my business management education as well as my hands-on experience related to sales, customer service, and operations management. I can provide excellent references at the appropriate time.

If your organization is committed to strong bottom-line results and needs a committed and well-educated young individual to join your team, I hope you will contact me to suggest a time when we might talk. My husband and I are frequently in the Maryland/ Washington area to locate housing, so I could make myself available at your convenience to meet with you.

Yours sincerely,

Jonathon Ogden

JONATHON OGDEN

1110½ Hay Street, Fayetteville, NC 28305   •   preppub@aol.com   •   (910) 483-6611

OBJECTIVE

I want to contribute to an organization that can use a resourceful young professional who offers strong problem-solving and customer service skills along with experience in sales, office administration, budgeting, as well as the management of people and operations.

EDUCATION

Bachelor of Science (B.S.) degree in Business Administration and Health Care Management, Boston College, Boston, MA, May 2001.
- Excelled academically with a 3.3 GPA.
- Persisted in obtaining my college degree despite frequent relocations with my husband; completed extensive coursework toward the degree at Methodist College, Boston, MA.
- Business coursework included Principles of Marketing, Economics, Accounting, Managerial Finance, Statistics, and many other courses.

Graduated from Walkersville High School, Walkersville, MD, 1996.
- Played field hockey and was active in drama.
- Was **Volunteer Counselor** for 6th and 8th graders; received numerous letters of appreciation.

EXPERIENCE

INSURANCE AGENT. Independent Order of Foresters of Ontario, Canada, Boston, MA (May 2001-present). Was recruited by this organization which has been in existence since 1874; the organization is committed to the philosophy of "members helping members" and offers insurance services, financial planning, benevolent assistance, and other services.
- After obtaining my Life and Health License, was assigned a customer base of 500 accounts; vigorously prospect for new accounts at schools and community events.

MEDICAL ADMINISTRATIVE ASSISTANT. Carolina Imaging Center, Boston, MA (2000-01). Resigned from this part-time position because I sought full-time hours; began with Carolina Imaging Center as a nighttime receptionist and then moved to days.
- Received superior evaluations of my performance in all areas; demonstrated my ability to handle multiple tasks and to produce top-quality results under tight deadlines.
- Trained the nighttime receptionist after I was asked to move to a daytime schedule.
- Worked with the Director of Marketing on marketing projects which increased revenue.
- Became knowledgeable of insurance coding and billing; refined my knowledge of medical terminology as well as Coding CPT-4/ICD-9 for Medicare and Medicaid reimbursements.
- Handled insurance billing and reviewed insurance denials; worked with insurers to resolve issues related to payment and eligibility.

INTERN. Pediatric Developmental Center, Boston, MA (2000). Excelled in a two-month internship while completing my college degree; gained knowledge of the health care delivery system while working with medical records, insurance recertification, insurance claims denial, and data entry.

RECEPTIONIST. *"The Daily Guide,"* Boston, MA (1999). For the city's daily newspaper, provided customer service; proofread legal notices; performed light bookkeeping.

Other experience: WAITER & WAIT STAFF MANAGER. Various restaurants in Baltimore, MD; Frederick, MD; and Missouri. Began working when I was 14 years old and worked in the hospitality industry while earning my high school degree and college degree.

LICENSE

Current Life and Health License in MA.

COMPUTERS

Proficient with Microsoft Windows, PowerPoint, Excel, Quicken 2000, other software.

Date

Mr. Tom Smith
Investor Services
PO Box 632
Whiteville, NC 28472

INSURANCE AGENCY MANAGER

Dear Mr. Smith:

With the enclosed resume, I would like to formally make you aware of my interest in exploring opportunities as an Investment Counselor with BB&T in the Savannah area. I am looking forward to seeing you in person on Thursday, 25th of September, at the BB&T office.

As you will see from my resume, I have excelled since 1996 in a track record of advancement with MetLife. I began with the company as a Sales Representative and achieved Leader's Conference Qualification in my first year. Then I was promoted to Sales Manager and in 1998 became Agency Manager. As Agency Manager, I have been recognized at the Management Leaders Council for leading my office to one of the top 15 among 139 sales offices in the southeast.

You will also see from my resume that, after graduating from the University of North Carolina, I became a Senior Officer and City Executive with a credit union and a Massachusetts bank.

With an outstanding personal and professional reputation, I am well known in the Charlotte community for my integrity and financial services knowledge. I have been active in numerous civic, church, and youth organizations as shown on my resume. I am licensed to sell insurance and annuities, and I hold the series 63 and 6. I would welcome the opportunity to obtain the series 7.

Best regards, and I'll see you Thursday.

Sincerely,

Scott Goidel

SCOTT GOIDEL

1110½ Hay Street, Fayetteville, NC 28305   •   preppub@aol.com   •   (910) 483-6611

OBJECTIVE   To become a valuable member of an organization that can use an outgoing and highly motivated financial services professional who offers a proven ability to produce a profit, develop new accounts, satisfy customers, as well as train and motivate employees.

EDUCATION   Received Bachelor of Science degree in **Business Administration** and a Bachelor of Arts degree in **Political Science**, University of North Carolina at Chapel Hill, NC, 1984.
Currently completing Certified Financial Planner Course.
Excelled in numerous training programs sponsored by MetLife Investment Institute.

LICENSES   Licensed to sell insurance and annuities in NC; also hold the series 6 and 63.

EXPERIENCE   **Have advanced to increasing responsibilities with MetLife, Savannah, GA (1996-present).**
2000-present: AGENCY MANAGER. Have been responsible for recruiting, training, and developing the sales force in the Savannah area.
- Coordinated target market approach of individuals to meet the needs of various groups in our market.
- Recognized at Management Leaders Council for leading the Charlotte office to top 15 out of 139 sales offices in southeastern US.
- Created, developed, and conducted training sessions to impart knowledge of variable life, variable annuities, and mutual funds.
- Am respected for my expert knowledge of financial services as well as for my proven ability to develop outstanding client relationships based on trust and quality service.

1998-00: SALES MANAGER. Became skilled in recruiting, managing, and motivating a sales force while guiding the office to one of the top 20 of 140 offices.

1996-98: SALES REPRESENTATIVE. Learned the insurance business at the ground level and excelled rapidly; developed leads and cultivated clients while providing financial needs analysis to prospects in order to help them prioritize financial planning needs of insurance, accumulation, and retirement programs.
- Achieved Leader's Conference Qualification in my first year with the company.
- National Quality Award Recipient, 1997 and 1998.

GENERAL MANAGER/COMPTROLLER. Cannon Enterprises, Tampa, FL (1991-96). Was recruited by this family business to serve as its General Manager and Comptroller; oversaw the operations of a chain of three restaurants, each of which had a unit general manager.
- Directed management team of food service operations primarily focusing on cost control, marketing, and financial operations in order to maximum profit while increasing sales and market share.
- Played the major negotiating role in the discussions which resulted in the company's being bought out by a larger restaurant chain.

CITY EXECUTIVE. NCNB, Boston, MA (1988-91). Produced exceptional growth in both commercial and consumer loan operations in order to reduce risk and improve profitability.

SR. LOAN OFFICER/CITY EXECUTIVE. State Employees Credit Union, Boston, MA (1984-88). Was promoted to Senior Loan Officer in 1987, and then to City Executive of the Clinton office; was in charge of opening the new office in Medford, MA.

Exact Name of Person
Exact Title
Exact Name of Company
Address
City, State, Zip

INSURANCE AGENCY MANAGER

Dear Exact Name of Person (or Dear Sir or Madam if answering a blind ad):

With the enclosed resume, I would like to make you aware of my interest in exploring employment opportunities with your organization and introduce you to my background and credentials related to your business.

Since 1991 until late 2001, I was involved in establishing and managing an independent insurance agency which I recently sold. The Professional Insurance Group which I founded grew to $5 million in revenue at its height and had relationships with most major carriers including CGU, Hartford, General Accident, Maryland Casualty, and others. I handled risk management work for the larger accounts and personally managed the agency's largest accounts. Throughout my years of managing and growing the agency, I was a top sales producer. I won an award every year from a major carrier based on my achievements in sales and profitability. Prior to founding my own company, I excelled as an Account Executive for an insurance company and handled all lines of personal insurance including health, auto, homeowners, life, and annuities. I am widely respected throughout the industry for my ability to resourcefully apply my expertise related to insurance, finance, and risk management, and I have established a vast network of contacts and relationships.

In prior experience outside the insurance industry, I worked in banking and finance. For four years with a large bank, I began as an Outside Adjuster and then moved into retail banking as a Loan Officer for small commercial accounts and individual loans. Previously as Business and Finance Manager for a major car dealership, I supervised the finance department in completing loan documentation.

With an excellent personal and professional reputation, I hold licenses which include the Long-Term Care Medicare Supplement, Life and Health License, and Property and Casualty License. I have held the Series 6 license, and I am confident of my ability to obtain the Series 7 or any other license which I might require in order to meet an employer's needs.

I am now seeking to apply my considerable knowledge of finance, banking, and insurance within a larger organization which can benefit from my experience in sales, customer service, and accounts management. If my background and skills interest you, I hope you will contact me to suggest a time when we could meet in person to discuss your needs. Thank you.

Yours sincerely,

Matthew Weiss

MATTHEW WEISS

1110½ Hay Street, Fayetteville, NC 28305   •   preppub@aol.com   •   (910) 483-6611

OBJECTIVE

To contribute to the growth and profitability of a company that can use a seasoned business executive with expertise related to insurance, financial consulting, and financial management as well as retail banking and commercial loan management.

EDUCATION

Bachelor of Science (B.S.) degree in Sociology and Business, Georgia Tech, Atlanta, GA, 1983.

Completed extensive coursework sponsored by the **American Institute of Banking,** Burlington Technical Community College, Burlington, ME.

• Later became an **Instructor of Banking** courses for the American Institute of Banking. Numerous training programs related to insurance, banking, finance, motivation, and sales.

LICENSES

Current Long-Term Care Medicare Supplement
Current Life and Health License
Current Property and Casualty License
Previously held Series 6 License

EXPERIENCE

FORMER OWNER/FOUNDER & AGENCY MANAGER. Professional Insurance Group, Clayton, GA (1991-01). Recently sold the company that I founded in 1991 which grew to $5 million in annual revenue with 10 employees and five agents licensed in property and casualty as well as life and health.

• Managed all aspects of the agency and was personally a major sales producer; every year since establishing the agency, I won an award, usually accompanied by a trip, from one of the major carriers based on my results in sales and profitability.
• Prospected for, secured, negotiated, and administered complex contracts.
• Handled risk management work for larger accounts; personally handled the agency's largest accounts.
• At one time, the agency handled the largest Workman's Comp premium in GA.
• Became widely respected throughout the industry for my savvy insights and ability to resourcefully apply my expertise related to insurance, finance, and risk management.
• Recruited, trained, and developed a top-notch sales force; created and conducted training sessions to impart knowledge of insurance products.
• Played the key role in developing relationships with major companies such as CGU, Hartford, General Accident, Maryland Casualty, and many others.

ACCOUNT EXECUTIVE. Smithson Insurance Co., Burlington, ME (1987-91). Handled all lines of personal insurance: health, auto, homeowners, life, and annuities.

LOAN OFFICER & OUTSIDE ADJUSTER. Wachovia Bank, Burlington, ME (1983-87). Began in the Sales/Finance Department and moved into retail banking as a Loan Officer.

• Handled small commercial and individual loans; actively recruited new commercial accounts while providing the highest level of customer service to established accounts.
• In my spare time, taught banking classes as an instructor for the American Institute of Banking program at FTCC.

AFFILIATIONS

Member, Independent Insurance Agents' Association and other affiliated industry associations
Member, LaFayette Baptist Church; former member, Insurance and Finance Committee
Moore County Hunt Club (Southern Pines)

PERSONAL

Highly motivated individual who desires to work in a larger corporation.

LOAN ORIGINATOR   Dear Ms. Smith:

With the enclosed resume, I am enthusiastically responding to your advertisement for a Financial Assistant.

As you will see from my resume, I offer strong computer skills and I enjoy using my computer skills and practical problem-solving ability to help office operations become more efficient and productive. I am seeking a job in which I can become the "right arm" of a busy executive such as you.

I can assure you in advance that my customer service skills are excellent. In my current job as a Loan Originator, I have refined my customer service and public relations skills while working with people from all social and economic levels. In a prior job, I managed an office and completed payroll for a 10-person office.

I am hoping you will look at my resume and feel that I am a definite candidate for interview because, as previously mentioned, the organization is truly one with which I would like to be associated, and I am confident that I could become an asset to your team. Please give me an opportunity to meet with you in person to show you that I am the candidate you are seeking.

Yours sincerely,

Petra Higgs

PETRA HIGGS

1110½ Hay Street, Fayetteville, NC 28305 • preppub@aol.com • (910) 483-6611

OBJECTIVE   To benefit an organization that can use an outgoing professional with excellent communication skills who enjoys dealing with the public in person and on the telephone.

EDUCATION   Completed three years of college course work in Communications/Mass Media, Salem State College, Salem, MA, 1995-98.

COMPUTERS   Experienced with Windows 3.1, 95, 97, Excel, Loan Handler, Calyx, and QuickBooks. Offer a proven ability to rapidly master new software and enjoy applying my technical knowledge and creativity in using computers to improve organizational efficiency.

EXPERIENCE   **LOAN ORIGINATOR.** First Security Mortgage Services, Inc., Medford, MA (2001-present). Work with customers to help them obtain a VA, conforming, or nonconforming loan.
- Prepare detailed submission worksheet to calculate customer's qualifying loan to value percentage and debt to income ratio.
- Prepare lending applications and calculate Good Faith Estimate and Truth in Lending statements.
- Work with customers face to face and on the telephone to explain out all benefits of their loan and to assure correct signatures on all documents.
- Order appraisal through a state certified appraiser.
- Interact with attorney to obtain title work and subordination.
- Process paperwork necessary to close loan; submit customer's loan package to lender.
- Accompany customer to attorney's office for loan closings.
- Meet all RESPA guidelines.

CUSTOMER SERVICE REPRESENTATIVE. GTE Mobile Net-Cellular One, Salem, MA (1999-00). Worked with customers to ensure service satisfaction and promote sales; received customer inquiries by phone or customer walk-ins.
- Helped customers decipher their bills; corrected billing errors and re-rated bills.
- Determined best service plan for customers; input account information into GTE Point of Sale computer program for customers transferring in and out of state.
- Promoted sales of service to customer by offering incentives to sign up for new and different services.
- Created an atmosphere of hospitality to ensure excellent customer relations.

OFFICE MANAGER. Beacon Financial Services IM&R, Salem, MA (1997-99). Managed office to accommodate the proper business environment.
- Computed and completed all aspects of payroll for a 10-person payroll roster; computed quarterly and annual payroll taxes.
- Reconciled four business bank accounts; maintained business budget in an effective manner.
- Maintained proper inventory to operate all office equipment.
- Managed all phones and mail operations; screened job applicants for interviews.

AUDIO-VISUAL TECHNICIAN. Salem State College, Salem, MA (1995-97). Worked with students, faculty, and school administrators to ensure proper use of audio visual equipment; organized, distributed, cataloged, and stored all school audio visual equipment.

PERSONAL   Excellent personal and professional references are available upon request.

LOAN PROCESSOR   Dear Sir or Madam:

With the enclosed resume, I would like to make you aware of the customer service background and office administration experience which I could put to work for your organization.

My husband and I have recently relocated back to Louisville because he is in a career field which is severely understrength. We are excited about being back in Louisville and I am seeking full-time employment. You will see that I excelled in an Office Assistant job previously with a Louisville company, and I most recently worked in Colorado Springs as a Loan Processor. In that position, I was recognized as one of the department's top three most productive employees.

As you will see from my resume, I have completed three years of college course work majoring in Finance at Louisville University. While carrying a full college load, I financed my college education working as an office assistant and then as a counselor for Louisville University. Unfortunately I was not able financially to complete my college education, but I am planning to complete my degree in my spare time while working full time. I began working while I was in high school and learned at an early age how to serve customers with a professional attitude. Even as a young high school student working at TCBY, I was commended for my attention to detail in handling cash and was entrusted with opening and closing the store. I also excelled in a part-time job as a Customer Service Representative for Sears while working toward my college degree.

Highly computer proficient, I have utilized PCs and mainframe computers with software including Microsoft Office, Quicken, Lotus, Excel, and numerous other customized software applications.

If you can use a hardworking young professional with experience in all aspects of office operations, I hope you will contact me to suggest a time when we might meet to discuss your needs. I can provide excellent personal and professional references.

Sincerely,

Christine Wynne

CHRISTINE WYNNE

1110½ Hay Street, Fayetteville, NC 28305 • preppub@aol.com • (910) 483-6611

OBJECTIVE

To benefit an organization that can use a results-oriented young professional with extensive customer service, computer operations, and office procedures experience along with excellent organizational skills and an eye for detail.

EDUCATION

Completed three years of college studies with a major in Finance, Louisville University, Louisville, KY.

COMPUTERS

Highly computer proficient; have utilized PCs and mainframes with software including Microsoft Office, Excel, Lotus, Quicken, and numerous customized applications; proven ability to rapidly master new software.

EXPERIENCE

LOAN PROCESSOR. Office Team/Wells Fargo Home Equity, Colorado Springs, CO (2001-present). Originally hired as a temporary employee, quickly built a reputation as a fast learner with excellent customer service skills and the ability to rapidly master the mortgage loan process while handling a pipeline of up to 250 files accurately and on time.
* Earned numerous certificates, commendations, and merchandise awards for performance and professionalism in a department undergoing high turnover.
* Trained and mentored new personnel while advancing ahead of the expected pace and acting as a senior loan processor.
* Was recognized as one of the department's top three most productive employees in a contest to increase the number of files being sent out.

ASSISTANT CONTROLLER. Vanguard Culinary Group Limited, Louisville, KY (1998-01). Handled general controller support functions as well as purchasing, accounting, and shipment/transportation arrangements.
* Served as a resource for information and general problem resolution.
* Screened, interviewed, and in-processed new hires.

OFFICE ASSISTANT. USPA & IRA - Family Financial Programming, Louisville, KY (1997). Answered a multi-line switchboard and was frequently commended for my gracious customer relations skills.
* Scheduled appointments; metered and distributed mail; utilized a computer to enter client information into a database; prepared correspondence.
* Prepared monthly spreadsheets for the District Advisor's taxes.

COUNSELOR & ADVISOR. Louisville University Housing and Residence Life Office, Louisville, KY (1994-96). Excelled in this job while pursuing my degree; on my own initiative, developed and implemented programs to enhance problem-solving, decision-making, interpersonal, social, and survival skills for 30 female students.
* Prepared weekly reports; administered check-in/checkout and security.
* Gained a reputation as a strong leader and effective motivator.
* Advanced after serving from 1993-95 as an Office Assistant while financing a major portion of my college education: answered phones; typed and filed correspondence.

Highlights of earlier experience: In two part-time jobs while attending college, refined customer service and problem-solving skills while controlling inventory and earning recognition for my accuracy and attention to detail in handling cash.

PERSONAL

Am known as a very outgoing, enthusiastic, and detail-oriented professional.

LOAN SPECIALIST   Dear

With the enclosed resume, I would like to make you aware of my interest in exploring employment opportunities within your organization.

As you will see from my resume, I have earned a reputation as a skilled problem solver and decision maker while working in the banking industry and in the U.S. Department of Agriculture (U.S.D.A.). Most recently as a Loan Specialist with the U.S.D.A., I evaluated credit risks and approved or disapproved housing loans and guarantees. In a previous job with the U.S.D.A. I assisted in managing farm ownership, equipment, and guaranteed livestock and poultry production loan programs for farmers in Sampson County.

In prior experience, I excelled in various jobs in the banking industry. As a Vice President and City Executive Officer, I opened a new branch office and handled the recruiting, training, and management of new employees. Previously as an Assistant Vice President, I trained numerous lending personnel to recognize the signs of deteriorating loan situations and to develop appropriate remedies. I managed dozens of employees and earned a reputation as a fair but firm manager who knew how to motivate employees to work toward common goals.

With a strong bottom-line orientation, I am confident I could become a valuable part of an organization that can use an experienced manager known for sound judgment as well as an ability to anticipate and avert problems before they happen.

If you can use a mature professional with a reputation for excellence and dedication to surpassing goals, I hope you will welcome my call soon when I try to arrange a brief meeting to discuss your goals and how my background might serve your needs. I can provide outstanding references at the appropriate time.

Sincerely,

Thomas Miller

THOMAS MILLER

1110½ Hay Street, Fayetteville, NC 28305 • preppub@aol.com • (910) 483-6611

OBJECTIVE	To contribute to an organization through my excellent management, communication, and negotiating skills as well as through my strong problem-solving and decision-making ability.
EDUCATION	**College:** Completed nearly two years of an associate-level Agricultural Science degree program, Lexington Community College, KY; the college terminated the program when I was only a few courses short of completion; completed additional courses at James Sprunt Community College in order to meet government Agricultural Specialist requirements. **Executive Training:** Completed extensive professional training related to banking and financial management, emergency disaster, human relations, appraisals, housing construction and inspections, customer service, credit and collections, and other areas. **Computers:** Completed training related to Word, Excel, and Windows.
EXPERIENCE	*Was promoted in this track record of advancement with the U.S.D.A. Rural Development (formerly Farmers Home Administration):* **2000-present: LOAN SPECIALIST & COMMUNITY DEVELOPMENT SPECIALIST.** Winston-Salem, NC. Processed single-family housing loan applications and determined eligibility and approval; at midyear review, was recognized as a top performer among eight loan processors. • Evaluated credit risk factors and approved/disapproved housing loans and guarantees. • Analyzed building lots, structures, topography, financial situation of applicants and borrowers, and other factors. • Advised and directed applicants and borrowers regarding possible actions to be taken, financial management of loans, debt servicing, and inventory property management. • Initiated actions to graduate eligible borrowers to other credit sources. • Applied my understanding of credit principles in assessing loan applications. **1988-00: ASSISTANT COUNTY SUPERVISOR.** Clinton, NC. Processed Farmer Program applications, both direct and guaranteed, from eligibility to approval. • Analyzed farm, home, family, and community situations; provided advice to the applicants and borrowers on selection, improvements, and use of farms. • Performed annual year-end analysis and helped prepare farm and home plans for annual operating borrowers; initiated and followed cases to conclusion. • Received Certificates of Merit for reducing severe backlogs. Became recognized as a leader in the banking industry in this record of advancement: **VICE PRESIDENT & CITY EXECUTIVE OFFICER.** Plymouth Savings & Loan, Columbia, SC (1987-88). Opened a new branch office and handled the recruiting, training, and management of employees; applied my extensive knowledge of state and federal banking regulations and laws related to insolvency, negotiable instruments, and consumer loans. **RECOVERY DEVELOPMENT MANAGER.** The East Carolina Bank, Columbia, SC (1984-87). Was responsible for the origination, processing, and collection of commercial and installment loans; established the terms of workout agreements and monitored adherence to agreements for all "problem" loans in the bank system. **ASSISTANT VICE PRESIDENT.** Bank of North Carolina NA, Columbus, GA (1971-84). Was promoted to **Assistant Vice President** after excelling as Problem Loan and Branch Specialist, Manager of Consumer and Mortgage Loans, and Collections Specialist.
PERSONAL	Outstanding personal and professional references available on request.

Date

Administrator
Muncy Medical Center
P.O. Box 449
Muncy, IN 89053

Medical Accounts Manager

Dear Sir or Madam:

In the first job on her resume, her skills are shown with a functional emphasis. Even though her previous jobs were not in the medical field, she shows her work experience without gaps. Don't leave off experience which you feel is unrelated. The employer is curious about all of your work experience. (The general rule is that you should go back at least ten years.)

I would appreciate an opportunity to talk with you soon about how I could contribute to your organization through my experience in the area of medical accounts management.

As you will see from my resume, I currently handle accounting and data entry for a company which has recently computerized its operations while experiencing a 20% growth in patient volume. I am skilled at accounts receivable/payable, billing/collections, insurance liaison, data entry, and customer service within a medical environment.

In previous jobs I excelled in a field dominated by fire and rescue professionals. I started out as a Fire Dispatch Operator for the City of Raleigh and was promoted to Telecommunications Supervisor of Wake County's Emergency Operation Center based on strong work performance and professional recommendations. A hardworking and highly motivated individual, I am always seeking to refine my skills and knowledge. I am certified as an Emergency Medical Technician and trained to provide CPR and other medical support.

You would find me to be a dedicated person who would pride myself on contributing to your goals and objectives. I can provide outstanding personal and professional references.

I hope you will call or write me soon to suggest a time convenient for us to meet and discuss your current and future needs and how I might best serve them. Thank you in advance for your time.

Sincerely yours,

Katie Eubanks

KATIE EUBANKS

1110½ Hay Street, Fayetteville, NC 28305 • preppub@aol.com • (910) 483-6611

OBJECTIVE   To contribute to an organization that can use a well-organized young professional who offers outstanding medical accounts management skills along with extensive data entry experience and expert understanding of medical terminology.

EXPERIENCE   **MEDICAL ACCOUNTS MANAGER.** U.S. Health Services, Raleigh, NC (2000-present). While balancing accounts totaling $190,000 monthly, mastered new computerized accounting procedures as the company expanded to a new automated accounting and billing system; continuously increased my efficiency as patient volume increased by 20%.
- *Accounts receivable:* Receive and post payments to patients' accounts.
- *Accounts payable:* Prepare a wide range of bills for companies and individuals.
- *Billing/collections:* Bill more than 150 patients monthly; follow up on past due accounts.
- *Insurance billing:* Prepare paperwork for Medicare, Medicaid, and commercial companies for insurance billing purposes.
- *Data entry:* Perform data entry for hundreds of accounts which require numerous entries weekly.
- *Customer service/public relations:* Have earned a reputation as a hardworking professional with a cheerful disposition and a helpful attitude toward the public.

TELECOMMUNICATIONS SUPERVISOR III. Wake County Emergency Operation Center, Raleigh, NC (1991-00). Was promoted to this job because of my excellent performance in the job below; was commended for remaining calm in emergencies and for my ability to soothe people in stressful situations while supervising the Emergency Operation Center.
- At a time when the emergency dispatch field was dominated by fire and rescue professionals, became a respected supervisor because of my significant contributions to the city/county when they were enhancing their 911 system.
- Monitored electronic telecommunications equipment; maintained detailed dispatch records for all emergency response.

FIRE DISPATCH OPERATOR. City of Raleigh Fire Department, Raleigh, NC (1989-91). Learned to operate complex communications equipment and acquired transcriptionist skills while monitoring multichannel fire and rescue dispatch equipment.
- Made decisions about appropriate equipment to dispatch to emergencies.
- Received a Letter of Congratulations from the Chief of Police and was promoted.

INSURANCE CLERK. Mainline Insurance Company, Dallas, TX (1985-89). While operating a wide range of office equipment and learning internal operations of an insurance company, determined correct charges for patients' premiums and distributed correct insurance policies to both companies and individuals.

EDUCATION   Studied Computer Programming, Wake Technical College, Raleigh, NC, 1998-99.
Completed Supervisory School, Wake Technical College, Raleigh, NC, 1986.
Certified Emergency Medical Technician; completed Basic Life Support studies, 1985.

SKILLS   *Medical equipment:* Skilled in oxygen setup and knowledgeable of equipment used to record vital signs; operate traction equipment.
Medical skills: Can provide basic life support, CPR, airway management, splinting, bandaging, hemorrhage control, and shock management.

CERTIFICATIONS   Certified as an EMT and in CPR, State of North Carolina, since 1985.

PERSONAL   Am a highly motivated person who strives to make a contribution in my job.

Exact Name of Person
Exact Title
Exact Name of Company
Address
City, State, Zip

MORTGAGE CONSULTANT   Dear Exact Name of Person (or Dear Sir or Madam if answering a blind ad):

With the enclosed resume, I would like to make you aware of my background as an educated finance professional with exceptional analytical, communication, and organizational skills who offers proven leadership abilities, a talent for building cohesive teams, and experience in mortgage sales as well as knowledge of financial products.

As you will see, I have earned a Bachelor of Science degree in Business Administration from Wayne State University, in Detroit, MI. Named to the National Dean's list, I graduated Summa Cum Laude with a 3.8 GPA from this rigorous degree program while working part-time as an assistant to several investment brokers.

In my most recent position, I have been excelling as a Mortgage Consultant for Freedom Mortgage Brokers while simultaneously serving as a Team Leader in the U.S. Army. I provide telephone direct marketing of home equity-based products and services, including mortgages, debt consolidation loans, home improvement loans, etc. Due to my exceptional sales ability, many of my prospects have produced loans that closed. With the U.S. Army, I have advanced to positions of responsibility, serving as a Team Leader in locations worldwide. I have been described as "an extremely perceptive and hardworking individual who takes charge and gets the job done."

Prior to my military career, I gained valuable experience in securities and investment trading, working as a Floor Operations Clerk at the Chicago Board of Trade, as an Institutional Broker at Multi-Bank Securities in Southfield, MI, and as an assistant to brokers with Merrill Lynch, Paine Webber, and Shearson Lehman. Although I have proudly served my country, I feel that my analytical skills and sales ability are better suited to a career in the financial services industry.

If you can use a mortgage and finance professional with highly-developed analytical and organizational abilities, then I hope you will welcome my call to arrange a brief meeting at your convenience. I look forward to speaking with you to discuss your current and future needs and how I might serve them. I can assure you that I have an excellent reputation and would quickly become an asset to your organization.

Sincerely,

Nimrod Frazer

NIMROD FRAZER

1110½ Hay Street, Fayetteville, NC 28305   •   preppub@aol.com   •   (910) 483-6611

OBJECTIVE	To benefit an organization that can use an educated finance professional with exceptional communication and motivational skills who offers proven leadership abilities, a talent for building cohesive teams, experience in mortgage sales, and knowledge of financial products.

EDUCATION   **Bachelor of Science in Business Administration**, Wayne State University, Detroit, MI, 1996.
- Graduated **Summa Cum Laude**, maintaining a 3.8 GPA in this rigorous degree program while working part-time to finance my education.
- Selected for National Dean's List in recognition of students in top 5% of senior class.
- Elected to Beta Gamma Sigma National Scholastic Honor Society.
- Participated in the AT&T College Investment Challenge, ranked in top 14% of all contestants.

Completed a number of courses related to financial products and services, including:

Options and Futures	Portfolio Management
Stock Markets and Investments	Business Finance
International Business Finance	Bank Management

Finished many military training courses, further honing my leadership abilities, such as the Ranger Indoctrination Program, Advanced Infantry School, Airborne School, and Combat Lifesaver course.

COMPUTERS   Familiar with Windows, Microsoft Word, Microsoft Excel, Lotus 1-2-3, and Paradox.

EXPERIENCE   **MORTGAGE CONSULTANT.** Freedom Mortgage Brokers, Mansfield, PA (2001-present). While serving in the U.S. Army, have continued to work in financial services, providing direct marketing of mortgage refinancing, debt consolidation, and equity-based financial products.
- Counsel homeowners on the benefits of refinancing existing mortgages due to lower interest rates and other incentives.
- Due to my sales ability, many of my telephone prospects have produced loans that closed.

TEAM LEADER. U.S. Army, 82ND Airborne Division, Fort Bragg, NC (1999-present). Responsible for the health, well-being, and safety of three personnel; manage, schedule, and direct all training for my team.
- While serving as arms room representative, provided support which led to my company receiving a 100% rating on an operational readiness survey of weapons and equipment.
- Received an Army Achievement Medal for dedication to duty and tactical knowledge and proficiency; due to my efforts, our squad was recognized as the best in the battalion.

TEAM LEADER and **MACHINE GUNNER.** U.S. Army, Korea (1997-1999). Improved the effectiveness of my team through dedication to personal excellence and willingness to push others to succeed at the highest levels of which they are capable.

FLOOR OPERATIONS CLERK. Refco, Inc., Chicago, IL (1996-1997). Relayed millions of dollars worth of orders to brokers on the floor of the Chicago Board of Trade.

INSTITUTIONAL BROKER. Multi-Bank Securities, Inc., Southfield, MI (1996). Provided high-quality, fixed-income investment products and up-to-the-minute market data to credit unions, banks, and other institutional investors.
- In my first month, was placed on the leader board for exceptional new account sales.

PERSONAL   Excellent personal and professional references are available upon request.

Date

Exact Name of Person
Title or Position
Name of Company
Address (number and street)
Address (city, state, and zip)

1ORTGAGE LOAN ORIGINATOR

Dear Exact Name of Person: (or Sir or Madam if answering a blind ad.)

With the enclosed resume, I would like to make you aware of an experienced finance professional with exceptional supervisory, communication, and organizational skills, who offers a track record of success in financial planning and loan origination as well as in sales and customer service.

As you will see from my resume, I have been in the financial services field since 1999, when I became associated with Norwest Financial as a Manager Trainee. I also worked in the financial services field as a Finance and Supply Management Officer with the U.S. Army Reserves.

In my current job as a Mortgage Loan Originator, I have excelled in all aspects of my job. In the past fiscal year, I closed loans totaling $239,700 in volume—the most loans closed in the branch; this allowed our branch to earn $1,765,700 in volume which put us in the top spot in our region. I have earned a reputation as a highly effective communicator with the ability to discuss sophisticated concepts with attorneys and industry experts as well as the ability to talk in "layman's language" and explain technical and abstract concepts to average consumers.

Although I am highly regarded by my present employer and can provide outstanding personal and professional references at the appropriate time, I would ask that you not contact my current employer until after we talk.

If you can use a sharp young professional with outstanding supervisory, communication, and organizational skills, I hope you will contact me to suggest a time when we might meet to discuss your needs and how I might serve them. I can assure you in advance that I have an outstanding reputation and would quickly become a valuable asset to your organization.

Yours sincerely,

David Smith

DAVID SMITH

1110½ Hay Street, Fayetteville, NC 28305　　•　　preppub@aol.com　　•　　(910) 483-6611

OBJECTIVE	To benefit an organization that can use an experienced finance professional with exceptional supervisory, communication, and organizational skills who offers a background in financial planning and loan origination as well as sales and customer service.
EDUCATION	**Bachelor of Arts** degree in Communications and Public Relations, Willamette University, Salem, OR, 1999. • Am a member of the local Kappa Alpha Psi fraternity alumni chapter, 1991-present.
COMPUTERS	Familiar with the operation of Windows, Microsoft Word, Excel, PowerPoint, and Access; Wordperfect; and Lotus 1-2-3. Able to quickly learn new programs.
EXPERIENCE	**MORTGAGE LOAN ORIGINATOR.** Norwest Financial, Salem, OR (1999-present). Provide customers with financial planning and consumer loan information for this mortgage broker.

- Process VA, FHA, conforming and nonconforming first and second mortgages while handling debt consolidations, refinancing and other financial arrangements.
- Perform research to assess property value, determine lien status, and assess credit worthiness of the prospective client.
- Consult with attorneys, VA and FHA officials, appraisers, and other construction and lending officials in matters related to loan conveyance and loan closings.
- Develop consumer mortgage loan programs and devise financial plans to assist the customer in regaining control over their financial situation.
- Demonstrate my exceptional communication skills while marketing and explaining to the customer products and services that are not well-understood by the consumer.
- Have the highest closing percentage (nearly 30%) on marketing leads provided by CMC.
- In the past fiscal year, I closed seven loans totaling $239,700 in volume – the most loans closed in the Branch; this allowed our branch to earn $1,765,700 in volume, to lead the region.

FINANCE and SUPPLY MANAGEMENT OFFICER. U.S. Army Reserves, Salem, OR (1999-present). As a 1st Lieutenant in the Army Reserves, provide finance, logistics and support, and transportation services; served in the Balkans during Operation Joint Guard.

- Supervised up to 30 employees, managing and tracking all cargo movements throughout the Western European theater.
- As Finance Officer, ensured the timely processing of per diem and finance issues.
- Provided technical assistance to all Department of Defense customers receiving outbound shipments of cargo.
- Served as Training Officer for the Directorate of Logistics, learning the training system and managing the training requirements for the organization.
- Processed more than 126 Transportation Movement Control Documents, 73 Hazardous Cargo Declaration forms, and 11 aircraft worth of equipment for deployment in three days, in support of a noncombatant evacuation mission to Zaire.
- Coordinated movement requirements for the US Army throughout Western Europe, providing sustainment operations and support in the Balkans for Operation Joint Guard.

MANAGER TRAINEE. Norwest Financial, Kansas City, MO (1995-99). Performed a variety of customer service, computer support, loan origination, and collections tasks for this busy national lender; held fiscal responsibility for over $300,000 in accounts; reduced the branch's exposure to losses while increasing our customer base.

Date

Exact Name of Person
Title or Position
Name of Company
Address (number and street)
Address (city, state, and zip)

Property Manager

Although the Objective on the resume is versatile and all-purpose, just in case she wishes to job-hunt outside the property management field, this junior professional likes what she does and is simply looking for advancement to greater responsibilities.

Dear Exact Name of Person: (or Dear Sir or Madam if answering a blind ad.)

With the enclosed resume, I would like to indicate my interest in your organization and my desire to utilize my management skills for your benefit.

As you will see from my resume, I offer extensive experience in property management and am known for my strong bottom-line orientation. You will notice that I have handled all aspects of property management including administration, maintenance management, public relations, inspection and inventory control, as well as collections and delinquency management.

I hope you will welcome my call soon to arrange a brief meeting at your convenience to discuss your current and future needs and how I might serve them. Thank you in advance for your time.

Sincerely yours,

Dianne Jones Weaver

Alternate last paragraph:
I hope you will call or write me soon to suggest a time convenient for us to meet and discuss your current and future needs and how I might serve them. Thank you in advance for your time.

DIANNE JONES WEAVER

1110½ Hay Street, Fayetteville, NC 28305 • preppub@aol.com • (910) 483-6611

OBJECTIVE	I want to contribute to an organization that can use a highly motivated self-starter who offers strong public relations and communication skills along with experience in managing people, property, finances, and daily business operations.
EXPERIENCE	**PROPERTY MANAGER.** Bladenboro Apartment Community, Canby, OR (2000-present). While managing this large apartment complex, raised and maintained occupancy by 17% in a 6-month interval.

- Collect rent, make deposits, and balance books at end of each month.
- Prepare activity, occupancy, and market reports for Broker-in-Charge and property owner.
- Maintain a monthly operating budget and explain any variances; manage a budget of $82,000.
- Coordinate with contractors and oversee all maintenance on units; lease apartment, process applications, and expedite lease agreements.

Began with The Affiliated Real Estate Consortium in 1992, and excelled in handling both sales/marketing and property management responsibilities on a large scale:
PROPERTY MANAGER. The Affiliated Real Estate Consortium, Property Management Department, Canby, OR (1992-2000). Excelled as a property manager for one of the area's most well-known real estate/property management firms; was responsible for an inventory of between 180 to 200 residences.

- *Maintenance Management*: Supervised maintenance activities; coordinated and scheduled staff and independent contractors; obtained estimates for work to be performed and monitored major repairs as work proceeded.
- *Public Relations*: Screened potential residents and conducted rental showings.
- *Inspections and Inventory*: Conducted biannual inspections of every property and conducted house inventories; ordered goods and materials as needed.
- *Administration*: Prepared reports for top management while also preparing lease renewals, inspection reports, and other paperwork.
- *Court Liaison*: Handled evictions and represented the company in small claims court.
- *Negotiation*: Mediated between owners and tenants as needed in situations where disputes arose over damages, security deposits, or rent owed.
- *Accomplishments*: Made significant contributions to office operations through my talent for organizing office policies and procedures; brought more than 125 new properties into management.

REALTOR. The Johnson Agency Realtors, Canby, OR (1990-92). Became a $1.2 million dollar producer within 12 months!

- Gained valuable skills in sales, marketing, and contract negotiating while acquiring expert knowledge of most aspects of the real estate business.

OFFICE ADMINISTRATOR. Killeen Real Estate Corp., Killeen, TX (1989-90). Handled a wide range of activities for this real estate company.

- Processed sales contracts and revisions; verified sales prices, financing, option pricing, and lot premiums with approved documents; deposited and accounted for all earnest money received; prepared sales, closings, and construction reports; maintained land files including settlement statements and title insurance commitments.
- Compiled information on approved houses for start of construction; handled building permits, color selections, and related matters; ordered trusses, brick, and cable; issued job assignments and construction schedules; assembled and evaluated plans and specifications for use by real estate appraisers.

PERSONAL	Can provide outstanding personal and professional references on request.

Exact Name of Person
Title or Position
Name of Company
Address (number and street)
Address (city, state, and zip)

PURCHASING MANAGER

Dear Exact Name of Person: (or Sir or Madam if answering a blind ad.)

In the first paragraph, this junior professional makes it clear that he is relocating to Seattle. Although his background will be of interest to food companies, his experience in sales and purchasing is transferable to many fields. Notice that, although he has a license to sell Life and Health insurance, he doesn't plan on approaching the insurance industry, so his license is shown in a low-key fashion in the Personal section of his resume rather than in a separate License section.

With the enclosed resume, I would like to make you aware of the considerable sales and purchasing experience which I could put to work for your company. I am in the process of relocating to Seattle, and I believe my background is well suited to your company's needs.

As you will see from my resume, I have been excelling as the purchasing agent for a large wholesale food distributor with a customer base of schools, restaurants, and nursing homes throughout the western states. While negotiating contracts with vendors and handling the school lunch bid process, I have resourcefully managed inventory turnover in order to optimize inventory levels while maximizing return on investment. I have earned a reputation as a prudent strategic planner and skillful negotiator.

In a prior position as a Sales Trainer and Sales Representative with a food industry company, I increased sales from $250,000 to $1.3 million and won the Captain Max award given to the company's highest-producing sales representative.

With a B.S. degree, I have excelled in continuous and extensive executive training in the areas of financial management, purchasing, contract negotiation, and quality assurance.

I can provide outstanding personal and professional references at the appropriate time, and I hope you will contact me if you can use a resourceful hard worker with a strong bottom-line orientation. I am in the Seattle area frequently and could make myself available to meet with you at your convenience. Thank you in advance for your time.

Sincerely,

Benjamin Brainerd

BENJAMIN BRAINERD

Until 12/15/01: 1110½ Hay Street, Fayetteville, NC 28305   (910) 483-6611
After 12/16/011: 538 Pittsfield Avenue, Seattle, WA 89023   (805) 483-6611

OBJECTIVE

To contribute to an organization that can use my exceptionally strong sales and marketing skills as well as my background in purchasing, inventory management, and contract negotiation.

EDUCATION

Bachelor of Science Degree, Business Administration, Denver University, Denver, CO.
- Majored in Health and Physical Education
- Minor in Business Administration

Graduated from W.G. DuBois High School, Denver, CO.
- Was named one of the "Ten Most Outstanding Seniors."
- Was selected to receive the Cayman Sportsmanship Award during my senior year. This award is presented annually to only one athlete in the Denver area.
- Earned varsity letters in football, basketball, and baseball.

EXPERIENCE

PURCHASING MANAGER. Culloughby Co., Denver, CO (2000-present). For this wholesale food distributor with a customer base of schools, nursing homes, and restaurants throughout the western states, purchase $750,000 of canned, dry, and staple goods.
- Am responsible for turning the inventory and maximizing return on investment (ROI); have resourcefully developed methods of purchasing products in a timely manner in order to optimize inventory turnover and ROI.
- Have earned a reputation as a skilled negotiator in the process of negotiating contract pricing as well as other terms and conditions with vendors.
- Have acquired eight years of experience with school lunch bid process; conduct product availability research, secure guarantee bid pricing, handle bid quoting.
- Utilize a computer with Target software for purchasing activities.

SALES REPRESENTATIVE. Mason Brothers, Denver, CO (1997-00). Sold portion control meat and seafood to established and newly developed accounts.

SALES REPRESENTATIVE. PYA/Monarch, Denver, CO (1995-97). Sold full-line food service products to restaurants, hospitals, and military procurement offices.

SALES REPRESENTATIVE & SALES TRAINER. Bryan Foods, Bodega Bay, CA (1991-94). Excelled in numerous positions of responsibility related to sales and sales management during my eight years with this company.
- As a Sales Representative, boosted annual sales from $250,000 to $1.3 million.
- As "Equipment and Supplies Specialist," initiated sales efforts in the western California region and helped produce sales in excess of $200,000 during the first quarter of the 1993 fiscal year.
- As "Sales Representative," produced growth of over $900,000 in annual sales revenue in my first year, which resulted in my winning the "Captain Max" Award, presented to the company's most outstanding salesperson.
- Managed and coordinated divisional sales meeting; trained sales personnel.

Other experience:
- As **Co-Manager** of a seafood restaurant in Denver, was in charge of hiring, training, scheduling, and supervising all employees.
- Worked as a **Sales Representative and Staff Manager** for Pilot Life Insurance Company in Los Angeles; sold life and health insurance products and served as Staff Manager at the Smithfield Branch.

PERSONAL

Can provide outstanding references. Have been licensed to sell **Life and Health** insurance.

Date

Exact Name of Person
Title or Position
Name of Company
Address (number and street)
Address (city, state, and zip)

PURCHASING MANAGER

This junior professional is approaching a wide range of companies, including some companies in her industry. Although it is not likely that a company she approaches will contact her current employer before talking with her, she explicitly requests in the second paragraph of her letter that the reader hold her initial expression of interest in confidence.

Dear Exact Name of Person: (or Dear Sir or Madam if answering a blind ad.)

I would appreciate an opportunity to talk with you soon about how I could contribute to your organization through my extensive background in purchasing parts and services for a manufacturing firm.

You will see from my enclosed resume that I have been with Goodyear Consumer Products, Inc., in St. Louis, MO, for several years. Although I enjoy this position and have advanced with the company from a Materials Buyer position to Purchasing Manager, I am interested in confidentially exploring opportunities within your company.

Because of my ability to reduce costs and negotiate product contracts with a wide variety of vendors, I have received numerous awards and honors recognizing my purchasing expertise and management ability. I believe that you would find me to be an enthusiastic and outgoing professional who offers strong organizational abilities and attention to detail.

I hope you will welcome my call soon to arrange a brief meeting at your convenience to discuss your current and future needs and how I might serve them. Thank you in advance for your time.

Sincerely yours.

Dean Hardwick

Alternate last paragraph:
I hope you will call or write me soon to suggest a time convenient for us to meet and discuss your current and future needs and how I might serve them. Thank you in advance for your time.

DEAN HARDWICK

1110½ Hay Street, Fayetteville, NC 28305 • preppub@aol.com • (910) 483-6611

OBJECTIVE	To offer my extensive background in purchasing and my aggressive bottom-line orientation to an organization that can use a positive and enthusiastic professional known for attention to detail as well as expertise in all aspects of purchasing both parts and services.
EXPERIENCE	**PURCHASING MANAGER & MATERIALS BUYER.** Goodyear Consumer Products, Inc., St. Louis, MO (2000-present). Began as a Materials Buyer and was promoted to Purchasing Manager in charge of a five-person department; provide oversight of the purchasing of a wide range of products valued at six million annually.

- Received a letter of appreciation from the company president in recognition of my accomplishments and contributions including my ability to continually reduce costs, January 2001.
- Wrote the standard operating procedures (SOPs) used by all purchasing department personnel, not only at the St. Louis central office but also at the 12 field offices.
- Oversee MRO (Maintenance, Repair, and Operating) purchasing contracts for plant services at 16 plants; negotiate contracts valued at $25 million annually.
- In 2000, negotiated a contract for additional commodities including labels and instruction books.
- Have acquired expertise in commodity buying including the purchasing of all electrical and electronic parts, fasteners, screw machine, and imported parts including finished goods.
- Chaired a task force which developed a new line of ceiling fans: the project was successfully completed ahead of schedule and within corporate budget guidelines and restrictions.
- On my own initiative, established a new buyer training program which has led to numerous efficiencies; set up a complete how-to system and oversaw the implementation of a new automated system used for tracking inventory and purchasing.

Highlights of previous experience: Refined skills as a Clerk/Typist and Secretary for a Human Relations/Equal Opportunity Office and the Director of Personnel and Community Affairs for an Army post in Germany.

- Earned several letters and certificates of commendation and a Sustained Performance Award in recognition of my professionalism and accomplishments as a government employee.
- Became familiar with the functions of a purchasing office as a Departmental Secretary, Goodyear Industries, Inc., St. Louis, MO.
- Gained experience in jobs as a Office Clerk/Claims Handler/Dispatcher for a trucking company and Real Estate Salesperson.

EDUCATION	Associate's degree in **Industrial Management Technology,** St. Louis Technical Community College, MO, 1996. Completed 60 credit hours in **Personnel Management** through a correspondence course. Attended Bohecker's Business College, Ravenna, OH: received training in the field of executive secretarial duties.
PERSONAL	Active in church activities, have served as vice president and secretary of the women's organization; served on the finance committee. Am a friendly and enthusiastic individual.

Exact Name of Person
Exact Title
Exact Name of Company
Address
City, State, Zip

REAL ESTATE APPRAISER

Dear Exact Name of Person (or Dear Sir or Madam if answering a blind ad):

With the enclosed resume, I would like to make you aware of my interest in exploring opportunities which will take advantage of my knowledge related to mortgage lending as well as my experience related to banking, credit unions, and financial services. As you will see from my resume, I am in the process of relocating to the Atlanta area. Although I am well-respected in my present position, I have made the decision to move closer to the area where many members of my extended family make their homes.

As you will see from my resume, I offer a distinguished track record of accomplishments with credit unions. As a Vice President with LaFayette Mutual Federal Credit Union, I enjoyed a history of promotion to increased responsibilities as a credit union executive. I was promoted to Vice President to handle a variety of strategic responsibilities for four branches with total assets of $31 million. Among my accomplishments were significantly outperforming the annual yields for all credit unions, diversifying the total loan portfolio, reducing delinquencies, and increasing capital. While achieving excellent results in all areas of operations, I was instrumental in leading the credit union to a five-star rating from Bauer Financial Reports, Inc., and a superior rating from I.D.C. Financial Publishing, Inc. Earlier as a Loan Manager, I played a key role in the rapid growth of assets of a credit union to $23 million from $10 million.

In 2001 I made a career change into real estate sales and then into the specialized field of real estate appraisal. This experience has allowed me to gain insight into the mortgage lending process from a different angle and has added to my strong background related to lending and financial services.

You would find me to be a congenial professional who is skilled at motivating employees to excel in their jobs and who is experienced in interacting with federal examiners, auditors, risk management professionals, and others with fiduciary responsibilities.

Because I am frequently in the Atlanta area exploring employment and housing options, I would be available for personal interviews at almost any time at your convenience. I hope you will contact me if you can make use of my experience and expertise.

Sincerely,

George Eddy

GEORGE EDDY

1110½ Hay Street, Fayetteville, NC 28305 • preppub@aol.com • (910) 483-6611

OBJECTIVE

To offer a versatile background which has included managing banking and credit union operations as well as real estate sales and appraisal to an organization that can use my ability to create new services, design software programs, and motivate employees to excel.

EDUCATION

Real Estate Appraisal and GRI Courses, Finger Lakes Community College, 2002 and 2001.
Credit Union Executive Program, Credit Union National Association, with course work in areas including accounting, marketing, credit/collections, business law, money and banking, and financial counseling. Other college courses in computers and trust services.
Associate's Degree, Business Administration, Kings College, Charlotte, NC.
Certified Financial Counselor, Florida State University.

EXPERIENCE

REAL ESTATE APPRAISER. Crestview and Associates, Weymouth, GA (2001-present). After achieving success in real estate sales, transferred my skills to this specialized area of appraising commercial properties as well as residential property, land, farms, and estates for banks, attorneys, and individuals for mortgage lending purposes.
- Developed expertise in the area of research, and became knowledgeable of USPAP regulations and laws governing the appraisal process.
- Expanded computer knowledge and skills with DOS and Windows using WordPerfect 4.1, Argus, Marshall and Swift, Appraise It, Deed Plotter, and Sketch-it programs.

VICE PRESIDENT. LaFayette Mutual Federal Credit Union, LaFayette, SC (1988-01). Began as Assistant Vice President and was promoted to handle varied strategic responsibilities while managing 10 employees and indirectly overseeing 29 people in a credit union with four branches and assets of $31 million.
- Developed written policies and procedures for approval by the Board of Directors while managing areas including credit union and office operations, loans and collections, cash flow, business development, insurance and credit card operations, and security.
- Produced an annual yield on loans of 14.95% which significantly outperformed the annual yield of 11.45% for all credit unions.
- Diversified the total loan portfolio: increased secured loans to 45%, decreased unsecured loans to 55%, and increased outstanding loans from $6 to $20 million.
- Became skilled in interacting with a wide range of professionals from federal examiners, to risk management professionals, to others with fiduciary responsibilities.
- Involved in the process of troubleshooting software programs used by the four branches, provided expertise during the conversion to a Data General system.
- Developed an insurance program to provide collateral protection.
- Was instrumental in achieving a five-star rating from Bauer Financial reports, Inc., and a superior rating from I.D.C. Financial Publishing, Inc.
- Reduced delinquencies to 1.06% and increased capital to 12.3%.

Other experience:
LOAN MANAGER. Marshall Federal Credit Union, Marshall, NJ. Was praised by the board of directors for "never less than excellent" performance; supervised up to 18 people including eight loan officers in a site with an annual loan volume of $14 million.
- Played a key role in the rapid growth of assets from $10 to $23 million.

AFFILIATIONS

Dispute Resolution Center Chairman. Chamber of Commerce board of directors.

Exact Name of Person
Exact Title
Exact Name of Company
Address
City, State, Zip

REGIONAL MANAGER   Dear Exact Name of Person (or Dear Sir or Madam if answering a blind ad):

With the enclosed resume, I would like to make you aware of my interest in exploring employment opportunities with your organization.

As you will see from my resume, I am excelling in my current position and am believed to be the youngest person in the history of the company to assume the job as Regional Manager. I was recruited for my position during my senior year of college and have made numerous contributions to the company's profitability while managing 12 individuals as well as a budget of approximately half a million dollars. After stepping into my position, I took over an underperforming operation which had experienced chronic sluggish performance for 13 years. Through innovative marketing, bulldog persistence, and skillful management, I have created one of the company's most profitable and efficient operations.

Although I am highly regarded in my current position and am being groomed for further rapid promotion, I have decided that I wish to embark upon a career in finance. I am confident that I will be very successful in the financial arena as I have been in management. With strong communication and motivational skills, I offer natural the drive and determination which I know is critical to success in a competitive marketplace.

I recently used my leadership ability in a volunteer role when I assumed the position as coach of a basketball team which had not won a game in two years. I completely transformed the skills and attitudes of boys aged 15-18, and the team I coached ended up second in the conference. In college at Texas Tech University, where I majored in Business Administration, I led my team to become the Intramural Basketball Champions. I recently played on an over-21 men's team which won the city championship. Through sports, I have learned how to compete, how to win, and how to persist.

If you can use a hard charger with unlimited personal initiative and a drive to become a part of a winning team with a championship company, I hope you will contact me to suggest a time when we might meet to discuss your needs.

Yours sincerely,

Scott Stanley

SCOTT STANLEY

1110½ Hay Street, Fayetteville, NC 28305　•　preppub@aol.com　•　(910) 483-6611

OBJECTIVE　　To contribute to a company that can use a resourceful and dynamic young professional with strong sales and communication skills along with an aggressive bottom-line orientation.

EDUCATION　　**Bachelor of Science (B.S.) degree in Business Management,** Texas Tech University, Simons, TX; graduated 2001; completed the degree in 3½ instead of four years.
- As **Rush Chairman,** recruited new member for Delta Sigma Phi leadership.
- Was recruited by numerous colleges and offered scholarships to play collegiate basketball, but I declined the offers in order to attend TX Tech's fine Business Management program.
- As a shooting guard, led my intramural team at NCSU to become the **2001 Intramural Basketball Champions.**

Professional Training: Obtained TX Real Estate Salesman License, 2001.

Graduated from high school at The High Water Academy, Simons, TX.

Sports leadership accomplishments:
- Was named **Player of the Year** for basketball accomplishments.
- As a shooting guard, helped my high school team become the **State Champions.**
- Was named **All Conference** and **All Tournament** and **MVP.**

LANGUAGES　　Strong working knowledge of **Spanish** (two years of college courses, three years in high school).

COMPUTERS　　Highly proficient in operating computers with software including Microsoft Word, WordPerfect, spreadsheets including Excel, and PowerPoint software for professional presentations.

EXPERIENCE　　**REGIONAL MANAGER.** United Management, Simons, TX (2001-present). Was recruited for a management trainee position by this property management company during my last semester of college; after three months of intensive on-the-job and hands-on training, was promoted to Regional Property Manager.
- Am the youngest person ever placed in this management role within a company which operates apartment complexes in Texas and Oklahoma; am being groomed for future rapid promotion.
- Supervise 12 employees who include maintenance technicians, site managers, and support service coordinators; handle hiring, training, and employee supervision and terminate employees when necessary.
- Manage seven apartment complexes with 322 units.
- Handle extensive financial management responsibilities including providing oversight for a budget of nearly ½ million dollars a year; am responsible for assuring tax credit management according to strict government guidelines.
- Handle financial planning which includes analyzing the previous fiscal year's expenses and calculating the budget for the next year; analyze trends and make projections for the upcoming year while estimating occupancy rates, payroll costs, and determining profitability projections.

Accomplishments:
- Took over one underperforming complex which had averaged a 34% vacancy rate for 13 years; replaced the site manager, revitalized marketing, and persisted until the problems were turned around: the complex is now at 100% occupancy.
- Took over six complexes which were successful operations and boosted their efficiency in numerous small but significant ways; have averaged 98% occupancy at five of the complexes, which has been a difficult accomplishment in a competitive market.

PERSONAL　　Highly motivated person with a talent for forming relationships. Excellent references.

Date

Patricia Smith
Administrative Office of the Courts
PO Box 2448
Raleigh, NC 27602

REVENUE FIELD AUDITOR   Dear Ms. Smith:

With the enclosed resume, I would like to make you aware of my interest in the position of **Accounting Specialist I with the Administrative Office of the Courts.** As you will see from my enclosed resume, I offer a background as a seasoned accounting professional with exceptional analytical, communication, and organization skills, and I have functioned essentially as a Financial Management Analyst in my role as a Field Auditor and Revenue Officer.

With the Department of Revenue, I have advanced in a track record of increasing responsibilities. In my current position as a Field Auditor, I analyze financial reports of businesses and individuals, reconciling various general ledgers, investment and checking accounts in order to accurately determine tax liability. Earlier as a Revenue Officer, I consulted with taxpayers to assist them in determining the validity of deductions and calculating the amount of individual income tax owed. In both of these positions, I trained my coworkers, sharing my extensive knowledge of Internal Revenue Service and Department of Revenue codes and laws as well as educating department personnel on correct procedures related to professional auditing and collections.

As you will see, I have earned an Associate of Applied Science degree in Accounting and a Bachelor of Science in Business Administration.

If you can use an accounting professional with highly developed analytical and organizational abilities and strong communication skills that have been tested in difficult situations requiring tact and diplomacy, I hope you will contact me to suggest a time when we might meet to discuss your needs. I can assure in advance that I have an excellent reputation and would quickly become an asset to your organization.

Sincerely,

Simon Lazarus

SIMON LAZARUS

1110½ Hay Street, Fayetteville, NC 28305   •   preppub@aol.com   •   (910) 483-6611

OBJECTIVE   To benefit an organization that can use an experienced accounting professional with exceptional communication and organizational skills who offers a background as a field auditor and revenue officer and experience in personnel management.

EDUCATION   **Bachelor of Science** degree in **Business Administration**, University of North Carolina at Wilmington, Wilmington, NC.
Associate of Applied Science degree in **Accounting**, Central Carolina Community College, Charlotte, NC.

EXPERIENCE   **REVENUE FIELD AUDITOR.** North Carolina Department of Revenue, Charlotte, NC (2000-present). Perform a wide variety of accounting, training, and administrative duties involved with ensuring and enforcing compliance with North Carolina Revenue laws.
- Conduct audits of taxpayers' records, checking the accuracy of all figures to confirm that all revenues owed to the state were paid.
- Analyze financial reports of businesses and individuals, reconciling various general ledgers, checking and investment accounts to verify tax liabilities.
- Examine taxpayer's records to ensure correct calculation of Sales and Use Tax, Corporate Income Tax, Franchise Tax, License Tax, and Inheritance Tax.
- Evaluate Individual Income Tax returns, judging the validity of deductions taken and confirming the accuracy of all figures.
- Provided training to my coworkers in professional auditing procedures.
- Possess extensive, detailed knowledge related to the laws and codes of both the Internal Revenue Service and the North Carolina Department of Revenue.

REVENUE OFFICER. North Carolina Department of Revenue, Charlotte, NC (1990-00). Provided education and assistance to taxpayers, as well as providing collections and enforcement and training personnel.
- Performed consultations with taxpayers to assist them in determining the validity of deductions and the correct amount of their tax liability.
- Contacted delinquent taxpayers, by telephone and in person in order to collect back taxes owed to the state.
- Provided training to my coworkers in all facets of the collections process.
- Enforced compliance with state revenue laws throughout Mecklenburg county.

PERSONNEL ASSIGNMENT MANAGER. U.S. Army, Personnel Command Headquarters, Germany (1985-1990). Performed human resource management and personnel assignments of enlisted personnel, ensuring adequate staffing of organizations and processing transfer requests.
- Designed a personnel assignment system that ensured that all units were staffed at 100% strength.
- Processed all requests for reassignment to stateside units, as well as requests for extensions of foreign service tours of duty in Europe.
- Determined appropriate duty assignments for enlisted personnel being transferred to Seventh Army or Headquarters, U.S. Army, Europe.

PERSONAL   Excellent personal and professional references are available upon request.

Date

Exact Name of Person
Title or Position
Name of Company
Address (number and street)
Address (city, state, and zip)

SALES FINANCE RELATIONSHIP MANAGER

Dear Exact Name of Person: (or Sir or Madam if answering a blind ad.)

    With the enclosed resume, I would like to make you aware of my exceptional skills in areas which include establishing strong customer relationships, providing top-notch financial support for businesses, and managing operations and accounts for maximum profitability.

    As you will see from my enclosed resume, I have excelled in a track record of accomplishment with Wellington Bank. In my current position I am the Relationship Manager to 55 active automotive dealerships in seven counties. Because of my strong customer service orientation as well as my ability to identify problems and opportunities, I have generated a commercial pipeline of $21 million during 2001, and I increased retail loan volumes from $250,000 to $120,000,000 a week.

    In a previous position with Wellington, I took over the management of a 10-employee branch and transformed it into a branch ranked at #1 in production status based on loans/deposits in a network of 9 branches. Prior to my taking over as manager, the branch was designated to be closed but, through my aggressive leadership and customer service, top management revised its strategic plan and the branch remains open and is prospering to this day.

    You will see from my resume that, in every job I have held, I have been ranked "the best" or in the top 5% of producers.

    If you feel you can use a dynamic producer who offers a sophisticated understanding of sales and finance as it relates to businesses of all sizes, I hope you will contact me to suggest a time when we could meet to discuss your needs. I can provide exceptional references at the appropriate time.

Yours sincerely,

John Ginman

JOHN GINMAN

1110½ Hay Street, Fayetteville, NC 28305   •   preppub@aol.com   •   (910) 483-6611

OBJECTIVE

To benefit an organization that can use a strong bottom-line producer who excels in developing relationships, delivering exceptional sales results, and solving business problems in ways that increase revenue, boost market share, and satisfy customers.

EXPERIENCE

With Wellington Bank, have excelled in a variety of challenging assignments that tested my sales ability, management skills, and executive problem-solving talents:

2001-present: SALES FINANCE RELATIONSHIP MANAGER. Wellington Bank, NA, New York, NY. Am the Relationship Manager to 55 active automotive dealerships with individual sales of more than $60 million annually; identify commercial lending opportunities and solicit dealer use of a competitive consumer retail/lease plan.

- Have generated a commercial pipeline of $21 million in wholesale and commercial portfolio (the previous territory record was $6 million); increased retail loan volumes from $250,000 to $1,200,000 a week.
- As of this year-to-date, my territory and I are ranked #2 among 78 counterparts in six states in production within the Sales Finance Division.
- Identify customer needs that would allow the integration of a complete financial services package; have excelled through my ability to identify and solve problems as well as my emphasis on customer service and building solid customer relationships.
- Within the Central Region of Wellington, have excelled at integrating other lines of business into my relationship base.

2000-01: SMALL BUSINESS RELATIONSHIP MANAGER. Wellington Bank, Boston, MA. Was ranked in top 5% in production among 75 relationship managers in three states.

- Generated more than $1 million a month in new small business credit; excelled in offering a broad range of credit, treasury services, and other instruments to businesses with sales of less than $2 million.

1999-00: BRANCH MANAGER. Wellington Bank, N.A., New York, NY. Managed and motivated 10 employees while establishing strong customer relationships.

- Achieved #1 production status in loans/deposits in a network of 9 branches; when I took over the management of this branch, it was ranked second to last.
- Although this branch was designated to be closed by mid-2000, I was credited with "turning around" a problem operation and restoring management's confidence.

1998-99: MORTGAGE (RESIDENTIAL) ORIGINATOR. Wellington Bank, NA, New York, NY. Generated an average of $1 million a month in residential mortgages, and learned the characteristics of residential mortgage underwriting.

1995-98: SALES FINANCE DEALER CREDIT MANAGER. Wellington Bank of GA, Atlanta, GA. Generated $6 million monthly in consumer loans from automotive dealerships in middle and northeast Georgia; this exceptional productivity occurred as I simultaneously maintained an unusually low loan delinquency ratio of .53%.

- Managed one employee and trained 60 employees in computer skills while serving as Computer Administrator responsible for internal computer training.
- Nurtured a territory producing $300,000 in monthly sales to $3 million in monthly sales.

EDUCATION

B.A. in Finance, minor in Business, Georgia State University, Atlanta, GA, 1998.
A.A. in Government, Louisburg College, Louisburg, SC, 1995.
Extensive financial and sales training sponsored by Wellington on business accounting.

February 29, 2000

National Specialty
ATTN: John Smith
630 United Drive
Durham, NC 27713

**SENIOR CLAIMS
REPRESENTATIVE**

Dear Mr. Smith:

I am sending you my resume upon the recommendation of Tom Smith, whom I recently assisted professionally in my capacity as an Adjustor with Nationwide Insurance Company. Mr. Smith suggested strongly that I approach you and make you aware of my strong sales skills and financial knowledge, and he has been complimentary about your company.

With a B.S. degree, I am currently excelling as an Adjuster with Nationwide. Based on exceptional results and strong communication skills, I was one of ten people selected in the state to teach a monthly Customer Service Program. In that capacity, I travel to cities all over Alabama to teach other adjustors and managers. I am constantly involved in continuing education as an Adjuster, and much of my continuing education focuses on medical subjects. For example, I have completed continuing education related to knee injuries, cervical and lumbar spine, fractures, and spinal disks.

For my previous job as an Adult Probation/Parole Officer, I was selected at an unusually young age because of the outstanding work and the reputation I had earned in my previous position. I handled a large case load of 134 individuals, nearly all of whom were older adult offenders. By applying my take-charge personality as well as my highly persuasive communication skills and motivational abilities, I reduced the normal rate of clients being returned to prison. I developed an extensive network within the judicial and medical services community and became known for my skill in developing and maintaining strong working relationships.

Although I am excelling in my current position and enjoy my colleagues very much, I wish to establish my career with a company that can make use of my strong sales and marketing abilities. My outgoing personality and confident nature are well suited to sales, and I have achieved exceptional results in my current job because of my ability to communicate, negotiate, persuade, mediate, and arbitrate. I partially financed my college education through jobs which helped me acquire experience in sales, customer service, and public relations.

If you are looking for a well-organized, highly motivated, aggressive young professional who could rapidly become an asset to your organization, I hope you will contact me to suggest a time when we could meet to discuss your needs. I can provide outstanding personal and professional references.

Sincerely,

Elizabeth Fair

ELIZABETH FAIR

1110½ Hay Street, Fayetteville, NC 28305 • preppub@aol.com • (910) 483-6611

OBJECTIVE	I wish to contribute to an organization that can use a motivated, dynamic, well-organized individual who offers exceptional sales and communication skills along with an ability to develop and maintain outstanding working relationships.
EDUCATION	**B.S. degree in Education,** Spring Hill College, Mobile, AL, 1999. • Received North Carolina Merit Scholarship and Greatest Gift Scholarship; Dean's List. • Was cast in the play "Pinnochio" in a singing and dancing role. • Earned a reputation as a campus leader and was active in the Student Education Association and the Student Council for Exceptional Children.
TRAINING	Certified as an Adjuster by AL Department of Insurance based on a statewide exam. • Medical Training: As part of continuous professional training, receive education on subjects including knee injuries, cervical and lumbar spine, fractures, and spinal disks.
HONORS	Am one of ten people in Alabama selected to teach a corporate Customer Service Program to adjusters and managers; travel to cities throughout the state to teach the course.
EXPERIENCE	**SENIOR CLAIMS REPRESENTATIVE.** Nationwide Insurance, Mobile, AL (2000-present). After claimants or policyholders call in a claim to the Alabama headquarters, I am responsible for conducting a face-to-face or on-site investigation within 24 hours. • Have consistently exceeded the company's objectives for customer service. • On claims lost to attorneys, the company average is 6% of total claims; I have lost only 2% and have become known as a highly effective negotiator, mediator, and arbitrator. • Closed more than 90% of claims initiated in 2000, which exceeds company standards. • In Nov 2000 and Feb 2001, won Claims Leadership Award; in 2001 was the First Quarter Winner for claims settled in comparison to all my peers in the Mobile office. • Routinely analyze and interpret medical reports, medical charts, and other documents. **ADULT PROBATION/PAROLE OFFICER.** Department of Corrections, Mobile, AL (1997-00). Was specially selected for this position at an unusually young age because of my outstanding work and the reputation I earned as a Deputy Clerk; became known for my efficiency in handling a large case load which involved supervising 134 adult offenders. • Became widely respected for my high success rate in working with troubled individuals. • Continuously coordinated with judicial officials including magistrates, attorneys, deputies and law enforcement officers, and others in both the public and private sector. • Performed investigations; prepared reports on activities of the 134 people I supervised. **DEPUTY CLERK.** Administrative Office of the Courts, Mobile, AL (1995-97). Developed an extensive network of contacts within the judicial system and became knowledgeable of the "inner workings" of the court system; handled data entry and conducted record checks. • Handled a wide variety of public relations and customer service responsibilities. **Other experience:** Refined my skills in dealing with the public in a gracious manner; excelled in these part-time and summer jobs while financing my college education. **TEACHER.** Braxton Child Care Center (1994). Developed and taught curricula. **HOSTESS.** Muriel's Seafood Restaurant (1993-94). Was known for my congenial personality while serving customers, coordinating work schedules, and training employees.
PERSONAL	Member, Junior League of Mobile. Known for my personality and highly creative nature.

Exact Name of Person
Title or Position
Name of Company
Address (number and street)
Address (city, state, and zip)

**SENIOR PERSONAL
BANKING OFFICER**

Dear Exact Name of Person: (or Dear Sir or Madam if answering a blind ad.)

With the enclosed resume, I would like to make you aware of my interest in joining your organization in some capacity which could utilize my banking industry background.

You will see from my resume that I offer a proven track record of accomplishment with the Bank of Nova Scotia in Canada, where I began as a Teller and was promoted into management responsibilities which involved selling mutual funds, supervising employees, and managing multimillion-dollar portfolios of mortgages, car loans, and student loans. I have excelled as a Consumer Credit Officer, Assistant Manager of the Consumer Credit Department, and Senior Personal Banking Officer. Prior to relocating to TX, I was being groomed for advancement to a more senior level responsible for handling liaison with the bank's most valuable customers and managing even larger portfolios.

In 1996 my husband, who is a Registered Nurse, was recruited by Central Texas Medical Center, so we relocated to Texas at that time. I have been in the process of establishing U.S. residency and obtaining a work permit so that I can resume my career in financial services.

With a reputation as a versatile professional with a proven ability to profitably manage a loan portfolio and provide outstanding service to VIP clients as well as others, I can provide outstanding personal and professional references. Just as you will notice my history of loyalty to the Bank of Nova Scotia, I am seeking to join a company where I could make long-term contributions and eventually become a valuable part of the management team.

If you can use a knowledgeable financial services professional known for my professional demeanor, commitment to quality service, and total attention to detail in all matters, I hope you will contact me to suggest a time when we might meet to discuss how I might fit into your organizational structure. I am a dedicated hard worker and can assure you in advance that I could rapidly apply my extensive knowledge and experience in ways that would produce valuable bottom-line results.

Yours sincerely,

Tonya McDowell

TONYA MCDOWELL

1110½ Hay Street, Fayetteville, NC 28305   •   preppub@aol.com   •   (910) 483-6611

OBJECTIVE   To offer financial expertise and sales experience gained in the banking industry as well as a strong reputation for possessing problem-solving skills and the ability to deal with people in an informative, helpful, and effective manner.

EDUCATION & TRAINING   Earned "Letter of Accomplishment Diploma" in Business, Institute of Canadian Bankers, Montreal, Quebec, Canada, 1994.
Excelled in corporate-sponsored management training courses.

EXPERIENCE   **VOLUNTEER WORKER/HOMEMAKER.**   Dallas, TX (2000-present). Relocated from Canada due to my husband's job as a Registered Nurse; have been raising a family, volunteering with various school and church organizations, and completing paperwork to establish U.S. residency and obtain a work permit which will allow resumption of my career.

Originally hired as a Branch Bank Teller and promoted to Senior Teller, built a track record of advancement and promotion with the Bank of Nova Scotia:
SENIOR PERSONAL BANKING OFFICER. Oakville, Ontario (1996-00). Developed and maintained high service levels while managing a $30 million portfolio of residential mortgages, car loans, and student loans as well as profitable retail business interests; sold mutual funds.
- Provided customer assistance with credit card accounts, student loans, and lines of credit.
- Provided assistance for retail loan and deposit portfolio administration.
- Was cited for displaying a highly professional demeanor and a talent for building strong customer relations through my knowledge and respect for the needs of the customer.
- Encouraged professional development of three people under my direct supervision and two other employees indirectly while supervising all aspects of their performance.

ASSISTANT MANAGER, CONSUMER CREDIT. New Toronto, Ontario (1993-95). Gained a great deal of knowledge and experience in selling mutual funds while also applying supervisory skills overseeing the performance of two departmental clerks.
- Emphasized the importance of collections and maintained branch delinquency rates which were consistently below the regional average.
- Handled daily responsibilities related to the processing and servicing of mortgages, loans, investments, and credit cards.

CONSUMER CREDIT DEPARTMENT ASSISTANT MANAGER. Etobicoke, Ontario (1992-93). Supervised two people and gained experience in a small bank environment while selling mutual funds and managing mortgages, loans, and credit card account services.

COLLECTIONS OFFICER and **CUSTOMER SERVICE REPRESENTATIVE.** West Etobicoke, Ontario (1991-92). Displayed a tactful, respectful but still firm manner of dealing with customers in order to make collections on overdue credit card and loan accounts.

ASSISTANT CONSUMER CREDIT OFFICER. Toronto, Ontario (1990-91). For the fourth largest bank in Canada with the largest volume of international business in the country, provided customer services for an upscale international customer base.

Highlights of earlier experience: Began as a Teller and became the Senior Teller.

PERSONAL   Offer expertise in office operations and a talent for utilizing computers and software.

Date

Mr. Vincent Nair
Human Resource Manager
Billows & Klein Recruiters
5881 North Delaware Street.
Miami, Florida 39023

SENIOR PURCHASING MANAGER

Notice the bold fourth paragraph, where he simply states that he has never been in a job where he didn't find ways to improve profitability and strengthen customer relationships. This ought to interest prospective employers in Florida!

Dear Mr. Nair:

With the enclosed resume, I would like to introduce myself and make you aware of the considerable experience in purchasing, contracting, property management, finance, and operations management which I could put to work for you. I am currently in the process of relocating to the Florida area where my extended family lives, and I would appreciate an opportunity to talk personally with you about how I could contribute to your organization.

With my current employer, I have been promoted to Senior Purchasing Manager. I am responsible for the property management of more than 5,000 houses and apartments, including a fleet of 72 service vans. I also prepare and resourcefully utilize a budget of more than $1.6 million annually for repair parts, outside services, support equipment, and materials. On my own initiative, I have totally streamlined the bidding process. In consultation with the System Manager, I implemented a new computer program to track bids, thereby transforming a previously disorganized manual process into an efficient computerized system. Additionally, I streamlined purchasing procedures while taking over a job which had previously been done by two people. Using available software, I have also established accounting and budgeting programs for a small business.

In all my previous jobs, I have been recognized—sometimes with cash bonuses— for developing new systems which improved efficiency and customer service. For example, while working for the U.S. Embassy in Miami, I created a computerized method of financial reporting which greatly enhanced the budgeting and fiscal accountability functions. In another job as a Purchasing Agent, I exceeded expected standards while handling critical functions including making decisions on the most advantageous sources, assisting in bidding solicitations, and evaluating quotations for price discounts and reference materials.

I have never been in a job where I did not find creative and resourceful ways to cut costs, improve bottom-line results, and strengthen relationships with customers.

I hope you will call or write me soon to suggest a time convenient for us to meet and discuss your needs and how I might serve them. Thank you for your time.

Sincerely,

Robert Rountree

ROBERT ROUNTREE

Until 12/15/01: 1110½ Hay Street, Fayetteville, NC 28305   (910) 483-6611
After 12/16/01: 538 Pittsfield Avenue, Orlando, FL 58401   (805) 483-6611

OBJECTIVE   To contribute to an organization that can use a resourceful purchasing manager who is skilled in contract negotiation, operations management, and personnel administration.

EDUCATION   Completed one year of **Master's degree work in Urban Management**, Texas State University, Mercerville, TX, 1995-96.
Earned **B.S. in Health Education**, University of Washington, Washington, DC, 1991.
Received **A.A. in General Education**, Miami Dale Community College, Miami, FL, 1986.
Completed executive development and non-degree-granting training programs in:

Cost Accounting	Managerial Accounting	Procurement
Computer Operations	Inventory Control	Budget Administration

COMPUTERS   Lotus 1-2-3, dBase IV, WordPerfect, Managing Your Money, Windows, others

EXPERIENCE   **SENIOR PURCHASING MANAGER.** Briley & Co., Ft. Hood, TX (2000-present). Have acquired a broad understanding of government contracting procedures while achieving an excellent track record of promotion in the finance and purchasing field.

- Was originally employed as a Purchasing Agent to replace two buyers; have been promoted to Senior Purchasing Manager in charge of five associates.
- Am responsible for an annual budget of approximately $2.1 million of which $1.6 million is used by me to purchase repair parts, outside services, support equipment, and materials.
- Responsible for property management: within a $150,000 monthly budget oversee maintenance and repairs performed on 5,000 housing units and a fleet of 72 vans.
- In a formal letter of appreciation, was commended for saving at least $400,000 annually by combining my extensive purchasing knowledge with my creative problem-solving skills.
- On my own initiative, streamlined the bidding process; developed a new system for obtaining price quotes from potential vendors and worked with the System Manager in developing a computer program to track quotes: this transformed the manual quotation to an efficient new process which reduced the time necessary to prepare quotes.
- Established excellent working relationships with vendors all over the country, and am known for my ability to quickly find difficult-to-obtain parts for critical needs.
- Knowledgeable of government contracting and new product testing.

CONSULTANT & VICE PRESIDENT OF FINANCE. Branson Enterprises, Dallas, TX (1994-00). Played a key role in helping the owner build a new business; established budgeting and accounting systems. Negotiated the details of the company's largest contract.

PURCHASING MANAGER. Contracting Division of the U.S. Air Force, Washington, DC (1989-93). Handled critical functions including making decisions on the most advantageous sources, assisting in bidding solicitations and acceptance, and evaluating quotations for price discounts as well as delivery/transportation costs. Developed outstanding relationships and received a Laudatory Best Operation performance appraisal with cash bonus.

PROCUREMENT OFFICER. The American Embassy in Miami (1986-89). Began working for the Embassy as a Warehouse Manager and, holding a **Top Secret** security clearance, excelled in managing warehouse operations and in relocating warehouse contents to new facilities.

- Because of my problem-solving ability, was promoted to Procurement Officer; took over a disorganized operation and created a computerized method of reporting Local Operational Funds (LOF) which enhanced efficiency of the budgeting and fiscal functions.

PERSONAL   Outstanding personal and professional references. Will cheerfully travel/relocate.

Exact Name of Person
Title or Position
Name of Company
Address (No., street)
Address (city, state, zip)

SITE FREIGHT COORDINATOR

Although he is "held in high regard" by his current employer, as he states in his cover letter, Mr. Palacios heard through the grapevine that his company was going to downsize and he didn't want to be caught without options. Developing options is what his resume and cover letter are designed to do.

Dear Exact Name of Person: (or Dear Sir or Madam if answering a blind ad.)

I would appreciate an opportunity to talk with you soon about how I could contribute to your organization through my experience in all aspects of traffic and transportation management. I offer extensive knowledge of LTL, TL, Intermodal, rate negotiations, pool shipments, and cost analysis to determine the most economical method of shipping.

As you will see from my resume, I am currently site freight coordinator for a Fortune 500 company, and I have continuously found new ways to reduce costs and improve efficiency while managing all inbound and outbound shipping. On my own initiative, I have recovered $10,000 in claims annually while saving the company at least 40% of a $10 million LTL budget. In addition to continuous cost cutting, I have installed a new bar code system in the finished goods shipping area and have installed a new wrapping system.

In previous jobs supervising terminal operations, I opened up new terminals, closed down existing operations which were unprofitable, and gained hands-on experience in increasing efficiency in every terminal area.

With a reputation as a savvy negotiator, I can provide excellent personal and professional references. I am held in high regard by my current employer.

I hope you will call or write me soon to suggest a time convenient for us to meet and discuss your current and future needs and how I might serve them. Thank you in advance for you time.

Sincerely yours,

Pedro Palacios

Alternate last paragraph:
I hope you will welcome my call soon to arrange a brief meeting at your convenience to discuss your current and future needs and how I might serve them. Thank you in advance for your time.

PEDRO PALACIOS

1110½ Hay Street, Fayetteville, NC 28305 • preppub@aol.com • (910) 483-6611

OBJECTIVE	To contribute to an organization that can use a skilled traffic management professional who offers a proven ability to reduce costs, install new systems, optimize scheduling, negotiate rates, anticipate difficulties, solve problems, and keep customers happy.
EXPERIENCE	**SITE FREIGHT COORDINATOR.** DuPont Corporation, Wilmington, DE (2000-present). For this Fortune 500 company, have continuously found new ways to cut costs and improve service while managing all inbound transportation as well as outbound shipping totaling in excess of one million dollars in finished goods daily; supervise ten people.

- Saved the company at least 40% of a $10 million LTL budget by resourcefully combining my technical knowledge with my creative cost-cutting skills.
- Recovered $10,000 annually in claims; prepare all cargo claims documents for corporate office and oversee all procedures for proper claims documentation.
- Installed a bar code system in Finished Goods Shipping, and also installed a new wrapping system.
- Reduced overtime by 90% while simultaneously cross-training some employees and improving overall morale.
- Became familiar with Total Quality Processes while analyzing transit times to ensure consistent and timely Just-In-Time delivery schedules.
- Am a member of the B & D corporate committee for North American rate negotiations; negotiate rates with various carriers on special moves.
- Justify capital appropriation requests for funding special projects; audit all freight bills and process them for payment.
- Prepare all documents for export shipments to Canada; also advise about the shipment of hazardous materials and maintain proper documentation placards and labels.
- Coordinate all site printing of product information and warranty cards.
- Am responsible for site switcher and equipment such as leased trailers.
- Have earned a reputation as a savvy negotiator with an ability to predict future variables that will affect traffic costs.

SUPERVISOR. International Freightways, Inc., Atlanta, GA (1993-00). Supervised up to 12 drivers while managing second-shift operations and controlling inbound and outbound freight at this terminal operation.
- Increased efficiency in every operational area; improved the load factor, reduced dock hours, and ensured more timely deliveries.

INVENTORY SPECIALIST. La-Z-Boy East, Inc., Florence, SC (1989-92). Learned the assembly process of this name-brand furniture manufacturer while managing replenishment of subassemblies for daily production.

Highlights of other experience:
- As Terminal Manager for Spartan Express, opened a new terminal in South Carolina; determined the pricing structure, handled sales, and then managed this new operation which enjoyed rapid growth.
- Gained experience in closing down a terminal determined to be in a poor location.
- As Operations Manager for a break bulk operation, supervised up to 12 people in a dock center while managing the sorting/segregating of shipments from origin to destination.

EDUCATION	Studied business management and liberal arts, Ohio State and LaSalle University. Completed extensive executive development courses in the field of transportation and traffic management sponsored by University of Toledo and Texas Technical University
PERSONAL	Can provide outstanding personal and professional references. Will relocate.

TELLER SUPERVISOR   Dear Mr. Holden:

With the enclosed resume, I would like to express my interest in the job as Senior Teller which we have discussed briefly.

As you will see from my resume, I offer a combination of customer service experience, clerical and computer skills, and public relations ability which could be useful to you. I am known for my cheerful and hardworking nature, and I would welcome the opportunity to be trained to do things your way.

In my current position at Nationwide Bank, I have been promoted to Back-up Teller Supervisor, and I am respected for my high levels of productivity and efficiency. I pride myself on my ability to make significant contributions to my employer through my technical knowledge as well as through my strong personal initiative.

If you would like to take our discussion to the next level of detail, I am certainly interested in doing so. I can provide excellent references at the appropriate time, but I would ask that you not contact my current employer until after we have a chance to talk. Thank you for your interest in my background and skills.

Sincerely,

Elizabeth Brewster

ELIZABETH BREWSTER

1110½ Hay Street, Fayetteville, NC 28305　　•　　preppub@aol.com　　•　　(910) 483-6611

OBJECTIVE　　To contribute to an organization through my cheerful and enthusiastic personality as well as through my computer skills and customer service experience.

EDUCATION　　Hamden Technical Community College, Hamden, CT.
- Completed one year of studies in Business Management.

First Citizens Bank, Hamden, CT.
- Completed training related to sales, customer service, computer operations, other areas.

Hamden Senior High School, Hamden, CT; graduated 1991; played on the softball team.

EXPERIENCE　　**TELLER SUPERVISOR BACK-UP.** Nationwide Bank, Hamden, CT (2000-present). Began as a Teller and was rapidly promoted to Back-Up Teller Supervisor; have assisted in training new employees.
- Am involved in a wide range of activities including cashing checks, making deposits, auditing other tellers, assuring the proper implementation of internal controls, controlling vault access, preparing daily reports, and updating information on the computer.
- Have gained a reputation as a cheerful hard worker known for the highest levels of efficiency and productivity.
- In an era when the bank is continuously implementing new software applications and programs, have demonstrated an ability to rapidly master new computer programs and applications.
- Routinely operate equipment including a Compaq V50 computer, fax machines, Pitney Bowes 8000, copies, Mita DC-1205, multiline phones, and other equipment.

SALES CLERK. Hecht's Department Store, Hamden, CT (1999-00). Excelled in all aspects of my job and won numerous awards for my sales and customer service skills; progressed from Gold Star, to Burgundy, to Ruby, to Diamond within the company's Mystery Shoppers competition.
- Became skilled in ringing and stocking merchandise.
- Conducted inventory and daily audits.
- Was entrusted with responsibility for ordering merchandise from other locations.

Other experience:
As a full-time homemaker from 1992-99, was very active in community activities including the PTA (six years) and Girl Scouts (three years) organizations; held numerous responsible volunteer leadership positions.
- Was honored as "Parent Volunteer of the Year, 1997."
- Through these volunteer leadership and service activities, refined my ability to work with others and to establish effective relationships.

PERSONAL　　Outstanding personal and professional references upon request. Strong work ethic.

Exact Name of Person
Exact Title
Exact Name of Company
Address
City, State, Zip

**UNDERWRITER
AND LOAN OFFICER**

Dear Exact Name of Person: (or Dear Sir or Madam if answering a blind ad):

With the enclosed resume, I would like to make you aware of my background as an articulate finance professional with exceptional communication and sales skills as well as a strong bottom-line orientation and a solid background in finance.

As you will see from my resume, I am currently excelling as an underwriter and loan officer, and I am skilled at handling every type of home mortgage product as well as specialized loan packages. In a previous job with First Security Mortgage, I maintained the highest sales average among all loan officers while excelling in originating home mortgage loans throughout 17 states and handling a residential and commercial portfolio in excess of $18 million.

While working in the manufactured home industry, I was involved in the sale and financing of manufactured home products. I have an excellent personal and professional reputation, and I have established a network of contacts throughout the lending industry. Later as a Sales Consultant with a Chevrolet dealership, I was groomed in the business management and financial aspects of the car dealership business.

You would find me in person to be a naturally outgoing individual who offers an unusually strong combination of sales ability and financial expertise. In financing the major assets in people's lives—homes and automobiles—both strong sales ability and a solid knowledge of lending are required in order to maximize profitability and market share.

I am confident that I offer experience which could make a valuable contribution to your business, and I hope we will have the opportunity to talk in person about my desire to join your finance and insurance team. I can provide excellent references at the appropriate time, and I am single and capable of relocating and working the strenuous hours which I am aware the job requires.

Sincerely,

John Miller

JOHN MILLER

1110½ Hay Street, Fayetteville, NC 28305 • preppub@aol.com • (910) 483-6611

OBJECTIVE	To benefit an organization that can use an articulate and resourceful professional with excellent communication skills who offers strong management abilities along with knowledge of finance, lending, underwriting, and mortgage banking.
EDUCATION	**B.S. degree in Investment Banking/International Economics** being completed in my spare time; completed courses at University of Virginia, Danville campus. Completed numerous professional development and executive training courses related to finance, investments, sales, mortgage banking, and lending.
EXPERIENCE	**UNDERWRITER & LOAN OFFICER.** Community Choice Mortgage, Danville, VA (2000-present). Perform extensive liaison with the lending community as well as with customers while expertly coordinating the underwriting of home mortgage loans; work with international, national, state, and local lenders to obtain financing. • Am skilled in handling FHA, VA, Fannie Mae, Freddie Mac, conforming, and nonconforming home mortgage products. • Have become knowledgeable of all types of mortgage and home equity loans including first, second, 125%, LTV, and debt consolidations. • Also handle specialized loan packages including venture capital loans; am skilled in prospecting for loans through private investors and funding groups, and have placed commercial loans of more than $200 million. • With an excellent personal and professional reputation, have established a network of contacts and friends throughout the lending industry whom I can call on for advice.

LOAN OFFICER. First Security Mortgage Corporation, Danville, VA (1998-00). Maintained the highest sales average among all loan officers for the third quarter of the 2000 fiscal year while also excelling in all administrative aspects of my job.
- Originated home mortgage loans throughout seventeen states; was responsible for a portfolio of residential and commercial loans in excess of $18 million.
- Handled processing of loans from origination to completion; assisted customers in obtaining the best possible loan for their personal needs.
- Maintained excellent client/bank relationships; personally underwrote loans via credit scoring, loan to value, and debt to income ratios.
- Trained junior loan specialists in techniques for loan origination, processing, and sales.
- Tracked in excess of 25 loans simultaneously at all times.
- Became skilled in the interpretation of loans as well as in sales.

SALES CONSULTANT & FINANCE SPECIALIST. Tom Benson Chevrolet, San Antonio, TX (1995-97). Communicated with lenders by phone and fax while obtaining financing for customers; worked with debt to income and trade-in values in determining optimal prices.
- Maximized the dealership's profit by maintaining an extremely high level of customer satisfaction; aggressively serviced customer needs.
- Assisted customers in selection of an appropriate vehicle; calculated monthly payments based on amount of down payment, price of vehicle, and approximate interest rate.

SALES & FINANCE CONSULTANT. Oakwood Homes, Danville, VA (1992-94). Continuously applied my sales and financial knowledge while assisting customers of manufactured housing in selecting and purchasing appropriate homes to suit their taste and budget.
- Worked with local lending institutions to obtain financing for customers.

PERSONAL	Am a naturally outgoing individual who believes in being involved in helping my community.

Senior managers and executives share unique advantages and disadvantages in a job hunt. Yet they face the common issues all managers face when they go out into the job market.

Problems faced by the senior manager and executive in a job hunt

Ask senior managers and executives what they believe to be their biggest problem in their job hunt and they will tell you this: They are afraid companies will discriminate against them because of their age, and they believe companies will hire the less expensive junior manager over the senior manager in many situations. Their fears are often based on reality.

Not emphasizing age on the senior manager's resume

Although it is never appropriate to misrepresent anything on a resume, it is often to the advantage of the senior manager to decrease the emphasis on his or her age. Generally it is recommended that a resume show the last 10 or 15 years of experience, and experience prior to that, if shown, can be highlighted in an "Other Experience" section without dates. When you look at the resumes in this section, you will see low-key techniques used to de-emphasize the age of many of these senior managers and executives. Since experience is often more important than education in terms of what the senior manager is offering, the Education section is usually near the bottom of the senior manager's resume, and sometimes the "year dates" showing when degrees were earned are omitted. The senior manager is not trying to disguise his age; he or she is simply trying to de-emphasize it and avoid being screened out because of seniority.

Seniority and experience can be a positive thing!

Experience, as they say, is the best teacher, and experience can be a valuable asset to any organization. Companies are not ignorant of that fact, and they know that experience usually comes with age, so the important facts to show on a resume are one's results, accomplishments, and achievements. Indeed, many companies actually seek the mature and seasoned employee. For example, a number of financial services firms say they look for individuals with "a little grey in their hair," because age and maturity seem to connote wisdom in that industry.

Senior managers can be in career change, too!

Several of the senior managers in this section are in the career-change mode. As we mentioned previously in this book, most of us working people are expected to have at least three different careers in our lifetimes. You will be seeing people in this section who are embarking on their third career!

Date

Exact Name of Person
Exact Title or Position
Name of Company
Address (number and street)
Address (city, state, and zip)

ASSISTANT VICE PRESIDENT, CONSUMER BANKING

Dear Exact Name of Person: (or Dear Sir or Madam if answering a blind ad.)

This aggressive young professional is on the "fast track" in his company, but he is feeling restless and wants to "see what's out there." The resume and cover letter are designed to interest employers in numerous fields.

With the enclosed resume, I would like to formally initiate the process of being considered for a position within your organization which can use my exceptionally strong marketing, communication, and consulting skills.

As you will see from my resume, since earning my B.S. degree in Business Administration with a Marketing major, I have enjoyed a track record of success in highly competitive banking and consumer product environments. Most recently I was named the top producer in my region based on my results in establishing the most new accounts, achieving the highest loan volume, and obtaining the most referrals. In an earlier position, I consistently led my office in sales and received the Sales Leadership award as well as other honors recognizing my aggressive marketing orientation and highly refined customer service skills.

Even in summer and part-time jobs while earning my college degree, I was selected for highly responsible positions at companies including R.J. Reynolds/Nabisco, where I managed 30 employees. My summer jobs prior to college graduation helped me acquire excellent skills in merchandising, marketing, and sales.

If you can use an ambitious, results-oriented marketing professional, I hope you will contact me to suggest a time when we might meet to discuss your needs and goals and how I might help you achieve them.

Sincerely,

Jason Vetter

JASON VETTER

1110½ Hay Street, Fayetteville, NC 28305 • preppub@aol.com • (910) 483-6611

OBJECTIVE	To offer strong marketing, managerial, and sales experience to an organization in need of a professional with the ability to motivate others to exceed expectations through excellent communication and consulting skills.
EXPERIENCE	**ASSISTANT VICE PRESIDENT, CONSUMER BANKING.** FirstBank, N.A., Seattle, WA (2000-present). In May, 2000, was ranked the Top Consumer Banker in the Central Washington Region based on my results in establishing the most new accounts, achieving the highest loan volume, and obtaining many referrals.

- Have achieved a record productivity for two years in a row.
- Assisted customers while educating them on the merits of different products such as checking and savings accounts, Certificates of Deposit, and IRAs.
- As a loan officer, met with customers and explained differences between types of loans available and made decisions on their qualifications for loans.

PERSONAL BANKER and **RETAIL MANAGEMENT ASSOCIATE.** Nations Bank of Washington, N.A., Seattle, WA (1995-00). Achieved record productivity while completing a comprehensive management training program with this major financial institution; maintained and managed a portfolio of approximately 1,000 customers.

- Increased the size of my customer base by 30%.
- Played a key role in achieving the highest number of loan and credit card sales and the highest dollar volume of any branch in the Seattle region.
- Learned all aspects of banking from teller operations to becoming familiar with investment and loan procedures as well as account management; continued to attend training classes to refine and add to my store of knowledge.
- Emphasized quality customer service and set an example for other bank employees while helping existing customers and selling the bank's services to new ones.
- Supervised teller staff and daily operations; conducted staff sales meetings.

ACCOUNT REPRESENTATIVE. Dictaphone Corporation/Pitney Bowes, Midlands, WA (1994-95). Managed more than 300 new and existing accounts while selling communications equipment including Dictaphone, voice mail, and time management equipment in a three-county area.

- Consistently led the office in sales: received the "Sales Leadership" award for achieving 206% of my quota two months ahead of schedule and later received recognition in the "Achievement Club" for 210% of quota.
- Worked mainly with medical and legal accounts while selling systems valued from $400 to more than $100,000 in a generally long-term sales process.
- Opened more than 25 accounts.

EDUCATION	**B.S. in Business Administration**, Seattle State University, Seattle, WA, 1993.

- Majored in Marketing; was a member of the American Marketing Association.
- Held leadership roles in Delta Chi Fraternity including vice president and rush coordinator; was honored as "Brother of the Year"; and currently serve as a trustee on the alumni board.

Completed professional development programs related to consumer finance and consumer loans sponsored by FirstBank, 1996-present.

PERSONAL	Have volunteered with the United Way, Hospitality House, and Watauga Hunger Coalition. Knowledgeable of Microsoft Word, Lotus 1-2-3, dBase III.

Exact Title
Company Name
Address (street and number)
Address (city, state, and zip)

CHIEF FINANCIAL OFFICER

With classic credentials
including the Harvard
Business School, this top
executive has worked
for only two companies.
He is seeking a new
challenge that will
further test his ability to
optimize efficiency
and maximize
profitability.

Dear Exact Name of Person: (or Dear Sir or Madam if answering a blind ad.)

Can you use an experienced top executive with a proven track record of success in transforming small business entities into large-scale, multiunit operations while assuring that all core systems are carefully designed and implemented to assure maximum profitability and efficiency?

With an MBA from the Harvard Business School, I have most recently led a small three-unit company operating in one state to become a major competitor in its industry while aggressively expanding into 12 states. Even though I am excelling in my job and am held in high regard by the board of directors, I am selectively exploring the possibility of joining a growth-oriented company which can use my proven ability to maximize profit and efficiency while building dynamic teams of highly motivated individuals. Although I can provide outstanding personal and professional references at the appropriate time, I would appreciate your holding my inquiry in confidence at this time.

Prior to assuming my current position, I refined my business skills in a track record of accomplishment in the retailing business. Throughout my more than 20 years of experience, I was effective in training and leading personnel to achieve historical sales records. Through my knowledge of marketing and merchandising, I increased sales and profits in every store and territory I managed and was successful in managing major expansion projects.

If you can use my considerable business acumen and experience, I hope you will call or write me soon to suggest a time when we might meet to discuss your current and future needs and how I might serve them. Thank you in advance for your time.

Sincerely,

Vincent Trossbach

Alternate last paragraph:
I hope you will welcome my call soon to arrange a time for us to discuss your current and future needs and how I might serve them. Thank you in advance for your time.

VINCENT TROSSBACH

1110½ Hay Street, Fayetteville, NC 28305 • preppub@aol.com • (910) 483-6611

OBJECTIVE   To benefit an organization that can use an experienced executive with a history of success in turning around unprofitable locations, designing and implementing cost control systems, and building teams of dedicated workers.

EDUCATION & TRAINING

M.B.A., Harvard Business School, Boston, MA, 1977
B.A. in English, University of North Carolina at Chapel Hill, NC, 1973

EXPERIENCE   **CHIEF EXECUTIVE OFFICER AND PRESIDENT.** Specialty Products, Inc., Chicago, IL (2000-present). Through my aggressive leadership of a privately owned retailing business, have transformed it from an operation with three stores in one state to 50 stores in 12 states; we are still expanding and I believe that savvy selection and thorough training of the right people is the key to continued growth and profitability.

- Was recruited by this company to assume the CEO position because of my reputation as an innovative leader and retailing executive with an aggressive bottom-line orientation.
- Worked closely with the director of operations to develop job descriptions and business plans, then hired and trained the management personnel for each location.
- While working closely with our advertising agency, have emphasized the creation of exciting sales promotions and advertising campaigns; hired and trained people whom I consider some of the world's finest merchandisers and retailers.
- Hired and worked closely with computer programmers who have established a point-of-sale and automatic replenishment system that is unique in the industry and which has dramatically lowered inventory carrying costs.

Advanced in the following track record of promotion, Gainey Corporation:
VICE PRESIDENT, SOUTHEAST REGION. Bentonville, AR (1993-00). On my own initiative, implemented numerous changes which boosted efficiency and profitability of the 120-store region which I managed and nurtured to its all-time high in sales and profitability.

TERRITORY MANAGER. Huntsville, AL (1990-92). Applied creative management skills which guided this territory to achieve more than $100 million in annual sales in 1989, a 9% increase over 1988.

STORE MANAGER. Decatur, AL (1984-89). Handpicked to take over an 85-90 employee store scheduled to be closed, implemented aggressive promotions and marketing which "saved" the store and subsequently led to a major expansion to 96,000 square feet; transformed it into a record-setting model store which is still in operation today.

- Guided a sales force which led the nation's 1,500 stores in sales; achieved an increase to $1.1 million from $580,000 in sales for the garden center.

STORE MANAGER. McMinnville, TN (1982-84). Challenged by the competition of having a Super K-Mart built only one-fourth of a mile away, increased profit margins 50% and sales from $2 million to $8.5 million during a two-year time period as manager of this 60,000-square-foot store with 55 employees.

Highlights of earlier experience: Advanced in retail management roles as Merchandise Manager and Assistant Manager where my accomplishments included setting up one store's POS system, developing assistant managers in a training store, and day-to-day management of an $18.5 million store.

- Was aggressively recruited by the Gainey Corporation upon graduation from the Harvard Business School; learned the ropes of retailing.

PERSONAL   Have a reputation as a detail-oriented and self-motivated individual.

Date

Exact Name of Person
Exact Title
Exact Name of Company
Address
City, State, Zip

CHIEF FINANCIAL OFFICER   Dear Exact Name of Person (or Dear Sir or Madam if answering a blind ad):

I would like to take this opportunity to make you aware of my background as an innovative young professional who offers a unique blend of managerial and accounting experience along with strong leadership, motivational, and communication skills.

Since graduating **summa cum laude** with a B.S. degree in Accounting, I have established a reputation as an excellent manager of fiscal and human resources who can be counted on to handle complex multiple responsibilities. I excel in producing measurable results while solving problems by applying my keen analytical skills and eye for detail. Although I am held in the highest regard by my current employer and can provide outstanding references at the appropriate time, I would appreciate your holding my expression of interest in your company in confidence until after we speak.

Since 2000 I have been the Chief Financial Officer for Client Behavioral Services (CBS) which was acquired by Greystone, Inc. Since the functional reorganization I have been achieving outstanding results in a dual role since I also am Greystone's State Accounting Manager. With offices in 22 cities, these two health care services companies provide mental health services for at-risk children and therapeutic foster care.

One of my greatest accomplishments has been building the CBS accounting and financial department from a one-person operation to its present level with eight employees. I have been a key factor in bringing about an impressive growth from $100,000 in annual income to the current $17 million by providing analysis of existing services along with recommendations of ways to enjoy major growth and expansion. I have designed, developed, and programmed management systems for billing and payroll for these related companies with more than 1,600 employees statewide.

In a previous position as an Auditor with Ernst & Young, I gained experience in accounting for cash, fixed assets, accounts receivables, income, and expenses while also developing spreadsheets which significantly aided in management decision making.

If you can use an articulate and resourceful young professional with exceptional communication and managerial abilities, I hope you will contact me soon to suggest a time when we might have a brief discussion about how I could contribute to your organization. I can provide excellent professional and personal references.

Sincerely,

Ashish Gupta

ASHISH GUPTA

1110½ Hay Street, Fayetteville, NC 28305　　•　　preppub@aol.com　　•　　(910) 483-6611

OBJECTIVE　　To offer a unique blend of managerial and accounting expertise to an organization that can benefit from my resourceful approach to business development, my ability to motivate and lead others to achieve excellent results, as well as my keen analytical skills and eye for detail.

EDUCATION　　**B.S., Accounting,** University of Wyoming, Cheyenne, WY, 1991.
- Graduated *summa cum laude* with a 3.5 GPA.
- Honors included **"Most Outstanding Student"** for the School of Business and Economics; recognition in the university's spring honors convocation each year; and an **American Institute of Certified Public Accountants Scholarship.**
- Completed two summer internships with ALCOA, played a key role in projects which resulted in significant reductions in county and investment credit taxes.

COMPUTERS　　Proficient with software programs including Microsoft Excel and Word, Lotus, Alpha 5, Business Works, MAS 90, Quick Books Pro, Turbo Tax, ADP, and NECS Data.

EXPERIENCE　　**I am applying exceptional time management and organizational skills in these simultaneous positions which require an innovative problem solver and manager:**
2000-present. CHIEF FINANCIAL OFFICER. Client Behavioral Services (CBS), LLC, Cheyenne, WY. Built the company's financial support from the ground up into an eight-person department which provides operations managers with customized services for a healthcare company that specializes in mental health services for 450 clients in 16 cities.
- Played a major role in the company's growth from $100,000 to $17 million in just three years by providing financial analysis used to evaluate possible new services as well as ideas for expansion after being acquired by new owners in 2002.
- Provide payroll support for 600 employees as well as overseeing billing, accounts receivable, and fixed assets.
- Generate weekly and monthly operational reports and divisional budgets.
- Designed, developed, and programmed the management information systems for billing and payroll as well as interfaces with the database.
- Apply excellent communication skills while dealing with a wide range of people ranging from customers, to division directors, to Medicaid representatives, to state authorities, in a service business with a client base of mostly at-risk children.

1999-present. STATE ACCOUNTING MANAGER. CBS, Inc., Cheyenne, WY. For a company which acquired CBS, handle similar duties: supervise 15 employees while overseeing all aspects of operations in the finance and accounting department.
- Control payroll accounting for more than 1,000 employees in 22 Wyoming cities.
- Developed and implemented a system for comparing key performance indicators to actual results as well as the system for billing $80,000 a month..
- Managed a $1.2 million new construction project during which two day care centers were built: oversaw all aspects of the project to include evaluating market research and dealing with contractors to ensure compliance with all applicable state standards.

Previous experience:
AUDITOR. Ernst & Young, Cheyenne, WY (1991-98). Polished analytical, accounting and auditing skills working with Fortune 500 clients and small business firms.
- Gained experience with cash, fixed asset, accounts receivable, income, and expense accounts; developed spreadsheets, analyzed data, and formulated conclusions.

PERSONAL　　Member, National Association of Black Accountants. Results oriented. Excellent references.

Exact Name of Person
Title or Position
Name of Company
Address (number and street)
Address (city, state, and zip)

CONTROLLER

Dear Exact Name of Person: (or Sir or Madam if answering a blind ad.)

An impressive background and a track record of exceptional results as shown on her resume ought to fetch numerous interviews.

With the enclosed resume, I would like to formally make you aware of my interest in exploring employment opportunities within your organization.

As you will see from my resume, I have excelled in a variety of assignments which required outstanding accounting, customer service, and management skills. In my current position as Controller, I prepare monthly financial statements and year-end financials while also supervising ten people in the accounting department including an assistant controller as well as the MIS and accounts payable/receivable personnel. I wrote this 30-year-old company's first policies and procedures manual. While in control of $5 million in inventory, I developed procedures which led the company to process inventory by barcode at its nine locations.

In my prior job, I rose to Chief Financial Officer for a diversified corporation with holdings in the construction industry and restaurant business. For one of the company's divisions, I was personally responsible for leading the limited partnership's reorganization out of Chapter 11 bankruptcy and, after leading the company out of bankruptcy, the company posted a 7% net profit within the first year.

I am knowledgeable of software including Depreciation Solution, Computer Systems Dynamics (CSD) programs, and Microsoft Office 97. I have demonstrated my capabilities in operational areas including contract development and negotiation, debt structure reorganization, and information systems/data processing administration.

If you can use a hardworking professional with knowledge in numerous operational areas, I hope you will contact me to suggest a time when we might meet to discuss your needs and how I might serve them. I can provide outstanding personal and professional references. Thank you in advance for your time, and I would appreciate your holding my interest in your company in the strictest confidence at this point.

Yours sincerely,

Michelle Bazaldua

MICHELLE BAZALDUA

1110½ Hay Street, Fayetteville, NC 28305 • preppub@aol.com • (910) 483-6611

OBJECTIVE   To contribute to an organization that can use a skilled accounting professional with experience related to financial analysis and financial statement preparation, auditing, cash management, AR/AP, general ledger, payroll, collections, and automated systems.

EXPERIENCE   **CONTROLLER.** Quality Building Supply, Springfield, VA (2000-present). Prepare monthly financial statements and year-end financials while supervising ten people in the accounting department including an assistant controller, AP and AR personnel, and the MIS Director.
- For this 30-year-old company, wrote its first policies and procedures manual.
- Implemented new computer systems for automated payroll with swipe cards.
- Am in control of over $5 million in inventory; developed procedures in processing inventory by barcode for the company's nine locations.
- Implemented new software called CSD, a program for the building supply industry.

For The Jason G. Roth Company, was promoted from Controller to Chief Financial Officer, and worked in two main divisions of the company (1985-93):

1991-99: CHIEF FINANCIAL OFFICER & GENERAL MANAGER. Stone Mountain, GA.
- For a chain of three premier restaurants, was personally responsible for leading the limited partnership's reorganization out of Chapter 11 bankruptcy; personally renegotiated the company debt structure and reduced food, labor, and liquor costs by as much as 12% within six months.
- After leading the company out of bankruptcy, achieved a 7% net profit within the first year.
- Supervised all business operations at three establishments which employed more than 150 employees while producing annual sales of $4.6 million.
- Was the hands-on manager in charge of daily operations, marketing and promotions, purchasing, inventory control, and alcohol management.
- Was in charge of transition planning as the businesses were readied for sale to a new management team; directed the liquidation of assets not included in the sale.

1985-1991: CONTROLLER and PROPERTY & PROJECT MANAGER. Lester Springs, GA. For the Real Estate Development Division, oversaw on-site and off-site construction of new buildings and tenant improvements in addition to performing all financial and property management functions for 32 industrial properties valued at $128 million.
- Collaborated with the owner and architects during the preliminary planning stages of each project; took bids, awarded contracts, and provided oversight of the construction phase through completion.
- Marketed properties, negotiated leases, and handled all property management duties.
- Was in charge of all accounting for this entire real estate portfolio; in addition to managing investment instruments, negotiated secured/unsecured loans up to $41 million.
- Oversaw cash management, mortgage management, and auditing.
- Served as liaison to company attorneys and accountants.
- Supervised projects valued at $61 million, saving $1.2 million as general contractor.
- Generated more than $7 million in net profits through the careful management of company-owned stocks, bonds, and mutual funds.

ACCOUNT CLERK II. County of Siddell, In-Home Supportive Services, Siddell, GA (1982-85). Prepared regular financial reports for the State of Georgia while also reviewing, auditing, and approving grants valued at $10.8 million on a bimonthly basis.
- Initiated and implemented the county's first computerized Medicare issuance system.

EDUCATION   **Associate of Arts Degree in Accounting,** Hazelton Junior College, GA.

PERSONAL   Knowledgeable of software including Depreciation Solution, CSD, and Microsoft Office.

Date

Exact Name of Person
Title or Position
Name of Company
Address (no., street)
Address (city, state, zip)

COST REDUCTION MANAGER

Dear Exact Name of Person: (or Dear Sir or Madam if answering a blind ad.)

I would appreciate an opportunity to talk with you soon about how I could contribute to your organization through my industrial engineering background including my experience in managing cost reduction programs, planning capital expenditures, and supporting new product design.

In my current job as an Industrial Engineer and Cost Reduction Manager, I have implemented the new manufacturing concept known as continuous process flow cells and have functioned as the "in-house expert" in training my associates in this area. While managing a $700,000 cost reduction program, I investigate and implement cost reductions through alternative materials and manufacturing processes as well as design modifications. I am involved on a daily basis in on-the-floor problem solving, costing of component processing, tooling and gaging, and capital equipment acquisitions. I have had extensive experience in project management.

Prior to graduating with my B.S. degree in Industrial Engineering, I worked my way through college in jobs in which I was involved in producing computer-aided drawings and participating in new product design. Although I worked my way through college, financing 80% of my education, I excelled academically and received the Outstanding Senior Award.

I am knowledgeable of numerous popular software and drafting packages. I offer a proven ability to rapidly master new software and adapt it for specific purposes and environments.

Single and willing to relocate, I can provide outstanding personal and professional references. I am highly regarded by my current employer and have been credited with making numerous contributions to the company through solving problems, cutting costs, determining needed capital equipment, and implementing new processes. I am making this inquiry to your company in confidence because I feel there might be a fit between your needs and my versatile areas of expertise.

I hope you will call or write me soon to suggest a time convenient for us to meet and discuss your current and future needs and how I might serve them. Thank you in advance for your time.

Sincerely yours,

Douglas Atkinson

DOUGLAS ATKINSON

1110½ Hay Street, Fayetteville, NC 28305 • preppub@aol.com • (910) 483-6611

OBJECTIVE

To add value to an organization that can use an accomplished young industrial engineer who offers specialized knowhow in coordinating cost reductions, experience in both manufacturing and process engineering, proven skills in project management, and extensive interaction with product design, quality control, vendor relations, and capital expenditures.

EDUCATION

Bachelor of Science (B.S.) degree, Industrial Engineering Major; concentration in manufacturing, Western Virginia University, Richmond, VA, 1988.
- Achieved a 3.5 GPA (3.8 in my major); inducted into National Honor Fraternity.
- Received Outstanding Senior Award in manufacturing concentration.
- Worked throughout college and financed 80% of my education.

Associate of Applied Science (A.A.S.) degree, Mechanical Engineering and Design Technology Major, Richmond Community College, Richmond, VA, 1986; 3.7 GPA.

From 1990-present, completed business minor at St. Simons Presbyterian College. Participated in continuing education sponsored by Ingersoll-Rand, Ford Motor Company, and the George Group in these and other areas:

ISO 9000 Internal Auditing	Root Cause Analysis
Total Quality Management	Value Engineering/Value Analysis
Continuous Flow Manufacturing	Synchronous Manufacturing

TECHNICAL KNOWLEDGE

Software: Quattro Pro, Freelance, Harvard Graphics, WordPerfect, Fox Pro
Drafting: VERSACAD, CADCAM, Cascade, Intergraph, Unigraphics Machining: **Knowledge of machining processes** and tooling and gaging equipment; experience in programming CNC equipment.
Certification: Certified Manufacturing Technologist; Certified ISO 9000 Internal Auditor

EXPERIENCE

INDUSTRIAL ENGINEER & COST REDUCTION MANAGER. Delbert Smith Co., Virginia Beach, VA (2000-present). Manage the processing of machined components from raw material to finished product while also coordinating a $700,000 annual cost reduction program; investigate and implement cost reductions by exploring the possibility of alternative materials, other manufacturing processes, and design modifications.
- Involved on a daily basis in on-the-floor problem solving, costing of component processing, tooling and gaging, and capital equipment acquisitions.
- Implemented and coordinated continuous process flow cells, a new concept in the manufacturing area; completed extensive training and trained my associates.
- Performed cost justifications and complete equipment installs for capital equipment acquisitions totaling half million dollars.
- Continuously interact with new product teams, problem-solving groups, purchasing specialists, vendors, as well as manufacturing and quality control personnel.
- Evaluated ergonomic equipment in assembly environment to reduce operator fatigue.

Other experience (1988-00):
- **DESIGNER.** For the Precision Controls Division of Dana Corporation, produced computer-aided drawings and actively participated in new product design while interacting with engineering and manufacturing. Was part of the team that introduced the first microprocessor controlled cruise control.
- **DEPARTMENT ASSISTANT.** On a part-time work scholarship, produced drawings on VERSACAD computer-aided drafting system for Richmond Community College.

PERSONAL

Society of Manufacturing Engineers, Roanoke Division; National Association of Industrial Technology; Epsilon Pi Tau International Honorary Fraternity for Education in Technology

Exact Name of Person
Title or Position
Name of Company
Address (number and street)
Address (city, state, and zip)

CREDIT CARD VICE PRESIDENT

Dear Exact Name of Person: (or Dear Sir or Madam if answering a blind ad.)

With the enclosed resume, I would like to indicate my interest in your organization and my desire to explore employment opportunities.

As you will see from my enclosed resume, in my current job as Vice President of Customer Service and Sales, I have supervised an 800-person workforce and improved customer satisfaction from 79% to 95%. Although I am held in high regard by my current employer, my wife and I have decided to relocate to the east coast to be closer to our aging parents.

If you can use an experienced credit card manager with extensive quality assurance knowledge, I hope you will welcome my call soon to arrange a brief meeting at your convenience to discuss your current and future needs and how I might serve them. Thank you in advance for your time.

Sincerely yours,

Denford Hanby

Alternate last paragraph:
I hope you will call or write me soon to suggest a time convenient for us to meet and discuss your current and future needs and how I might serve them. Thank you in advance for your time.

DENFORD HANBY

1110½ Hay Street, Fayetteville, NC 28305 • preppub@aol.com • (910) 483-6611

OBJECTIVE
To add value to an organization that can use an energetic and innovative executive who offers a dynamic communication style, superior motivational skills, as well as problem-solving and decision-making abilities refined as a corporate executive.

EDUCATION
Completed **Graduate Management Training Program**, MasterCard.
M.B.A., San Diego State University, CA, 1990; Led a team of MBAs to earn honors in a state competition solving profitability problems of real companies.
B.S. in Business Administration, Georgia State University, SC, 1983.
• Received a full athletic scholarship; was captain of the track team.

EXPERIENCE
VICE PRESIDENT, CUSTOMER SERVICE & SALES. MasterCard, San Diego, CA (2000-present). Lead and develop strategies for one of three major customer service and sales centers located in the United States; responsible for serving over 20 million cardmembers with exclusive relationship management responsibilities for customers that hold co-branded MasterCard cards like the Travelers Group product while controlling a $36 million annual operating budget.
• Supervise 800-person workforce; improved customer satisfaction from 79% to 95%.
• Achieved best annual employee satisfaction scores in the company's history to date.
• Improved revenue attainment by 6% in customer service "concept test."

REGIONAL SALES DIRECTOR. Sprint, Huntington Beach, CA (1994-00). After excelling as Regional Sales Director in Huntington Beach from 1994-96, was handpicked to manage the consolidation of two offices with a total of more than 300 employees which involved managing sensitive customer relations for Sprint residential customers while controlling a $35 million annual budget.
• Supervised 1,100 employees operating out of two remote customer contact centers.
• Improved revenue attainment 15% and customer satisfaction 10% while meeting a $190 million revenue objective.
• Provided the leadership which allowed the region to achieve first-place honors in tough competition with the seven other regions throughout the country.
• At Huntington Beach, improved revenue attainment 20%, customer satisfaction 5%, and productivity 30% while managing customer service and sales relationships with more than 200,000 small business customers; supervised 200 employees located in a remote business sales center operating on a $9 million budget while working as a key member of a team to achieve a $40 million corporate revenue objective; cut expenses by $300,000.

Previous MasterCard experience: Was promoted in this track record:
1990-94: **RE-ENGINEERING DIRECTOR**. Managed re-engineering project portfolio worth $3 million in savings; redesigned work flows and eliminated activities that did not add value to the process of delivering excellent customer service.
• Aggressively managed re-engineering projects, reaping over $2 million in savings; consulted with retailers on streamlining credit card operations to improve customer service.
• Developed innovative concept for resolving customer inquiries that saved $500,000.

1984-90: **CUSTOMER SERVICE DIRECTOR**. Began as a Customer Service Manager managing 85 employees, settling cardholder-retailer disputes, and controlling a $2 million budget; then was promoted to manage customer relationships with over 400,000 retail merchants nationwide to develop strategies for improving service levels and re-engineering workflows.
• Re-engineered workflows; reduced by 50% the correspondence time for selected retailers.

Date

Exact Name of Person
Title or Position
Name of Company
Address (number and street)
Address (city, state, and zip)

DIVISION CONTROLLER   Dear Exact Name of Person: (or Sir or Madam if answering a blind ad.)

With the enclosed resume, I would like to initiate the process of **exploring** employment within your organization.

As you will see from my resume, I offer experience as a controller, staff accountant, and cost accountant. In my current position as Division Controller, I manage 12 people while preparing a 12 million dollar annual budget and overseeing accounting functions in a division of a publicly traded company with $875 million in sales. Through my initiative and leadership, we have cut inventory losses in half by proper monitoring, and we have reduced accounts receivable from a high of 20% to 6%, an expected industry norm. I have played a key role in increasing gross profit by 2% since I assumed this position. Although I am held in high regard and can provide outstanding references at the appropriate time, I am selectively exploring other opportunities. I would ask that you hold my interest in your company in confidence at this time.

As you will see from my resume, I hold a Bachelor's degree in Business Administration, an Associate's degree in Data Processing, and have completed more than 30 hours of Accounting course work. I have completed course work related to COBOL, Basic, and RPG, and I am skilled in using popular software including Excel, Lotus, DACEASY, and other programs.

It is my desire to become a permanent asset to an organization which can benefit from my considerable skills in consulting, management, and accounting. If you can use my experience and knowledge, please contact me to suggest a time when we might meet to discuss your needs and how I might serve them. Thank you in advance for your time.

Sincerely,

Harold Hafner

HAROLD HAFNER

1110½ Hay Street, Fayetteville, NC 28305 • preppub@aol.com • (910) 483-6611

OBJECTIVE   To benefit an organization that can use a detail-oriented professional with a strong bottom-line orientation who offers experience in management accounting and business management.

SKILLS   **Computer programming: COBOL, BASIC,** and **RPG** languages.
Software: Excel, Lotus, and DACEASY; familiarity with Solomen IV and GAP software.
Accounting: Data processing, payroll, purchasing, cost estimates, tax return preparation, preparation of P&L Statements.
Management information systems: Utilized the Retail Flooring Management System (RFMS).

EDUCATION   B.A. degree, **Business Administration,** 1982; and A.A.S., **Data Processing,** 1990; University at Albany, NY.
Completed 30 hours of course work in **Accounting** at Albany Technical Community College.

EXPERIENCE   **DIVISION CONTROLLER.** Textiles Unlimited, Albany, NY (2000-present). For the a division which consists of four retail locations with sales of $12 million divided between a customer base of retail builders and commercial contractors, I am the Division Controller reporting to the Region Vice President.
- Supervise 12 people who include a payroll clerk, job cost clerks, inventory clerks, and accounting technicians.
- Am highly regarded by this company which is publicly traded and does an annual overall sales volume of $875 million.
- Have increased gross profit by 2% to date compared to when I assumed the position.
- Cut inventory losses in half by proper monitoring.
- Reduced mill claims by 50% over prior years through astute problem solving and skillful claims and credit management.
- Have reduced accounts receivable from a high of 20% to 6%, an expected industry norm.
- Am closely involved with accounts receivable, payroll, and checking account reconciliations and ensure accurate and timely preparation and approval.
- Prepare monthly financial statements and interpret them for management; meet month end deadlines, tax deadlines, and other governmental and regulatory deadlines.
- Prepare and monitor the annual budget of 12 million dollars.

CONTROLLER. Braxton, Inc., Albany, NY (1991-00). Was recruited to supervise accounting functions for a $97 million project which involved maintaining general ledger, accounts receivable, and accounts payable; this firm liquidated its assets.

CONTROLLER. Delaby's Products., Albany, NY (1986-91). Handled all accounting functions associated with operating this two-location, 60-employee business that processed soil and bark products sold primarily to large chain stores, including Lowe's, Food Lion, etc. •
- Coordinated and supervised two clerks in the home office.

Highlights of other experience:
STAFF ACCOUNTANT. Supervised four clerks for this construction materials firm with annual revenues in excess of $15 million.
STAFF ACCOUNTANT. Analyzed corporate books for compilations and preparation of financial statements. Prepared individual/corporate tax returns. Participated in field audits.

PERSONAL   Can provide outstanding personal and professional references upon request.

Date

Exact Name of Person
Exact Title
Exact Name of Company
Address
City, State, Zip

SENIOR VICE PRESIDENT   Dear Exact Name of Person: (or Dear Sir or Madam if answering a blind ad):

With the enclosed resume, I would like to make you aware of my background as an articulate, experienced finance industry professional who offers an extensive background in loan department operations, supervision and development of staff, and account relationship development.

As you will see from my resume, I have served Meredith Savings Bank with loyalty and distinction, advancing from Loan Officer to Assistant Vice President, to Vice President, and finally to my most recent position as Senior Vice President, where I managed up to 15 personnel, providing direct supervision to five employees. In this job, I oversaw the operation of the Loan Department, managing a portfolio of $46 million in mortgage loans as well as $15 million in consumer loans. In addition, I originated, processed, and underwrote mortgage and consumer loans in amounts up to $650,000, and established "from scratch" the bank's consumer loan department and correspondent lending program.

Although I was highly regarded by everyone at Meredith Savings Bank and can provide outstanding personal and professional references at the appropriate time, this venerable institution has recently been purchased by a major northeastern financial conglomerate. While I could have continued under the new management, I have decided to pursue my long-term career objectives in an environment where I can better make use of my strong customer focus and extensive industry knowledge. I feel that there is a good "fit" between your organization's needs and my unique combination of ability and experience.

If you can use a loyal and experienced finance professional, I hope you will welcome my call soon when I try to arrange a brief meeting to discuss your goals and how my background might serve your needs.

Sincerely,

Robert Dran

Alternate Last Paragraph:
If you can use a loyal, articulate, and experienced finance professional, I hope you will write or call me soon to suggest a time when we might meet to discuss your needs and goals and how my background might serve them.

ROBERT DRAN

1110½ Hay Street, Fayetteville, NC 28305   •   preppub@aol.com   •   (910) 483-6611

OBJECTIVE

To benefit an organization that can use an experienced professional with exceptional supervisory and customer service skills who offers a background of excellence in account relationship management and loan development.

EDUCATION

Earned a **Bachelor of Arts** from the University at Buffalo, Buffalo, NY.
Extensive additional professional development schools, conferences, and workshops.

EXPERIENCE

With Meredith Savings Bank, Meredith, AL, have advanced in the following "track record" of increasing responsibilities while excelling in customer service and loan development at this local institution:

1985-2002: SENIOR VICE PRESIDENT.
Started with Meredith Savings as a **Loan Officer** and was quickly promoted to **Assistant Vice President**, and **Vice President**; served loyally and with distinction in these jobs before advancing to my most recent position.

Loan Department:
- Oversaw the operation of the Loan Department, managing a loan portfolio of $46 million in mortgage loans and $15 million in consumer loans.
- Originated loans up to $650,000; originated and processed traditional conforming and nonconforming mortgage loans.
- Established the bank's consumer loan department, increasing overall loan volume by actively developing relationships with new clients.
- Created and established the correspondent lending program.
- Underwrote mortgage and consumer loans for the bank.

Supervision, Training, and Operations:
- Managed as many as 15 personnel, providing direct supervision to five employees.
- Served as Security Officer, conducting quarterly meetings with all bank personnel to instruct employees in security policies and procedures.
- As Compliance Officer, ensured that all bank departments and employees maintained strict adherence with all state and federal laws.

Marketing:
- Promoted the products and services offered by Meredith Savings through creation and refinement of effective newspaper and radio advertisements.

**CIVIC
ACTIVITIES**

A respected member of the community, I have been active in a number of church and government positions, charitable organizations, etc., including:
- Served as an elected member of the Meredith City Council from 1992-1996; was mayor pro-tem from 1992-1994.
- Member of the Meredith Chamber of Commerce; served as Director from 1990-1992, as well as chairing the Governmental Affairs Committee and the Transportation Committee.
- Director of the Meredith County United Way, 2001-present and 1988-1992.
- Received the Distinguished Service Award from the Meredith Jaycees, 1983.
- Appointed Director of the Meredith Airport, 1984-1986.
- Ruling Elder, Meredith Presbyterian Church.
- Volunteer my time for the Boy Scouts of America.

PERSONAL

Excellent personal and professional references are available upon request.

Exact Name of Person
Exact Title of Person
Exact Name of Organization
Address
City, State zip

VICE PRESIDENT

Banks and financial
institutions in Houston
should be happy to meet
this accomplished
banking professional
who is relocating.

Dear Exact Name (or Dear Sir or Madam if answering a blind ad):

I would appreciate an opportunity to talk with you soon about how I could contribute to your organization through my extensive management experience in most functional areas of accounting, human resources, operations, and banking.

As you will see from my resume, I have enjoyed a track record of promotion with National Consumer Bank, one of the leading financial institutions in the South. I have often worn multiple "hats" and am known for my ability to oversee complex responsibilities in numerous areas simultaneously. For example, in my current position as a vice president, I oversee the Operations and Compliance areas for the bank, and I actually developed the bank's Deposit Compliance Program.

If you feel your management team could benefit from my in-depth experience, creative problem-solving style, and reputation as a strategist and visionary, I would be delighted to make myself available at your convenience to discuss your needs and goals and how I might help you achieve them. I do wish to point out that I will be relocating to the Houston area in order to be closer to my family who all live in or near Houston.

I hope you will welcome my call soon to arrange a brief meeting to discuss your current and future needs and how I might serve them. Thank you in advance for your time.

Sincerely,

Anne Wade

ANNE WADE

Present:	1110 Hay Street, Fayetteville, NC 28305	(910) 483-6611
Permanent:	1605 California Street, Houston, TX 78345	(823) 522-3400

OBJECTIVE　To contribute to an organization that can use an innovative manager who believes that "the sky is the limit" when persistence, creativity, and attention to detail are combined with superior planning, time management, communication, and problem-solving skills.

EXPERIENCE　*For more than 14 years, have built a "track record" of accomplishment in positions of increasing responsibility at National Consumer Bank, Virginia Beach, VA;*
VICE PRESIDENT, OPERATIONS & COMPLIANCE (2000-present). Was promoted to handle additional responsibilities related to consumer compliance while continuing to handle responsibilities described in the Assistant Vice President job below.
- Developed Deposit Compliance Program for consumer law and regulation.
- Personally conduct compliance testing (audits) and the training program; have trained approximately 40 employees in this specific area.
- Have become very experienced in internal auditing for compliance.

ASSISTANT VICE PRESIDENT OF OPERATIONS & HUMAN RESOURCES. (1995-00). In this highly visible, fast-paced position reporting to the bank president, wore "three hats," balancing multiple responsibilities in human resources, operations, and investments.
- *Management:* Directly supervised five people, ensuring that assigned responsibilities were executed in a systematic and effective manner.
- *Operations:* In coordination with top management, developed/implemented plans and policies that affected accounting, bookkeeping, and data processing of main office and two branches.
- *Human Resources:* Applied my expert knowledge to develop, maintain, and administer all personnel policies as they applied to 40 bank employees; oversaw EEO compliance, recruitment, safety & health.
- *Benefits Administration*: Oversaw all salary and benefit functions, including 401(k) pension plan and Blue Cross/Blue Shield health plan.
- *Finances*: Managed an investment portfolio utilizing excess funds per day while efficiently planning and administering the department's budget.
- *Training:* Coordinated in-house programs on personnel policies; organized training on compliance with demand deposit, direct deposit, bank privacy, and other regulations.

OPERATIONS OFFICER. (1991-1995). Excelled in directing all aspects of the Operations Department because of my versatile management skills; supervised five employees.
- Reviewed surveys of community banks and made recommendations on competitively pricing various banking products.
- As a member, Strategic Planning Committee, offered input on personnel and operations.
- Managed all day-to-day bookkeeping functions and monitored the bank's cash position, making investments or borrowing funds as appropriate.

HEAD BOOKKEEPER. (1989-1991). Ensured the highest standards of customer service while supervising and reviewing the work of five assistants; balanced general ledger accounts; processed overdrafts, returns items, and ACH debits and credits.

EDUCATION　B.S., **Accounting**, Virginia State University, Virginia Beach, VA, 1991.
Excelled in courses in Accounting, Introduction to Computers, Banking & Finance, Business Communication, Supervision, and Principles of Management.
Attended seminars on sexual harassment, interviewing & hiring, state and federal wages, personnel policies (developing/implementing), public speaking, and check processing.

PERSONAL　Self-motivated, dedicated professional with a reputation as a team leader.

ABOUT THE EDITOR

Anne McKinney holds an MBA from the Harvard Business School and a BA in English from the University of North Carolina at Chapel Hill. A noted public speaker, writer, and teacher, she is the senior editor for PREP's business and career imprint, which bears her name. Early titles in the Anne McKinney Career Series (now called the Real-Resumes Series) published by PREP include: *Resumes and Cover Letters That Have Worked, Resumes and Cover Letters That Have Worked for Military Professionals, Government Job Applications and Federal Resumes, Cover Letters That Blow Doors Open,* and *Letters for Special Situations.* Her career titles and how-to resume-and-cover-letter books are based on the expertise she has acquired in 20 years of working with job hunters. Her valuable career insights have appeared in publications of the "Wall Street Journal" and other prominent newspapers and magazines.

PREP Publishing Order Form

You may purchase any of our titles from your favorite bookseller! Or send a check or money order or your credit card number for the total amount*, plus $3.50 postage and handling, to PREP, Box 66, Fayetteville, NC 28302. If you have a question about any of our titles, feel free to e-mail us at preppub@aol.com and visit our website at http://www.prep-pub.com

Name: _____

Phone #: _____

Address: _____

_____

E-mail address: _____

Payment Type: ☐ Check/Money Order ☐ Visa ☐ MasterCard

Credit Card Number: _____ Expiration Date: _____

Check items you are ordering:

☐ $16.95—REAL-RESUMES FOR FINANCIAL JOBS. Anne McKinney, Editor
☐ $16.95—REAL-RESUMES FOR COMPUTER JOBS. Anne McKinney, Editor
☐ $16.95—REAL-RESUMES FOR MEDICAL JOBS. Anne McKinney, Editor
☐ $16.95—REAL-RESUMES FOR TEACHERS. Anne McKinney, Editor
☐ $16.95—REAL-RESUMES FOR CAREER CHANGERS. Anne McKinney, Editor
☐ $16.95—REAL-RESUMES FOR STUDENTS. Anne McKinney, Editor
☐ $16.95—REAL-RESUMES FOR SALES. Anne McKinney, Editor
☐ $16.95—REAL ESSAYS FOR COLLEGE AND GRAD SCHOOL. Anne McKinney, Editor
☐ $25.00—RESUMES AND COVER LETTERS THAT HAVE WORKED.
☐ $25.00—RESUMES AND COVER LETTERS THAT HAVE WORKED FOR MILITARY PROFESSIONALS.
☐ $25.00—RESUMES AND COVER LETTERS FOR MANAGERS.
☐ $25.00—GOVERNMENT JOB APPLICATIONS AND FEDERAL RESUMES: Federal Resumes, KSAs, Forms 171 and 612, and Postal Applications.
☐ $25.00—COVER LETTERS THAT BLOW DOORS OPEN.
☐ $25.00—LETTERS FOR SPECIAL SITUATIONS.
☐ $16.00—BACK IN TIME. Patty Sleem
☐ $17.00—(trade paperback) SECOND TIME AROUND. Patty Sleem
☐ $25.00—(hardcover) SECOND TIME AROUND. Patty Sleem
☐ $18.00—A GENTLE BREEZE FROM GOSSAMER WINGS. Gordon Beld
☐ $18.00—BIBLE STORIES FROM THE OLD TESTAMENT. Katherine Whaley
☐ $14.95—WHAT THE BIBLE SAYS ABOUT... *Words that can lead to success and happiness* (large print edition) Patty Sleem
☐ $10.95—KIJABE An African Historical Saga. Pally Dhillon

_____ **TOTAL ORDERED (add $3.50 for postage and handling)**

PREP offers volume discounts on large orders. Call us at (910) 483-6611 for more information.

THE MISSION OF PREP PUBLISHING IS TO PUBLISH
BOOKS AND OTHER PRODUCTS WHICH ENRICH
PEOPLE'S LIVES AND HELP THEM OPTIMIZE THE
HUMAN EXPERIENCE. OUR STRONGEST LINES ARE
OUR JUDEO-CHRISTIAN ETHICS SERIES AND OUR
BUSINESS & CAREER SERIES.

Would you like to explore the possibility of having PREP's writing
team create a resume for you similar to the ones in this book?

For a brief free consultation, call 910-483-6611
or send $4.00 to receive our Job Change Packet to
PREP, Department Financial, Box 66, Fayetteville, NC 28302.

QUESTIONS OR COMMENTS? E-MAIL US AT PREPPUB@AOL.COM